Violence, Society, and the Church

Violence, Society, and the Church

A Cultural Approach

Gerald A. Arbuckle, S.M.

LITURGICAL PRESS
Collegeville, Minnesota

www.litpress.org

1	2	3	4	5	6	7	8	9

Library of Congress Cataloging-in-Publication Data

Arbuckle, Gerald A.
    Violence, society, and the church : a cultural approach / Gerald A.
Arbuckle.
        p. cm.
Includes bibliographical references and index.
ISBN 0-8146-2926-1 (alk. paper)
1. Violence—Religious aspects—Catholic Church.   I. Title.

BX1795.V56A73   2004
261.8'3—dc22

                                                                    2003014499

For

Those who courageously name violence no matter from where it comes.

Whenever I must speak, I must cry out, violence and outrage is my message . . . (Jer 20:8)

Contents

Acknowledgments

No book comes unaided from the mind of a single writer. Rather, it is encouraged and shaped by the advice and assistance of many others. This book is no exception to that pattern.

This book is a sequel to three earlier publications on the relationship between culture, society, and Church: *Earthing the Gospel: An Incultura-tion Handbook for Pastoral Workers* (1990); *Refounding the Church: Dissent for Leadership* (1993); and *Healthcare Ministry: Refounding the Mission in Tumultuous Times* (2000). Many readers from different parts of the world have commented on these books, and I have frequently used their insights in the development of this text.

I am grateful to Mark Twomey, editorial director of the Liturgical Press, for his encouragement and willingness to publish the book; to my colleagues Michael Mullins, S.M., Patricia Moroney, and Kerry Brettell for their challenging questions on the themes of this book; to Catherine Duncan and Patricia Kent, R.S.M., for their detailed reading and commenting on the text; to Geri Vaughan, for her patient expertise with computer advice. These people, however, are in no way respon-sible for the book's inadequacies.

Gerald A. Arbuckle, S.M.
1 January 2003

Introduction

> The essence of [violence] is the destruction of human beings. This includes not only killing but the creation of [cultural] conditions that materially or psychologically destroy or diminish people's dignity, happiness, and capacity to fulfill basic material needs. (Ervin Staub[1])

> [Violence is] unacceptable as a solution to problems. . . . [It] destroys . . . the dignity, the life, the freedom of human beings. (John Paul II[2])

There is no lack of raw material for a book on the relationship of cultures to violence. Last century humankind witnessed violence to an extent never seen before—an estimated 130 million killed. At the beginning of the new century the world remains divided, weighed down with violence: ideological conflicts, terrorism in increasingly violent forms, pathological forms of nationalism, racial violence, ethnic cleansing, famine, domestic violence, workplace abuse, cyberspace violence, intercultural violence, and accepting violence as normal. We who gasped at Hitler's or Stalin's genocidal policies now live in a world where the destruction of all living species on the earth is a real possibility. It is a universe "groaning in travail" (Rom 8:22).

Not only individuals, but cultures act violently because they facilitate and legitimize individuals, groups, and institutions to demean and subjugate people. This book searches for the roots of such violence. It seeks answers to questions like: What is there in a culture that facilitates

---

[1] Ervin Staub, *The Roots of Evil: The Origins of Genocide and Other Group Violence* (Cambridge: Cambridge University Press, 1989) 25.

[2] John Paul II, at Drogeha, Ireland, cited in the review *Books and Culture* (January 1996) 13.

and legitimizes violence? Why do certain cultures legitimize particular types of violence?

Violence

The term "violence" does not have a standard or set definition. Ideas of what constitutes violence can vary not only between different societies, but also between different groups within the same society at different times and in different situations. Violence, however, in this book means every action or lack of action of persons or cultures (including customs, institutions, structures) that are insensitive to and oppressive of human persons who have been created according to the divine image and likeness.[3]

Violence involves *force* or *violation*. It may be physical, emotional, verbal, theological, cognitive, sexual, visual, institutional, structural, economic, political, social, ecological. It can be sensational or hidden, intermittent or ongoing, intentional or unconscious, but there is still the violation of the victim.[4]

Violence is not about damaging or destroying things. It is about abusing *people*. The tragedy is that it lowers their self-esteem, self-confidence; they experience a sense of powerlessness and subjugation. Violence crushes the spirit of people and makes them submissive to violators for their purpose. The psalmist describes the effects of violence in poignant terms: "An enemy is in deadly pursuit, crushing me into the ground . . . My spirit is faint, and within me my heart is numb with fear" (Ps 143:3-4, 7). Consider for example poverty as a form of violence. A fifth of the world's population goes hungry every night, a quarter lacks access to even a basic necessity like safe drinking-water, and a third lives in abject poverty. It is impossible to enjoy a sense of self-worth or human dignity, freedom and equality without food, health or shelter. Are there entrenched processes in a culture which legitimize institutions and individuals to act as their exploiters and degrade the poor, rendering them powerless to do anything about their situation?[5]

[3] See Alain J. Richard, *Roots of Violence in the U.S. Culture* (Nevada City: Blue Dolphin, 1999) 14.

[4] See Jeff Hearn, "The Organization(s) of Violence," *Violence and Gender Relations: Theories and Interventions*, ed. Barbara Fawcett and others (London: Sage, 1996) 43.

[5] See John Gledhill, *Power and Its Disguises: Anthropological Perspectives on Politics* (London: Pluto Press, 1994) 7.

Causes of Violence and the Focus of This Book

Psychologists have different views about the origins of violence. Some attribute violence to innate human predisposition. Some assume culture is its root. For psychoanalyst Melanie Klein violence is instinctual and inborn; violators project their own inner fears and inadequacies on to other people and society. Erich Fromm, on the other hand, opts for a Freudian frustration hypothesis by claiming that violence is due to the constrictions of civilized society.

It is not the task of this book to explore different psychological approaches to violence. Instead, the emphasis is particularly on culture and its power to cause violence. The main conceptual instruments come from cultural anthropology, though the insights of other disciplines will be used where appropriate, e.g., Scriptures, history, theology, psychology. Cultural anthropology's contribution is twofold: to examine cultural and historical pressures which have strong and unappreciated roles explaining violence; secondly, to examine social realities in a cross-cultural frame of reference. For the anthropologist violence is preeminently collective rather than individual, usually culturally structured and always culturally interpreted. The cultural anthropological approach in this book focuses not on individual violent behavior, but on identifying entrenched processes in cultures that foster or allow violence to occur.

Culture and Power

Some introductory explanations of culture and power will be helpful to the reader. The word "power" means the capacity of an individual or a culture to influence others. It is both positive and negative. It is positive when it directs people and institutions to act in favor of human dignity and justice, negative or abusive when it dominates, manipulates, or unduly coerces others. The distinction between unilateral and reciprocal power can be useful. In the case of the former, a person (e.g., a terrorist), group, or culture refuses to receive the influence of others, rendering dialogue impossible. In the case of reciprocal power there is an openness to receive the influence of others. Nonviolent movements exercise both positive and reciprocal power.

Culture simply means the ways in which a people is empowered to feel, think, and act in particular ways, as expressed in its symbols, myths, and rituals (chapter 1). Negative and positive power in a culture primarily reside in its mythologies (i.e., an interconnected set of myths) and through them in individuals, structures, and institutions. Myths are a type of narrative that seeks to express in an imaginative form a belief about the person or group, the world or deity, which simply cannot adequately be expressed in ordinary language. They are like the inner structures of a house, unseen from the outside, but they hold the building together. Through myths people are "lifted above their captivity in the ordinary, attain visions of the future, and become capable of collective actions to realize such visions."[6] Consider one example. Slobodan Milosevic's ability to inspire people with the Serbian national mythology, with its roots as far back as the fourteenth century, led to the contemporary disasters in the Balkans. Trying to describe the power of mythology for good or evil the anthropologist Bronislaw Malinowski says that myth "is not merely a story told but a reality lived." It is "not an idle tale, but a hardworking active force."[7] Mircea Eliade believes myth is "saturated with being . . . and *power*."[8]

Since myths contain an inner power to facilitate and legitimate people to be violent, this book aims to identify and uncover cultural mythologies that have this destructive power.

Culture Models

Culture models can help to identify the mythologies that have the potential to facilitate and legitimize violence in predictable ways. A model aims to illuminate reality by highlighting emphases and downplaying details or nuances that might interfere with the clarifying process. A model is modified or put aside in the light of the data being reviewed. A model is simply a way of helping us explore very complex processes and we should expect no more from it.

The four culture models contained in the chapters are: "premodern," "modern," "postmodern," and "paramodern." In the first three models, their particular mythologies and expressions of violence are identified; the fourth describes people's efforts to counter violence. The models are not necessarily historically sequential. Nor are they exclusive of each other. Stressing a particular element in a model is not to imply that

[6] Peter L. Berger, *Pyramids of Sacrifice: Political Ethics and Social Change* (Harmondsworth: Penguin, 1977) 32.

[7] Bronislaw Malinowski, *Magic, Science and Religion* (Glencoe: Free Press, 1980) 100–1.

[8] Mircea Eliade, *The Sacred and the Profane* (New York: Harcourt, 1959) 95.

it is not present in others. It merely indicates that it is more dominant in one model than in others. While perhaps favoring one model as a dominant source of identity, a person can move in the space of a day or less from one framework to another, e.g., from modern to paramodern, to premodern, to modern. Cultural identity is "situational" for individuals, that is, the choice of a set of meanings (culture model) depends on the particular context in which people find themselves.

A Guide for Inculturation

Roman Catholics see inculturation as an *exchange* or *dialogue* between the Gospel and cultures, in which both are positively affected in some way or other. Inculturation is an exercise of ongoing reciprocal power. Inculturation is "the expression of one's faith through one's own culture . . . [It] means that faith must somehow become an integral part of the cultural community's cognitional, emotional and motivational way of life. Christ must become an integral and fully functional part of the local culture and hopefully, its very heart and center."[9] There are four stages in the inculturation process:

Clarifying reality—what is happening in the culture.

Identifying what conforms or does not conform to Gospel values.

Choosing how to bear witness to Gospel values in the context of violence.

Actually implementing the plan that is chosen.

The first requirement of inculturation is that people actually know the culture. It is not as simple as it immediately sounds. It is easier in fact to discuss the theology and spirituality of inculturation than to grasp the complexities of cultures. This book primarily focuses on the latter.

By "Gospel values" are meant the foundational principles of Catholic social teaching. They form the evaluative assumptions behind judgements in this book, e.g.:

every person is created in the image of God and redeemed by Jesus Christ;

[9] Louis Luzbetak, quoted in *New Directions in Mission and Evangelization*, ed. James A. Scherer and Stephen B. Bevans (Maryknoll: Orbis Books, 1999) 5.

all human life is sacred from conception;

all people have equal dignity and the right to be treated equal;

the powerless must be our particular concern.

Fr. John Langan, S.J., professor of philosophy at Georgetown University, while applauding the development of Catholic social teaching, believes that there is a tendency to underestimate "the power of nationalist and secessionist movements in political life and to be less attentive to the task of discerning and denouncing the evils which they can produce." He concludes that the Church "can fall short by offering no more than moralistic denunciations; its teaching needs to offer historically and socially informed criticisms."[10] This book attempts to do so by reviewing the impact of globalization on ethnicity, the rise of political and religious fundamentalism, ethnic cleansing, etc.

Though this book draws on several disciplines—for example, theology, Scripture, and history—the main models of analysis are derived from cultural anthropology. Like a surprising move on a chessboard, anthropology offers a new way of looking at the causes of violence. Anthropology is about how people feel and communicate with one another within and across cultures. It is often about laying bare the cultural forces that motivate people, though they are so often unconscious of these forces' existence and their power to control behavior.[11] The book is written for the nonspecialist in anthropology.

The book has a handbook format, with frequent use of headings and summaries, so that readers—college students, pastors, and members of their congregations, bishops, leaders of religious congregations—can more effectively participate in the process of inculturation in their communities. In particular, through the use of concrete examples, it provides readers with ways to understand the links between culture and violence in society and the Church. With this understanding readers will be better able to lead in proactive ways and not be paralyzed by the negative forces within cultures. Each chapter ends with discussion questions.

[10] John Langan, "Issues in Catholic Social Thought," *Origins*, vol. 30, no. 3 (2000) 47–8.

[11] For an introductory summary of the role of cultural anthropology, see James L. Peacock, *The Anthropological Lens: Harsh Light, Soft Focus* (Cambridge: Cambridge University Press, 1986) 4–7.

The use of models aims to provide analytical instruments to assist readers to understand their experience of cultures at the local and global levels. A wide range of case studies is used throughout the text. A case study is a detailed description of a particular human experience of individuals and/or groups that illustrates theoretical principles of a chapter. Through case-study analysis it is possible to see in a focused way the impact of violence on particular people and groups. It is also possible that case studies from cultures different from one's own are able to throw unexpected light on one's own local cultural experience.

The Catholic Church as a Culture

From time to time the Roman Catholic Church is used as a case study to illustrate theoretical analyses. Readers of other Christian traditions, though their histories may differ, will discover in this case study many relevant lessons for themselves.

Only those who assume that the Church is a pure spirit can claim that it does not form a culture or have the capacity to legitimize violence against people. As Fr. Henri de Lubac, S.J., writes, the Church is no "misty entity."[12] In recording instances of cultural abuse I follow the example of Pope John Paul II. Millions of non-Catholics and Catholics have been moved by an ailing and courageous pontiff offering long-delayed apologies for the Church's participation in violence in the past, e.g., against Jews, Muslims, indigenous peoples.

There is much to apologize for in the present Church also—gaps between the Church's cultural life and Gospel-based tradition. The hopes that collegial interaction and dialogue between Rome and the local churches would develop have not always been realized. Local churches feel that their rights at times are not always respected. As Cardinal Walter Kasper writes, "the relationship between the universal and the local Church has become unbalanced."[13] The fact is that the Church "is much more authoritarian and uniformist than the Church of the Middle Ages ever was."[14] The Church is lagging behind in acknowledging the changing role of women; as long as their involvement in

[12] Henri de Lubac, *The Splendour of the Church*, trans. M. Mason (London: Sheed and Ward, 1956) 114.

[13] Walter Kasper, "On the Church," *The Tablet* (23 June 2001) 927.

[14] Walter Kasper in 1988, cited by Terence L. Nichols, *That All May Be One: Hierarchy and Participation in the Church* (Collegeville: The Liturgical Press, 1997) 330.

decision-making and Church administration remains minimal women are unappreciated and intimidated.[15] Then there is the additional massive breakdown of trust in the institutional Church through the on-going revelations of sexual abuse by clergy and religious. We now know that the Church cultivated a culture of concealment and the rights of victims have been ignored.

There are also attempts to restore the Church to the cultural ghetto or opposition-to-the-world mentality of the pre-Vatican II Council era. Restorationism is an ill-defined, but nonetheless powerful, movement within the Church towards the uncritical reaffirmation of pre-Vatican II structures and attitudes. Some Vatican officials and their departments continue to employ theological and administrative violence to support the restorationist and fundamentalist movements in the Church (see chapter 8).

A significant theme in this book is that a culture has within itself forces that resist change. When the status quo is threatened people fearing the unknown seek to hold on to the security of the familiar. The forces of resistance are so strong that it is rare that the appointment of a change-oriented new leader, e.g., a CEO, a prime minister, president, can alone alter the situation. The culture of the Catholic Church illustrates this point. Efforts have been made by popes since Vatican II to reform the structures of the Church, but they have met significant resistance.

Structure of This Book

Chapter 1 defines culture and explains elements and dynamics of culture that legitimize violence. Part of this chapter is devoted to an updated analysis of the nature and power of symbols, myths, and ritual that I first wrote about in my book *Earthing the Gospel* in 1990.

Chapter 2 analyzes the relationship between violence and premodern cultures. The Church is used as a case study of such a culture (chapter 3). Chapter 4 concentrates on particular potential sources of violence in premodern cultures, namely, gossip, shame, honor, and humor. This chapter also looks at how the issue of shame encouraged the concealment of the sexual failings of clergy and religious in the Church.

[15] See an excellent study commissioned by the Australian Bishops Conference, *Woman and Man: One in Christ Jesus*, ed. Marie MacDonald and others (Sydney: HarperCollins, 1999).

Chapter 5 examines a culture model of modernity. The emphasis is on the mythology of modernity as a legitimating source of violence. Chapter 6 analyses the relationship of envy, jealousy, and scapegoating as forces of violence in modernity. In chapters 7 and 8 postmodernism is examined as a source of "anti-order" and "pro-order" violence. These two categories of violence are reactions to the cultural revolution of the 1960s, Vatican II, and globalization. Examples of "anti-order" violence are what John Paul II called "cultures of death," e.g., societies that approve abortion, euthanasia. Among "pro-order" reactions are right-wing political and religious movements, e.g., Thatcherism, Reaganism, restorationism in the Catholic Church.

Terrorism has always existed, but its ability to intimidate and kill is dramatically growing in consequence of new technology. Religious fundamentalism and fanaticism are behind contemporary international terrorism, but they cannot be understood without grasping their cultural roots (see chapter 8).

Chapter 9 describes the paramodern culture model notable for positive movements in the secular and religious worlds which emphasize collaboration, ecological and human interdependence, nonviolence, and reconciliation. Particular emphasis is given to the positive power of nonviolence to prod the oppressor to reflect on the evil of his or her actions. Nonviolence has a Gospel quality, since it transcends more human expressions of power.

The epilogue is a meditative reflection on the parable of the Good Samaritan. The story contains several types of violence, e.g., racial, physical, ritual, occupational, and Jesus invites his followers how they should respond to them.

Personal Reflection

I began this book as a personal journey in search of answers to troubling questions about the nature of violence and its causes. In 1960 I visited the former notoriously cruel concentration camp of Mauthausen in the hills beyond Linz, Austria. In the late afternoon of a summer's day there was a haunting stillness I can never forget. What part did culture have in encouraging people systematically to starve, torture, and gas millions of innocent people? Thomas Merton had the same disquieting question after his visit to the concentration camp of Auschwitz.[16] Since

---

[16] See Thomas Merton, *Thomas Merton on Peace* (London: Mowbrays, 1971) 80.

that visit to the camp I worked in Papua New Guinea where intertribal violence is common. I also witnessed what happens when the restraints of tribal cultural life breakdown in cities and towns freeing people to act violently against others and property. I have observed the oppression of the Marcos regime in the Philippines. The same question kept coming to me: what does culture have to do with such violence?

More recently I found bullying in white-collar and voluntary organizations. Some cultures, I discovered, encouraged this intimidation while others restrained it. Then the horrific terrorist attacks on New York and Washington, D.C., on 11 September 2001. What part did culture play in this? It is too simplistic to say that the terrorists are exceptionally violent by nature. I have also observed the paradox that a culture may tolerate nonpolitical violence, such as gang warfare and interethnic clashes, but remain for the most part free of political violence. The United States is one of the most violent nations, yet political violence is not tolerated. France and Germany, on the other hand, have a low cultural tolerance for violent crime, but a tradition of political violence.[17] These experiences needed analysis. What is there in cultures that encourages people to act violently?

I have in my journey at the same time met people who have resisted violence with courage and patience. Many have fearlessly spoken out against violence, even within the Church. They were CEOs of corporate systems who did not tolerate in their organizations intimidating tactics toward staff members and clients. They were people helping the poor in the midst of violence in the Philippines. They were women who refused in nonviolent ways to be classed as second-class people in patriarchal cultures. And Pope John Paul II vigorously condemning communism, oppressive aspects of capitalism, and anti-life legislation. What gave them the strength to do this? I invariably found they were people who had taken to heart the call of John: "Let us love, then, because Christ first loved us" (1 John 4:19). I have seen in their actions a light shining in the darkness of violence, "and darkness could not overpower it" (John 1:5). It is to people like this that I dedicate this book.

---

[17] See David J. Whittaker, *The Terrorism Reader* (London: Routledge, 2001) 21.

Chapter 1

Violence, Power, and Culture

> By myths we mean the value impregnated beliefs that [people] hold, that they live by or live for. Every society is held together by a myth system, a complex of dominating forms that determines and sustains all its activities. (Robert M. MacIver[1])

This chapter explains:

- the nature of culture and that the potential for negative and unilateral power resides in a people's symbols, myths, and rituals;

- the capacity of mythology to encourage violence;

- the capacity of ritual to express violence;

- other ways in which cultures sanction people to act violently;

- four models of culture; subsequent chapters describe how models relate to violence.

The purpose of this chapter is to explain why cultures have inbuilt tendencies to foster and legitimize violence. The manner in which culture is conceptualized will affect how we view violence and its relationship to culture. It is a difficult concept to define because the reality the word tries to embrace is complex.[2] The process of globalization has

---

[1] Robert M. MacIver, *The Web of Government* (London: Macmillan, 1947) 4.

[2] In postmodern anthropology culture is approached in different ways, e.g., as "text," "drama," "narrative," "performance." See discussion by Robert Layton, *An*

ɔologists to rethink the traditional approach to cul-
ʳpes of culture are developing with new ideas about
, for example, an individual, a citizen, a member of

fined as: a pattern of shared meanings and values,
ᴄₘᵇₒᵈₗₑd in a behavioral network of symbols, myths, and rituals,
created by a particular group as it struggles to adjust to life's challenges
and educate its members about what is considered the orderly and
correct way to feel, think, and behave.[4] Negative and positive power,
that is the capacity to facilitate violence or to empower people for good
actions, resides in a people's symbols, myths, and rituals.

Explanation

1. Impact on Feeling

Culture shapes people's emotional reactions to the world of people,
events, and things. It permeates the deepest recesses of the human
group, and individuals, in particular their feelings. Hence this is the
reason for defining culture not as "what people *do*," but rather as "what
people *feel* about what they do."[5] It is the task of cultural anthropologists to identify and analyze the dynamics of feeling in a culture.

2. A Process

The definition emphasizes the developmental and survival function
of culture for a people, in a world of change, prejudice, and discrimination. In the following incident, when I reidentified with the founding
story of my nation, I became re-energized and determined not to be

---

Introduction to Theory in Anthropology (Cambridge: Cambridge University Press,
1997) 184–215; Chris Jenks, *Culture: Key Ideas* (London: Routledge, 1993); Robert J.
Schreiter reflects on the weaknesses and strengths of integrated definitions of
culture, *The New Catholicism: Theology Between the Global and the Local* (Maryknoll:
Orbis Books, 1999) 46–61.

[3] See Henrietta L. Moore, "Anthropological Theory at the Turn of the Century,"
Feminism and Anthropology (Oxford: Polity, 1988) 11.

[4] This is an adaptation of a definition by Clifford Geertz, *The Interpretation of Cultures* (New York: Basic Books, 1973) 89, and Edgar H. Schein, *Organizational Culture
and Leadership* (San Francisco: Jossey-Bass, 1985) 9.

[5] See Roger Keesing, *Cultural Anthropology* (New York: Holt, 1981) 68–9.

intimidated into inaction.[6] My culture had helped me to survive in the midst of a hostile environment.[7]

Culture: A Case Study

In the summer of 1959, I and a fellow priest traveled from Rome to Forli to visit a New Zealand war cemetery. Forli and the surrounding area at this time were well known for their communist sympathies, so we did not expect a warm reception from the local people. We were not disappointed. Our Roman collars attracted scowls, even verbal abuse, particularly from taxi drivers, who refused to take us to the cemetery. Weary after a long journey from Rome in third-class rail coaches, we became increasingly angry at the unwillingness of the taxi drivers. We felt publicly humiliated and bullied by strangers. After two hours, as the sun was setting, one driver reluctantly agreed to take us. On arrival at the cemetery, I suddenly noticed on a gravestone my national New Zealand emblem, a fern leaf. Without thinking, my companion and I fell on our knees and embarrassingly broke into tears. In our feelings of confusion and chaos this symbol reminded us of all that was dear and familiar to us: memories of great heroes who had built a thriving democracy thousands of miles away, family, friends, and the hundreds of unknown countrymen buried around us who had fought and died far from their own land.

Our self-pity and sense of being lost in an unfamiliar world disappeared. If the heroes of my nation, including the deceased soldiers in the cemetery, had faced incredible difficulties, then so could we. With that we stood up determined to respond with courage, self-reliance, and resourcefulness to the demands of the strange and fear-evoking culture around us. Our self-esteem would not be crushed. We would not fall victim to the deadly chaos of self-pity. Refusing to be intimidated by the driver's obvious distaste for being with us, we took our time to pray in the

continued on next page

---

[6] See Pierre Bourdieu, *The Logic of Practice*, trans. Richard Nice (Stanford: Sanford University Press, 1990).

[7] I first used and partially commented on this experience in my book *Out of Chaos: The Refounding of Religious Congregations* (London: Geoffrey Chapman, 1988) 11–4.

cemetery, then told him in clear and confident voices that we needed a hotel and refused to be over-charged for the journey, his final attempt to bully us.

This simple event describes most of the important elements of our definition of culture: symbol, myth, ritual, and the inherent power in them which can legitimize violence. What follows is an explanation of these elements, aided by the lessons on the above incident.

Symbols and Power

Symbols are at the heart of all cultures. As anthropologist Clifford Geertz argues, cultures are webs of meaning or significance; they establish *symbolic* templates or blueprints that define the limits of behavior and guide it along predictable routes.[8] A *symbol*, for example, the fern leaf for a New Zealander, the White House for Americans, is any object that by its very dynamism or power makes one think about, imagine, get into contact with, or reach out to a deeper reality, through the dynamism of the symbol itself, and without additional explanations.[9]

A symbol is more than a sign. Signs only point to the object signified, but symbols by their very dynamism *re*-present the object. They carry meaning and values in themselves that permit them to articulate the signified rather than merely announce it.[10] The fern leaf did not point to New Zealand; it brought the nation alive in our imagination in a way that restored our sense of belonging.

There are three aspects to any symbol: the meaning, the emotive and the directive levels. The *meaning* aspect allows a symbol to make a statement about something, e.g., the fern leaf said to us "We are New Zealanders." A symbol has *emotive* power because it speaks primarily to the hearts or the imagination of people, giving rise to positive or negative feelings of power. We can never be neutral in the presence of symbols. A symbol *directs* us to do something as a result of its meaning and its emotional impact. Consider the taxi drivers in Forli—our Roman

---

[8] See Geertz, *The Interpretation of Cultures*, 216–8.

[9] I am grateful to Adolfo Nicolas, s.j., for this definition.

[10] For a fuller explanation see Gerald A. Arbuckle, "Communicating through Symbols," *Human Development*, vol. 8, no. 1 (1987) 7–12.

collars evoked in them the feelings of a strongly anticlerical culture, leading them to discriminate against us.

A symbol has also the capacity to absorb meanings around two semantic poles, one affective or emotional value, the other cognitive or moral. An interchange between the two poles occurs and in the interaction they strengthen and enhance each other. The social norms and values gain greater force through saturation with emotion, and the basic emotions are ennobled through contact with social values or norms. For example, the Pentagon building in Washington, D.C., symbolizes the moral commitment of the government to defend the nation's values. But the building, following the terrorist attack, now evokes strong feelings of shock, loss, and outrage that reinforce in Americans their support of the military's role to defend the nation's integrity. Because of their affective dimension, symbols have the power to grip the allegiance of people over a long period of time.

In this study "dominative" and "pivotal" symbols are particularly important. Dominative symbols are those that evoke in people undue fear of being intimidated. For example, just the presence of a bully or some reminder of him or her can cause fear in a victim and the feeling of being terrorized. Pivotal symbols contribute to the uniqueness of a culture, e.g., a flag, language.

Since symbols relate primarily to people's hearts, logical or rational attacks do not necessarily destroy them. It would have been quite useless to have argued with the taxi drivers at the Forli railway station that it was wrong for them to refuse to take us to the cemetery. They would not have been impressed with our protestations that we were not Italian priests, that we had not contributed by our behavior to the rift between the local population and the Church!

Myths: Narrative Symbols

Definition

Myths are value-impregnated beliefs or stories which bind people together at the deepest level of group life, and which they live by and for. Without myths people have no reason to be or act. Contrary to popular belief, myths are not fairy tales or fallacies. A myth is a story or tradition that claims to reveal in an imaginative or symbolic way a fundamental truth about the world and human life. This truth is regarded as authoritative by those who accept it.

Mythologies respond to four basic needs:[11]

- A *reason for existence*, that is, a need to find some satisfying reason for why things exist.

- A *coherent cosmology*, that is, an explanation of where we fit in a comprehensible and safe world.

- A *social organization*, that is, a framework which allows us to work together in some degree of harmony and thus avoid chaos.

- An *inspirational vision*, that is, an overall view that inculcates a sense of pride and belonging. For example, myths inspire people to acts of patriotism.

Myths are concerned about the meaning of human existence at the deepest possible level, about the problems of evil, the source of creation and order, the origins of different cultures. By mythically defining and structuring the world, the human person and group are able to grasp to some degree or other the regions beyond human control which influence well-being and destiny. Like sacred icons, myths are the medium of revelation handed down from the gods or heroes of the past,[12] so they are not to be lightly put aside or questioned. Like all symbols, myths can evoke deep emotional responses and a sense of mystery in those who accept them, simply because they develop out of the very depths of human experience of birth, life, death. No matter how hard we seek to deepen our grasp of the meaning of myths, they still remain somewhat ambiguous and mysterious, because they attempt to articulate what cannot be fully articulated.

Myths are symbols in narrative form. At the cemetery the fern leaf restored my feelings of belonging and it brought back to consciousness the founding story of my nation—the incredible navigation skills of the indigenous peoples centuries ago as they voyaged over thousands of miles of dangerous seas, and of my ancestors from Britain who developed an agricultural economy in the midst of a mountainous and remote countryside in the nineteenth century. Identification with these people gave me renewed vigor; as they and their successors had

---

[11] See Joseph Campbell, *The Masks of God* (4 vols.; New York: Viking Press, 1970).

[12] See Thomas Fawcett, *The Symbolic Language of Religion* (London: SCM Press, 1970) 101.

triumphed with limited resources, so could we New Zealanders in the hostile culture of Forli. The action of standing up and giving directions to the surprised taxi driver with revitalized determination, was the ritual expression of identification with the founding mythology.

In the mythologies of every group there will be founding myths that are the ultimate binding forces of identity and hope in the future. All other myths will be linked to these founding myths, e.g., the founding myth of the United States is that it is the new Israel, the new promised land where democracy will protect its citizens. A culture will continue only if the founding myths are able to be repeatedly retold. Oppressors will prohibit people retelling their myths and passing them on to their descendants because as long as this is done the oppressor can never succeed. Such was the case, for example, in Ireland under the British government. Every effort was made to destroy the Irish language and therefore Irish mythology and identity but without success.

Myths and History

Myths can contain or have solid foundations in historical reality. But the purposes of myth and history differ; myth is concerned not so much with a succession of events as with the moral significance of these happenings. A myth is a "religious" commentary on the beliefs and values of a culture. Thus, Abraham Lincoln can be viewed historically or mythologically. As seen from the historical perspective, he is depicted as fitting into a definite time period, influencing and being influenced by events around him. If, however, he is evaluated as a person who exemplifies the virtues of zeal for the rights of the individual, honesty, inventiveness in the face of difficulties, and hard work, then we are measuring him by the founding mythology of the nation.

Myths can be a mixture of remembering, forgetting, interpreting, and inventing historical happenings. For example, people in Serbia in their mythology may recall that Bosnian Muslims were Christians in former times, prior to the Ottoman conquest, but overlook or deny that the Bosnians' conversion was deeply serious. Jews may recall that they had a state in Palestine over two thousand years ago but forget or deny that their sovereignty was lost and that the country had become subsequently settled by other peoples. In the Apostolic Age (ca. 27–70 C.E.), ministry was considered a duty common to many, including laypeople, but following the Peace of Constantine (313 C.E.) ministry became restricted to clerics.[13] Whatever is remembered or reinterpreted in myths is impregnated with powerful meaning that deeply affects people's feelings about themselves and others. Myths become charters legitimizing for themselves a people's identity and actions.[14]

Myths and Power

Among the many types of myths three are particularly relevant here:

- A *public* myth is a set of stated ideals that people openly claim bind them together, e.g., the mission statement of an organization; in practice these ideals may have little or no cohesive force.

- An *operative* myth is what actually gives people their felt sense of identity; the operative myth can and often does differ dramatically from the public myth.

- A *residual* myth is one with little or no daily impact on a group's life, but which at times can become a powerful operative myth, as the following examples illustrate.

Example: Residual Myths and Violence

Slobodan Milosevic, the Serb leader, manipulated Serbian public opinion in his incendiary speech of 28 June 1989 when he invoked a residual myth of humiliation that had remained dormant for centuries: Yugoslavia belonged to Serbs, he argued, despite the fact that they had been defeated in Kosovo by Muslims on 28 June 1389, and revenge for six hundred years of subjugation had now to be sought in bloody warfare. A reminder of the same defeat had inspired a Serb in 1914 to assassinate Archduke Franz Ferdinand of Austria, so lighting the touchpaper for the First World War.[15]

continued on next page

---

[13] See David McLoughlin, "Authority as Service in Communion," *Governance and Authority in the Roman Catholic Church*, ed. Noel Timms and Kenneth Wilson (London: SPCK, 2000) 123–5.

[14] See Jack D. Eller, *From Culture to Ethnicity to Conflict* (Ann Arbor: University of Michigan Press, 1999).

[15] See Chris Hann, *Social Anthropology* (Abingdon, Tenn.: Teach Yourself, 2000) 141; "Nations and their Past," *The Economist* (21 December 1996) 73.

The Provisional IRA (Irish Republican Army) in Northern Ireland in January 1970 needed to bring the Catholic minority together through the power of an inspirational myth. They felt they could not look to the Irish Government in Dublin because they believed that it had abandoned the Catholic minority in the North to British rule. The IRA openly reclaimed the residual myth of Irish republicanism, a myth that had ceased, they believed, to be operative in the Irish Government's relationship with the British: "we take our inspiration and experience from the past."[16] It is the republican myth that has inspired so much violence on the part of the IRA in Northern Ireland and Britain for the last three decades.

Myths, Change, Memory, and Violence[17]

Myth Change

New myths are created and old ones are maintained, revised, or completely lost because of forces such as changing needs, new insights into history, and new ways of seeing things. This process of change is called *myth management* and it occurs in several ways, e.g., myth extension, substitution, drift, and revitalization.

1. Myth Substitution

The process of myth substitution can often lead to abuse in various forms, as the following examples illustrate.

Soviet Union

Marxist Soviet leaders sought to manipulate their people, often under the threat of violence, by inventing new myths to legitimate their power and supremacy. For example, massed formations of people—marching, parading, flag swinging, performing gymnastics—were common on major national festive occasions. The

continued on next page

[16] Quoted by Paul Arthur, "'Reading' Violence: Ireland," *The Legitimization of Violence*, ed. David E. Apter (London: Macmillan Press, 1997) 257.

[17] See Gerald A. Arbuckle, *Earthing the Gospel: An Inculturation Handbook for Pastoral Workers* (Maryknoll: Orbis Books, 1990) 36–44.

leaders aimed through these rituals to impose, even with violence, a myth of nationwide solidarity, that is, the integration of the individual and different ethnic groups into the collective. They ultimately failed because the Soviet Union broke apart into many different political and ethnic groups based on pre-Soviet mythologies.[18]

Ireland

A central point of Irish republican mythology has been that the Great Famine of 1847 happened because of evil Protestant politicians and merchants exporting corn to England while Catholics were left to starve. Research now shows this is an oversimplification of history; many members of the Irish middle class benefited financially from the starvation of their compatriots and some of the worst Poor Law administrators were not Protestant landlords, but Irish Catholics. From these facts a new myth is painfully emerging. It is difficult to put aside a historically flawed myth when it conveniently placed the blame on others.[19]

Catholic Church

It is common to hear it said that the Church is not a democracy, never has been, and never will be. Since it is assumed to be integral to the founding myth of the Church no argument is possible. In accordance with this myth, it is correct for Rome to appoint bishops without any consultation with local churches. Yet, this behavior ignores not only the values of participative and consultative leadership fundamental to Vatican II, but also the custom during a significant period of history. The choice of bishops by clergy and laity was customary until the twelfth century. Indeed, as late as the beginning of the twentieth century, fewer than half of the

continued on next page

---

[18] See Christel Lane, *The Rites of Rulers: Ritual in Industrial Society—The Soviet Case* (Cambridge: Cambridge University Press, 1981) 276.

[19] See Inga Clendinnen, *True Stories* (Sydney: ABC, 1999) 12–3; Cathal Poirteir, *The Great Irish Famine* (Dublin: Mercier, 1995) 64, 91.

world's bishops were chosen by the Pope.[20] The fact is that in the early New Testament times the Church was very much a decentralized network of communities. Over time, the Church's administrative structures began to mirror secular ones, e.g., those of the Roman emperors, Byzantine suzerains, feudal lords, the courts of medieval kings.[21] The present monarchical structure of the Church is thus an example of myth substitution. The founding myth emphasized hierarchical roots with at the same time strong emphasis on democratic principles (see chapter 3).

Islam

The religion of Islam developed in the seventh century C.E., and integral to its founding mythology is the doctrine of *jihad* (that is, waging holy war on behalf of Islam as a religious duty). Jihad is appealed to as a means to social and political justice. Throughout jihad's complicated history the moderate interpretation has been dominant throughout the centuries. For the reform of society it was assumed that violence could be used, but only as a last resort and with certain constraints, e.g., women and children, the old and the sick are to be spared. Since the 1970s, however, a process of myth substitution has developed. Osama bin Laden, for example, declared that perpetual war must exist between Islam and the West, especially the Americans who represent the greatest evil. It is legitimate, according to this view, to terrorize even noncombatants such as women and children with whatever type of force is considered most useful, including the use of suicide bombing. Most Islamist religious authorities have rejected this attempt at myth substitution.[22]

---

[20] See Leonard Swidler, "Democracy, Dissent, and Dialogue," *The Church in Anguish*, ed. Hans Küng and Leonard Swidler (San Francisco: Harper & Row, 1986) 310; *A Democratic Catholic Church: The Reconstruction of Roman Catholicism*, ed. Eugene C. Bianchi and Rosemary Radford Ruether (New York: Crossroad, 1992), passim.

[21] See George B. Wilson, "'The Church Isn't a Democracy'—Meaning?" *America* (22 September 1990) 158; Terence L. Nichols, *That All May Be One: Hierarchy and Participation in the Church* (Collegeville: The Liturgical Press, 1997) 95–170.

[22] See Abdullah Saeed, "Jihad and Violence: Changing Understandings of Jihad among Muslims," *Terrorism and Justice*, ed. Tony Coady and Michael O'Keefe

2. Myth Drift

Drift occurs when myths change, degenerate, or disappear without deliberate planning on the part of individuals or groups. In the creation mythology of the United States God, for example, or some extra-ordinary destiny, calls Americans to participate in a new exodus, a new journey from oppression to justice, to build a new Promised Land. Over time this call by God has been reinterpreted to condone atrocious political actions, e.g., slavery, oppression of non-Americans. "With God on our side we can do no wrong" is now the operative myth. In an operation code-named "Just Cause," American troops invaded Panama to kidnap the notorious drug-dealer, President Noriega. In the process between three and seven thousand people, mainly innocent civilians, were killed. Few Americans publicly objected to this drifted myth of their founding story being used to legitimize this violence.

3. Myth Revitalization

Myths can speak about how chaos became cosmos, or an orderly world. When a people or culture is threatened or experiences dis-integration (i.e., chaos), people feel the urge to rediscover the original creation myth(s) (today sometimes referred to as "roots"), and to relive the energizing creation experience. In reliving the myth, people hope to achieve identity, courage, and self-worth once more. This repeatedly happened to the Israelites. When they would admit to their feeling of lostness—their sinfulness, idolatry, or injustices—they would retell their creation story when Yahweh made them his chosen people in the desert (e.g., see Psalm 107). President George W. Bush, in his address to Congress following the terrorist attacks of 11 September 2001, used the chaos of the experience to reaffirm America's founding identity and mission: "And in our grief and anger, we have found our mission and our moment. Freedom and fear are at war. . . . Our nation, this generation, will lift the dark threat of violence from our people."

Myths: Reservoirs of Memory

Myths are the memory bank for people, as the above examples illus-trate. Because myths tell of past defeats and victories they are the poten-

---

(Melbourne: Melbourne University Press, 2002) 72–86, and Malise Ruthven, *Islam* (Oxford: Oxford University Press, 1997) 116–42.

tial source of violence. Myths recounting former defeats can arouse in people the desire to revenge the humiliation. The mythology of the Croats contains the memory of their oppression by Serbian communists, while Serb myths recall Croatian fascism, its links with Nazism, and their own sufferings in the Second World War. Little wonder that the recent war between Croatia and Serbia was so violent on both sides.

Mythologies that recount past successes can also stir up feelings of resentment and violence in the defeated. The annual Orange parades in Northern Ireland, recalling the defeat of the Catholics by William of Orange in 1691, hearten the participants but feed the feelings of anger and powerlessness of the Catholic minority. These mythologies build barriers down through the years between the defeated and the victors, making them forever suspicious of one another; any new actions, no matter how well intentioned, are judged with these in mind.[23]

Ritual: Control and Violence

Ritual: Definition

> Ritual, the third constituent element of culture, is the repeated symbolic behavior of people belonging to a particular culture. It is the external expression of myths and symbols. It is the capacity of rituals to transform people and their social environment that gives them their positive or negative power. A ritual may create a well-behaved school pupil or a brutal terrorist, a devoted employee or a dictator. Some rituals are particularly relevant here: "models for" and "models of" behavior.

The function of "models for" rituals is to impose, reaffirm, and strengthen value consensus or conformity to the status quo, as desired by leaders of a particular society. For example, Hitler, supported by his ritual experts, ruthlessly created and manipulated public rituals to express his distorted mythology of Germanic racial superiority. In the former Soviet Union the great civic rituals such as the May Day parades in Moscow's Red Square, aimed to reinforce the power of the Marxist leaders to dominate the people, the message being "dissenters will not be tolerated."

---

[23] See Jonathan Glover, *Humanity: A Moral History of the Twentieth Century* (London: Jonathan Cape, 1999) 146–7.

"Models of" rituals exist where there is already a strong value consensus in a culture; the consensus does not have to be imposed, but is reaffirmed or strengthened and expressed through rituals. For example, for Americans the flag is such a powerful symbol of national identity that its raising carries considerable ritual importance, especially in times of national tragedy, such as when it is draped on the coffins of soldiers killed in the line of duty. Following the terrorist assaults on the United States in 2001 the whole country was aflutter with flags, huge ones decorated the damaged Pentagon and sports stadiums, tiny flags were attached even to baby carriages. Their display was a ritual of defiance and reaffirmation of identity signifying that Americans would not be coerced into submission.[24]

Rituals, therefore, are the means by which we seek, establish, and preserve or celebrate order and unity for ourselves and for society. Rituals make the mythic values of a culture concrete and experiential; they act out these values in social relations. While rituals can have beneficial effects, they can be used to unjustly coerce people into conformity.

Rituals of Violence

Ritual can be a powerful way to degrade people. For example, when the hostages taken at the American embassy in Iran in 1979 were paraded through the streets of Teheran they symbolized the humiliation of the American nation. Rituals can also prompt violence. During the Catholic-Protestant tensions in France in the sixteenth century, Protestants were commonly so enraged by the music, dancing, and costumes of the Catholic rites that they would attack the celebrants. Such is also the case in Northern Ireland today.[25] The annual summer parades of the Protestant Orange Order through Catholic suburbs in Northern Ireland are ritual acts of symbolic warfare to Catholics reminding them that their minority status will continue to be enforced.[26]

[24] See *The Economist* (22 September 2001) 35.

[25] See David I. Kertzer, *Ritual, Politics and Power* (New Haven: Yale University Press, 1988) 130.

[26] See R. Scott Appleby, *The Ambivalence of the Sacred: Religion, Violence, and Reconciliation* (Lanham: Rowman and Littlefield, 2000) 173.

Ritual and "Rebounding Violence"

Anthropologist Maurice Bloch in his analysis of rites of passage focuses on the second of their three stages. In the first stage people turn aside from ordinary living and in the second stage they make contact with the founding mythology of the group, e.g., clan, tribe, nation. The mythology has transcendental power to revitalize them. (By "transcendental" he means that mythology is greater and more powerful than any individual; it is "god-like" in its ability to draw people beyond themselves.)

So energizing is this mythological power that when people move into the third and final stage of the ritual they are tempted to act violently towards people they blame for problems in their lives. Bloch calls this "rebounding violence." His thesis is important because it highlights the "greater-than-human" power of mythology, and its ability to incite people to violence. This is evident in Hitler's ability to arouse massive support through the mythology of anti-Semitism, or in Milosevic's skill in inspiring Serbs to ethnic cleansing on the basis of a mythology dating from the fourteenth century. Hitler portrayed the Jews as an "evil transcendental power," and for the Serbs, Muslims were "invaders" of centuries ago.[27]

Cultures: Roots of Violence

The processes in a culture which foster or allow people to be violent are to be found ultimately in its symbols, myths, and rituals. In the following section some processes are more precisely identified and summarized in a series of axioms which are further explained and applied in subsequent chapters.

Axiom 1: Groups see their culture as "clean" or "pure" and others as "dirty" or "impure," and therefore dangerous—to be avoided, changed, or eliminated.

Cultures through their symbols, myths, and rituals have an inbuilt tendency to create boundaries with powerful feelings like "us and them"

---

[27] See Maurice Bloch, *From Blessing to Violence* (Cambridge: Cambridge University Press, 1986) and Fiona Bowie, *The Anthropology of Religion* (Oxford: Blackwell, 2000) 180–1.

and in the form of "they" are not as good as "us"! The poet Rudyard Kipling describes ethnocentrism in this way: "All nice people like Us are We, and everyone else is They."[28] Anthropologist Mary Douglas explains this behavior by focusing on a people's understanding of "purity" and "pollution."[29] Every human society and organization subscribes, most often unconsciously, to rules of purity and pollution in some form or other. A culture is a purity system—that is, it tells people what is pure and clean, or evil and therefore dangerous or polluting. The fear of pollution defines and protects the boundaries of a group. In the time of Christ touching lepers or eating with tax collectors and sinners made one "polluted" because these people were considered unclean and without social identity.

Pollution, as opposed to purity, interferes with the acceptable equilibrium, destroys or confuses desirable boundaries, and evokes destructive forces or conditions. As Douglas writes: "In short, our pollution behavior is the reaction which condemns any object or idea likely to confuse or contradict cherished classifications."[30] The potential for violence is unlimited. Islamic fundamentalists regard Western civilization as a polluting force to be kept at a distance and/or destroyed (see chapter 8). Hitler considered that particular peoples—Jews, people with disabilities, and gypsies—endangered the purity of the Aryan race and had to be eliminated. In possibly the most horrible expression of this logic of pollution, he cleansed the fatherland by turning "dirty" Jews into "clean" soap.[31]

Case Study: Ethnocentrism in Action

My experience at Forli, though positive in many ways, had a negative side. I continued for a long time in my ethnocentric dislike of Italians in that part of the country. Ethnocentrism is a dynamic at work in every culture and subculture. In its mild

continued on next page

---

[28] Rudyard Kipling, "We and They," in *Debts and Credits* (London: Macmillan, 1926) 327–8.

[29] See Mary Douglas, *Purity and Danger: An Analysis of the Concepts of Pollution and Taboo* (London: Routledge and Kegan Paul, 1966).

[30] Ibid., 36.

[31] See Alan Dundes, "A Study of German National Character through Folklore," *Journal of Psychoanalytic Anthropology*, no. 4 (1981) 265–364.

forms, ethnocentrism is normal, reasonable, and serves a useful purpose. Cultural identity requires that people feel pride in their group's achievements, and believe that other cultures have something to learn from their group. Unchecked, this group pride can go over the brink into prejudice and discrimination against people who are different, and then it ceases to be a positive value. It leads to an assumption that "our way of life is *the* way to live" to be protected at all costs. "Members of other subcultures and cultures have nothing of value to offer us!" Pejorative and divisive expressions like "dirty," "unreasonable," "uppity," and "crude" are used of them; the often unspoken assumption is that the speaker is "clean," "reasonable," "polished." I left Forli with prejudices strongly reinforced about its citizens. It took me years to recognize this and the need for me to go deep into history to discover that there were good reasons for their anticlericalism.

Axiom 2: Since myths most often dominate thoughts, feelings, and behaviors in unconscious and seductive ways, it is easy for them to be manipulated in ways that exploit and oppress people.[32]

When we speak of the "culture unconscious,"[33] we simply mean that because symbols and myths are so much part of our inner selves, their existence and influence are apt to escape our conscious awareness. Social reality is so complex and ambiguous that insights that might threaten the security of our cultural myths are readily ignored or distorted in an effort to make it simple and unambiguous. At best we are frequently manipulated by our culture, and at worst exploited.

Walter Wink speaks of the "myth of redemptive violence" in Western society. By this he means it is taken for granted that violence is necessary for a society's continued existence. Violence is presented as something that solves conflicts. Even the threat alone of violence is able to stop aggressors; the more power one has the more effective the threat.[34] Violence is redemptive in the sense that it restores society to a state of peace and justice. Television, cartoons, comic strips all reinforce this

[32] See Robert M. MacIver, *The Web of Government*, 4.

[33] See Peter Berger and Thomas Luckmann, *The Social Construction of Reality* (Harmondsworth: Penguin, 1967).

[34] Walter Wink, *Engaging the Powers: Discernment and Resistance in a World of Domination* (Philadelphia: Fortress, 1992) 13.

belief.[35] The fact that the myth is pervasive, seductive, and unquestioned in Western cultures is an encouragement to bullying in intergroup relationships.

Hidden Potential to Dominate: Views

Psychologist Max Lerner, in a moving passage composed as Hitler was preparing for war, was extremely disturbed by the unquestioning support evoked by the Fuehrer, and prophetically warned that while the power of dictators derives from the "symbols that they manipulate, the symbols depend in turn upon the entire range of associations that they evoke. The power of these symbols is enormous. Men *[sic]* possess thoughts, but symbols possess men."[36] Michel Foucault claimed to find configurations of unnecessarily coercive power relations in such particular social situations as the professions, churches, police, and social welfare agencies. He associated the developing power of these organizations with the production of ever more specialized knowledge which, in turn, has been able to control more and more spheres of private life. The control is exercised by imposing classifications which result in developing progressively finer distinctions between acceptable and unacceptable ideas of what a normal individual is like. In categorizing people these professionals, e.g., doctors, religious ministers, unduly force individuals into "social boxes" and society uncritically accepts this domination.[37]

Axiom 3: Since people tend to fear the unknown, cultures have an in-built resistance to change, and this can lead to violence against people or groups who advocate change. Cultures serve as defenses against individual and group anxiety.

Sociologist Peter Berger explains this axiom. He calls culture *nomos* (i.e., "felt order" or "the predictable") because it protects us from what

[35] See ibid., 25; see also Peter Ackerman and Jack Duvall, *A Force More Powerful: A Century of Nonviolent Conflict* (New York: Palgrave, 2000) 457–9.

[36] Max Lerner, *The Ideas of the Ice Age* (New York: Viking, 1941) 235. See comments by David I. Kertzer, *Ritual, Politics and Power* (New Haven: Yale University Press, 1988) 5–6.

[37] See Michel Foucault, *Power, Knowledge: Selected Interviews and Other Writings*, ed. C. Gordon (Brighton: Harvester Press, 1980); Stewart R. Clegg, *Frameworks of Power* (London: Sage, 1989) 154–6.

we most fear—the awesome insecurities of *anomy* (chaos, or the radical breakdown of felt order). *Nomos*, Berger writes, is "an area of meaning carved out of a vast mass of meaninglessness, a small clearing of lucidity in a formless, dark, almost ominous jungle."[38] Culture, in this sense, is a human creation that protects us from the fear-evoking dark abyss of disorder. Little wonder, says Berger, that an innovator can become the object of violence such as scapegoating or marginalization: "the individual who strays seriously from the socially defined programs can be considered not only a fool or a knave but a madman."[39]

From experience we know that individually and corporately we so dread the pain of chaos that we often commonly resist it. We may readily say we are open to change, but in practice there are powerful inner forces that move us to resist it, even in matters of seemingly little importance. Think about how you feel when someone dares to sit in your favorite armchair in front of the television! Or how do you feel when the pots and pans are not in the "right" place? When cultural predictability is seriously threatened or disintegrates, we can experience the darkness of meaninglessness, a crushing taste of chaos, just as I did in Forli. The poet Dante Alighieri describes chaos as "a forest dark . . . So bitter is it, death is little more."[40] Change, even at times the faintest whisper of it, substitutes ambiguity and uncertainty for the known, and we yearn for the predictable. As Margaret Wheatley comments, "We are not comfortable with chaos, even in our thoughts, and we want to move out of confusion as quickly as possible."[41]

Cultures have been also defined as "defenses against anxieties," "containers of anxieties,"[42] even "psychic prisons,"[43] in an effort to describe their inner power to resist change and to bully would-be change agents into conformity. Shirley P. Lowry concludes her study of myths with this assertion: "Most mythic systems agree on this basic point:

---

[38] Peter Berger, *The Sacred Canopy: Elements of a Sociological Theory of Religion* (New York: Doubleday, 1969) 23.

[39] Ibid., 23.

[40] Dante Alighieri, *The Divine Comedy*, trans. Henry W. Longfellow (New York: Charles C. Bigelow, 1909) 15.

[41] Margaret Wheatley, *Leadership and the New Science* (San Francisco: Berrett-Koehler, 1994) 149.

[42] See Isabel Menzies Lyth, *The Dynamics of the Social: Selected Essays* (London: Free Association Books, 1989) viii.

[43] See Gareth Morgan, *Images of Organization* (Beverly Hills: Sage Publications, 1986) 199–231.

What promotes cosmic order, harmony, and life is good, and what promotes chaos, disintegration, and death is evil."[44]

Axiom 4: A mythology that tolerates or normalizes violence will legitimize people who act violently; these people have the qualities of a bully.

The more society endorses the use of physical and other forms of violence to attain socially approved ends such as crime control, sports entertainment, economic success, or international dominance, the greater the likelihood that this legitimization of force will be generalized to other areas of life where force is less socially approved, such as the school, family, relations between sexes, the workplace. For example:

- The entertainment media frequently exaggerates and even praises violence: children in the United States see 8,000 murders and 100,000 other acts of violence on television before they end elementary school.[45]

- The "male solution (fighting) permeates the media, and this may endorse this behavior for individual men and may promote it as the best way of solving social problems."[46]

- A nation that has adopted a mythology of economic rationalism sends the message to workplace managers that it is acceptable to bully employees provided this leads to economic success.

Example: Impact of Mythology on Violence

Criminologist Joan McCord proposes that mythological factors are making American cities more violent than those in other developed nations. The mythology of the American Revolution and the Civil War, with their violent overthrow of a colonial

continued on next page

---

[44] Shirley P. Lowry, *Familiar Mysteries: The Truth in Myth* (New York: Oxford University Press, 1982) 131.

[45] Quoted by Marvin L. Krier Mich, *Catholic Social Teaching and Movements* (Mystic, Conn.: Twenty-Third Publications, 2000) 236; see also Joel Federman, *National Television Violence Study* (Thousand Oakes: SAGE, 1998) 7.

[46] Michael O'Shaughnessy, *Media and Society* (Melbourne: Oxford University Press, 1999) 210; see also Helen L. Conway, *Domestic Violence and the Church* (Carlisle: Paternoster Press, 1998) 61–84; *Bullying and Peer Pressure*, ed. Kaye Healey (Sydney: Spinney Press, 1998) 10–1.

power and defeat of the South, lives on. Two researchers conclude that "the United States has had the bloodiest and most violent labor history of any industrial nation in the world."[47] Americans have often used unremitting violence in a cause considered to be a good one. The mythology of the nation also contains the belief that all are equal and can be materially successful. The poor in the inner cities bitterly recognize that discriminatory policies have blocked opportunities for success; there is a clash between the myth of democratic equality and the harsh reality that oppresses them. Some urban violence and destructive riots, therefore, may be due to "Resentment, rather than jealousy [and] displaced rage in response to unfair treatment."[48]

Bullies seek to force others to do what they want them to do and will try all kinds of intimidation or terrorization to achieve this. They aim to degrade and subjugate their victims to make them feel powerless and worthless. The behavior of the bully can range from the threat or use of physical violence to the use of abusive language and unilateral/negative power, passive aggression, public or private humiliation, persistent nitpicking. This form of violence is so widespread that it has been called "a hidden epidemic of intentional aggression."[49] It is estimated that in Western societies one-third to one-half of all stress-related illnesses are due to bullying at the workplace; in the United States businesses are losing an annual five to six billion dollars in decreased productivity alone, due to real or perceived abuse by employers. The personal consequences of bullying can be devastating; for example, feelings of despair, depression, memory loss, even post-traumatic stress disorder.[50]

[47] Philip Taft and Philip Ross, "American Labor Violence: Its Causes, Character, and Outcome," *The History of Violence in America*, ed. H. D. Graham and T. R. Gurr (New York: Bantam Books, 1970) 281.

[48] Joan McCord, "Placing American Urban Violence in Context," *Violence and Childhood in the Inner City*, ed. Joan McCord (Cambridge: Cambridge University Press, 1997) 102, 79.

[49] Peter Randall, quoted by Ruth Hadkin and Muriel O'Driscoll, *The Bullying Culture* (Oxford: Butterworth-Heinemann, 2000) 10.

[50] See David Kinchin, *Post-Traumatic Stress Disorder: The Invisible Injury* (London: Success Unlimited, 1998).

Bully: Psychoanalytical Description

In the Kleinian model bullying is a defense against unbearable anger and destructiveness due to a person's hatred of his or her own inner inadequacy. Bullies are inadequate people, fearful of losing face, overly sensitive to criticism, deeply lonely within themselves. According to Melanie Klein, bullies experience an inner rage over their personal inadequacy and project it on to some other object, in this case the victim. The victim chosen to contain the inner rage becomes the "bad object" to be shattered. She argued: "Original aggression is expelled as a danger and established elsewhere as something bad, and then the object invested with dangerousness becomes a target at which aggression arising subsequently can be discharged."[51] The "bad object," the victim, is then considered persecutorial and its destruction becomes permissible.

There are many forms of bullying: terrorism (see chapter 8); vertical (i.e., abuse of power by superiors); horizontal (i.e., abuse by peers); serial (i.e., one victim after another); ecclesiastical (see chapters 3 and 8); corporate (see chapter 5); cultural, and client (i.e., being abused by one's clients).

Case Study: Israelites as Client Bullies

Recall the reactions of the Israelites when confronted with the chaos of the desert. They leave Egypt with enthusiasm inspired by the leadership of Moses and the vision of the Promised Land, but they are suddenly overwhelmed by the fear-evoking starkness of the desert. They exemplify client bullying because they vigorously blame Moses for their troubles and want to return to Egypt; better the order of an oppression they know, than the chaos of uncertainty in the desert (Exod 14:11-12).

---

[51] Melanie Klein and Joan Riviere, *Love, Hate and Reparation* (New York: Norton, 1964) 13.

Axiom 5: Bullying is more likely to occur in hierarchical cultures than in cultures with a mythology of collaboration.

Power distance can be defined as the extent to which less powerful members of organizations accept that power is distributed unevenly. In hierarchical organizations, in which the power distance between superiors and members is considerable a small number of superiors often control the avenues of communication. Members who have complaints feel oppressed and cynical about ever being impartially listened to. They can feel demeaned, of little importance in the system, and there is nothing they can do about it. An example of power distance, with its unfortunate accompanying potential for intimidation, is the Curia of the Church. When the Congregation for the Doctrine of the Faith in the Church pursues suspected theological nonconformists, it simultaneously holds the positions of judge, prosecutor, and investigator. In addition, there is no presumption of innocence and secrecy surrounds all trials.[52]

In organizations in which interdependence is a pivotal symbol the power distance is minimal, power is shared, channels of communication are open, members feel they can communicate about misunderstandings or the misuse of power in an atmosphere of trust, and bullying is less likely to occur.[53]

Axiom 6: Cultures, like individuals, decline in vigor or undergo times of uncertainty or chaos during which they either collapse into destructive dysfunctionality or rediscover the creative energy of their mythology; this can lead to a positive or negative reintegration.

In cultural chaos people are left without familiar symbols, myths, and rituals. The only positive way out is for them to reenter the sacred time of their founding under inspiring leaders who can rearticulate the founding mythology in ways that relate to the changing world. The founding mythology again becomes generative, a process well described by Malinowski as "a narrative resurrection of a primeval reality."[54]

---

[52] See Paul Collins, *From Inquisition to Freedom* (Sydney: Simon and Schuster, 2001) 43.

[53] See Angela Ishmael, *Harassment, Bullying and Violence at Work* (London: Industrial Society, 1999) 131–5.

[54] Bronislaw Malinowski, *Magic, Science and Religion, and Other Essays* (Glencoe, Ill.: Free Press, 1948) 101.

For example, my companion and I in Forli were at first overwhelmed by the unfamiliar environment. We felt anger, blamed Italians for our lostness, and experienced a sense of panic. Everything changed for the better when we noticed the fern leaf on a gravestone and were able to re-own the founding event of our nation. A more profound example is the Great Depression for Americans, a time of widespread socio-economic chaos. President Franklin Delano Roosevelt used the experience to develop the New Deal to benefit the poor. To be true to the nation's founding myth, Roosevelt argued, the nation had to detach itself from excessive individualism and embrace a collaborative approach to solving problems of unemployment and poverty.

On the other hand, people can become so overwhelmed by chaos that they fall victim to the paralyzing influence of dysfunctional intimidating behavior such as scapegoating (see chapter 6), feuding (see chapter 2), and cynicism; or, they can turn to a political or organizational messiah to return them to an assumed golden age of the past that encourages dangerous nationalism, fundamentalism, and dictatorships to emerge, as was the case in Germany under Hitler, the Philippines under Marcos, Indonesia under Suharto, Chile under Pinochet. Dictators destroy the normal political systems of accountability, often suppress all dissent through violence, and build a system of civil and military patronage to maintain themselves in power, as happened with the dictators above.

Axiom 7: The process of "splitting" can encourage violence.

"Cultural splitting" is a common method of containing political, social, or economic chaos, but a method that is not life-giving. Splitting is "a cultural and psychodynamic process whereby individuals and groups, in an effort to cope with the doubts, anxieties and conflicting feelings caused by difficult work" [or cultural breakdown] "isolate different elements of experience, often to protect the perceived good from the bad," the clean from the unclean.[55] As noted earlier, when people feel threatened or inadequate they project their feelings and impulses onto others. This projection then forms a social defense, that is, a way of relating which protects them from cultural disintegration or loss of meaning. Melanie Klein discovered that the unconscious dynamic of splitting begins very early in life; in early infancy a child separates

---

[55] Gareth Morgan, *Images of Organization*, 206.

good and bad experiences of the same object (breast) or person (mother).[56]

Examples: Cultural Splitting and Violence

The contemporary resurgence of extreme nationalism in Western democracies, with its anti-immigrant dynamic, is an example of splitting. People feel threatened by rapid social and economic changes generated by globalization. They want to feel good again. The more immigrants are marked as "bad," the more the locals feel good. Likewise, "ethnic cleansing" in the former Yugoslavia, the "dirty war" that occurred in Argentina to "cleanse" the fatherland of subversion,[57] and the genocide in Rwanda where prior to the killings, Tutsi women were condemned by Hutus as oversexed seductresses. Not surprisingly, they were subjected to widespread rape and considerable sexual humiliation during the conflicts.[58]

Understanding the inner structuring of myths also helps to clarify the process of cultural splitting and violence. Myths often contain opposite meanings.[59] However, founding myths do not spell out how the opposites are to be balanced in reality and so there is a built-in ambiguity or vagueness in all founding mythology that inevitably leads to tensions. Political factions can form around each pole, one faction claiming that it has the correct understanding of the mythology and demanding respect for its position; the faction around the other pole can do the same. This ideological polarization can call forth bitterness, even violence at times. The creation myth in Genesis contains the polar opposites of male and female, with the female perceived as of secondary importance. This unequal relationship has caused untold suffering to

[56] See Klein and Riviere, *Love, Hate and Reparation*, 58.

[57] See Marguerite Feitlowitz, *A Lexicon of Terror: Argentina and the Legacies of Torture* (New York: Oxford University Press, 1998).

[58] See Marcelo M. Suarez-Orozco and Antonius C. Robben, "Interdisciplinary Perspectives on Violence and Trauma," *Cultures Under Siege: Collective Violence and Trauma*, ed. Antonius C. Robben and Marcelo M. Suarez-Orozco (Cambridge: Cambridge University Press, 2000) 30.

[59] See Claude Lévi-Strauss and his notion of "Pairing" in Edmund Leach, *Claude Lévi-Strauss* (London: Fontana, 1970) 36–53.

women down through the centuries. The founding myth of the United States contains several sets of polar opposites; for example, the dignity of the individual and his or her freedom, and on the other pole the rights of the community over the individuals. The latter pole in the tension is neglected so that the individual has an unqualified right to own guns despite the violent consequences for the community.

Axiom 8: If a mythology indiscriminately expects all to achieve success, and legitimate means to realize this are inadequate, people are encouraged to resort to violence to achieve results.

This is a restatement of Robert Merton's thesis.[60] Merton assumed that in America there is an overriding cultural goal of material achievement. At the same time since there is an unequal availability of lawful means for people to attain this goal, many are tempted to resort to violence because they lack the resources to compete legitimately.

Axiom 9: Every culture consists of subcultures all of which share to varying degrees common myths, symbols, and rituals, while at the same time having their own distinctive qualities. Relationships between subcultures may range from mutual respect to distrust, suspicion, fear, extreme hostility, rejection, and oppression.

Each subculture will have prejudicial stereotypes of other subcultures which help maintain a sense of difference and identity and generate feelings of superiority or inferiority, which may lead to violence. Before the civil rights movement in the United States the popular stereotypes among many Anglo-Americans of blacks were that they were lazy and not to be trusted. Such negative images fostered violence towards blacks. Describing the stereotypes of Protestants and Catholics in Northern Ireland Ruth Edwards writes: "To the most bigoted Protestants, Catholics are dirty and untidy; to bigoted Catholics, Protestants are obsessively house-proud and fail to understand that life is for living."[61] Stereotypes like these reinforce the divisions between these two groups and contribute to the intergroup violence.

[60] See Robert Merton, "Social Structure and Anomie," *American Sociological Review*, vol. 3, no. 6 (1938) 672–82. For a recent adaptation of Merton's thesis see S. F. Messner and R. Rosenfeld, *Crime and the American Dream* (Belmont: Wadsworth, 1994).

[61] Ruth Dudley Edwards, *The Faithful Tribe: An Intimate Portrait of the Loyal Institutions* (London: HarperCollins, 2000) 98.

A significant source of identity for some subcultures or minority groups can be a common experience of oppression by the dominant subculture(s); their resulting anger is exacerbated by the fact that they lack the social, economic, or political power to interact with equality with those who dominate. Such is the history of the Catholic minority in Northern Ireland or poor minority subcultures in the United States. On the other hand, subcultures may have similar power in a society, but maintain separate identities through periodical rituals of violence. For example, when British football fans fight against the followers of another nation's team to defend their territory or their favorite team they are also reinforcing their group solidarity and identity.[62]

Myth-Based Models of Culture

Models of Cultures

As explained in the introduction, a model aims to illuminate complex social reality by highlighting emphases and downplaying details or nuances. Nuanced explanations or details are omitted to allow us to grasp a little more clearly what is in fact a highly complex situation. Any particular culture is then compared with the model to see to what extent it resembles it or not. In the application of models, five cautionary comments are necessary:

- In a particular society it is possible for all the models to be observable at the same time, with one model more influential than others.

- When a particular behavior, e.g., scapegoating, is defined as belonging to one model it may still also be operative in other models but less dominant.

- Models are not necessarily historically sequential, that is, it is not inevitable that a premodern culture predates a modern culture. The types can coexist.

- Within a short space of time a person may draw on one model and then on another, depending on the situation. For example, a person may in business matters be postmodern, but in the practice of religion premodern. This shifting is termed "situational identity," that

[62] See Nigel and Joanna Overing, *Social and Cultural Anthropology* (London: Routledge, 2000) 381–2.

is, a person's or a group's behavior depends on the particular context in which they find themselves (see figure 1.1).

• Because a model is a simplification of reality, it must not be forgotten that in practice systems of social relationships function in complex and subtle ways, and free choice has considerable play.[63]

Figure 1.1 Situational Identity

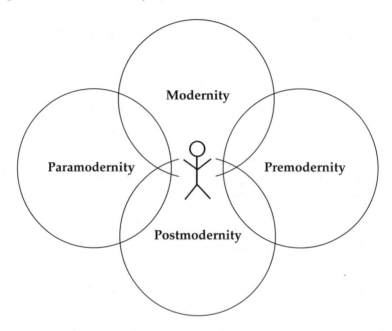

Myth-Based Models

Four models of culture are developed in this book, each having a unique mythology and potential for violence, except the last. The four culture models to be explained in the following pages are: "premodern," "modern," "postmodern," and "paramodern." They are summarized in table 1.1.

---

[63] See James L. Peacock, *The Anthropological Lens* (Cambridge: Cambridge University Press, 1986) 38.

Table 1.1 Culture models

	Premodern	Modern	Postmodern	Paramodern
Founding Myth:	Ancestors Tradition	Progress Human perfectibility Materialism	Progress questioned chaos	Humankind and universe: Interdependent
Pivotal Symbols:	Group Tradition Fate	Individual Progress Orderly world Rationality Western superiority	Narcissism Cynicism Despair Chaos Authority Globalization	Interdependence Collaboration Nonviolence Otherness Reconciliation Systems Hope
Culture Images:	Organic whole: humankind & universe	Mechanistic Impersonal	Violence	Organic whole: humankind & universe
Individual Identity Source:	Group	Autonomous self	Self: fiction	Relationships freely chosen
Language:	Concrete: imagination story-telling	Rational: abstract concise	Feelings: intellect distrusted	Intuition and reason
Cosmology:	Sacred & profane are one: life subject to fate/magic	Sacred & profane are separate	Real world unknowable	Life: interconnected processes
		Orderly knowable controllable universe	Order questioned	Patterns in chaos
	Humankind & environment interdependent	Environment separate from and subject to humankind	Environment to be used at will	Humankind & environment: interdependent
	Sin: social	Sin: individual guilt	Sin: failure to achieve	Sin: social and ecological
Social Priority:	Group Order Kinship	Individual Sovereign nation states Capitalism	No consensus Globalization Neocapitalism Ethnic groups	Interdependence Collaboration Multiculturalism Internationalism People power

Social Control:	Order over justice Informal sanctions: honor, shame, gossip	Justice over order Formal sanctions Informal sanctions: envy, jealousy, scapegoating	Struggle for rights Fear of violence	Consensus on values Dialogue Arbitration Reconciliation
Economic Structures:	Subsistence: personalized small trading	Capitalism: extreme or modified Bureaucratic: specialization and impersonal rules	Extreme capitalism: economic rationalism	Equality of opportunity Social justice
Minorities:	Tribal societies: oppressive	Oppressed: survival of fittest Assimilationist	Struggle for minority rights	Multiculturalism
Gender emphasis:	Male dominant	Male domination reinforced	Male domination questioned	Equality
Education:	Experience based	Institutional Rational Abstract	Institutional questioned	Experience based
Theology:	God-centered secrets of universe belong to God Salvation: obey commandments	Universe: coherent intelligible, law-abiding system God's existence knowable through reason God: transcendent	Reason not able to know God: faith alone Scripture centered Reason downplayed Incarnational theology	Particular theologies: liberation, creation, feminine Breakdown of patriarchal theology
Church:	Hierarchical Patriarchal	Rejection of Enlightenment Ghetto Patriarchal Hierarchical Power at Center	People of God Restorationist	Pilgrim People of God Small faith communities Participatory Collaborative Gender equality

Significant Events:		Renaissance Science Reformation Englightenment Social Darwinism	Holocaust Hiroshima Vietnam War Expressive Revolution Vatican II Globalization	Deconstruct -ionism New sciences Nonviolent movements
Significant People:	Aristotle Aquinas	Descartes Newton Bacon Locke Hume Darwin Marx Nietzsche Hitler Stalin Ford	Nietzsche Freud Sartre Warhol Marcuse Greer Schussler Reagan Thatcher	Gandhi Chardin Derrida Foucault Cory Aquino Martin L. King John Paul II Radford Ruether Mandela

Summary

- The constituent elements of a culture are symbols, myths, and rituals. Myths, especially founding myths, tell us that we are a unique group in the world, with a particular destiny. It is through myths that we are raised above the ordinary things of life; they give us powerful visions of what can be and the energy to do what must be done to realize them.

- Little wonder that people are prepared to act violently against those who dare to question or suppress their myths. This helps to explain the brutal break-up and interethnic violence of the former Yugoslavia and the long-standing internal disorder in Northern Ireland. Nor is it surprising if people are confused and tempted to violence because their myths disintegrate or cease to be operative in their lives. One significant cause of the current protests against globalization is that the latter is threatening the identities of traditional nation-states causing people to feel lost and angry (see chapter 8). Individuals and institutions exercise power in violent ways when the mythologies of their cultures legitimize them to do so. Hence, we speak of "violent cultures."

- Ritual is the stylized or repetitive symbolic use of bodily movement and gesture within a social context to express and articulate meaning. The meaning of a ritual comes from a people's myths; that is, ritual is the external expression of myths. An act of violence is itself a ritual expressing in outward ways a violator's commitment to a particular myth-based vision of what reality should be. For example, the terrorist attack on the World Trade Center was a ritualized action motivated by the violators' myth-based hatred of America's (and the West in general) own mythological system.

- The following eight chapters examine three culture models and the potential of their unique mythologies to facilitate and legitimize violent behavior.

Discussion Questions

1. What are the key symbols in your culture? Do they clash with Gospel values?

2. Reflect on Psalm 107. What does it tell you about the symbols and myths of the Israelites?

3. What are the operative myths in your workplace culture? Do they respect or oppress human dignity? If they oppress people, what can you do about it?

4. What symbols in your Church encourage you to pray to God?

Chapter 2

Premodernity and Violence

> Mythologies . . . provide systems of interpreting individual experience within a universal perspective, which may include the intervention of suprahuman entities as well as aspects of the natural and cultural orders. (William G. Doty[1])

This chapter explains:

- the mythology of premodern culture;

- loyalty to family and ancestors, conformity to sacred tradition, sensitivity to the power of spirits;

- the nature and power of the extended family and kinship ideology;

- the potential abuse of kinship ideology;

- the nature of "fictive" kinship systems, e.g., Mafia, patronage and crony systems, and gangs, and their potential to encourage violence.

The aim of this chapter is twofold: to describe the mythology of the premodern culture model and how it generates and legitimizes violence. Chapter 3 looks at the Church as a case study of a premodern culture. In chapter 4 shame, honor, and humor in premodern cultures are examined in view of their relationship to violence. Examples from a

---

[1] William G. Doty, *Mythography: The Study of Myths and Rituals* (Tuscaloosa, Ala.: University of Alabama Press, 1986) 11.

wide variety of societies and times are given in these chapters to illustrate that qualities of the premodern culture are not confined to any
particular period of history.

By way of introductory summary: in this type of culture the founding myths exalt group harmony, cohesiveness, togetherness, interdependence, stability, and the sacredness of tradition; the culture is a
gift of the gods/ancestors so it must not be questioned or significantly
changed. The fear of being mocked, gossiped about, shamed, and punished by spirits if one goes against tradition informally enforces conformity to the group's norms. To be expelled from the group (as Cain
found after murdering Abel [Gen 4:10, 12-13]) is a most severe form of
punishment, because the individual loses a sense of identity and rights.
Respect for patriarchal values is also a strong force in maintaining the
status quo. To avoid shame and maintain a sense of male honor,
women must be kept in an inferior status. Key points of this summary
will now be further explained.

The Sacredness of Tradition and Violence

The word "sacred" is used broadly here to mean that which must be
protected against defilement or violation. A wide variety of practices,
places, customs, and ideas may acquire a sacred, inviolable character.
In this model, a people's most important duty is to respect tradition
or the status quo. What the ancestors have given cannot be changed
or questioned. Among the Kwaio people in the Solomon Islands, the
ancestors have immediacy as members of one's group and are participants in daily life. *E abu* ("it's taboo") is one of the commonest sayings
heard from adults. It means that the ancestors have declared that there
must be no change to the Kwaio way of doing things. Otherwise, the
ancestors will punish the transgressors.[2]

Examples: Western Societies

In Western societies, although few things and places are sacred
by contrast with other parts of the world, in the United States

continued on next page

---

[2] See Roger M. Kessing, *Kwaio Religion: The Living and the Dead in a Solomon Island
Society* (New York: Columbia University Press, 1982) 30–1.

pivotal symbols in the mythology evoke a sense of reverence, e.g., the White House, Congress buildings. On the other hand, people can exploit the awe that the sacred evokes. President Richard Nixon sought to stop investigations into his involvement in the Watergate scandal by frequently complaining that they would undermine the sacredness of the presidential office. Government and Church officials can use the same technique to intimidate people into submission, for example, by the manner in which they speak, write, or use the trappings of power.

Rites of Rebellion and Reversal: Managed Violence

Violence may serve at times to maintain the sacredness of the social order. Anthropologist Max Gluckman describes rites of reversal, in which men and women exchange clothes and commoners show disrespect to chiefs, as examples of stylized reaffirmation of the order of things. Rituals of rebellion and license function as a mechanism of psychological/cultural catharsis because they discharge real social tensions connected with rigid hierarchical relations and, as a symbolic protest, they reduce the possibility of real violence destroying the status quo.[3]

Political cartoonists in Western societies also fulfill a function of expressing hostility within the status quo. Anger, ridicule, and opposition can be released without endangering the system. Parliamentary oppositions likewise are not out to destroy the democratic processes, despite at times the viciousness of their verbal abuse thrown at the government benches. There are rules to avoid excessive abuse and their breaking constitutes an act of violence.

Rites of Feuding: Channeling Violence

Feuding is not uncommon in societies of this culture type. A feud can be defined as relations of mutual animosity among intimate groups in which a resort to limited physical and verbal violence is anticipated on both sides.[4] Feuding is thus a way of channeling physical or verbal violence through ritual so that an uneasy peace is maintained between

[3] See Max Gluckman, *Custom and Conflict in Africa* (Oxford: Basil Blackwell, 1956) 109–36.

[4] See Jacob Black-Michard, *Feuding Societies* (Oxford: Basil Blackwell, 1975).

hostile groups. In certain Eskimo societies there is a *nith*-song contest which permits both sides to air their grievances in an open arena, but only by way of song and dance. After both sides have abused each other in melody and movement and collapsed into exhaustion, one side will emerge with more public acclaim than the other, but both have had the chance to give vent to their tensions within safe limits.[5] The relationship that prevailed between the former Soviet Union and the United States or between contemporary mainline China and the United States could also be classed as feuding.

Kinship and the Extended Family: Potential for Abuse

Kinship terminology consists of terms which designate social relationships that mandate rights and obligations. "Biological relationships," writes anthropologist Robert Lowie, "merely serve as a starting point for the development of sociological conceptions of kinship."[6] For example, in some cultures all people at the level of one's biological parents or grandparents are called "mother," "father," "grandmother," and "grandfather" respectively, even if there is little or no biological relationship. All "grandparents" must relate to "grandchildren" as "grandparents" should and vice versa.[7] The identity of an individual in such cultures is primarily obtained from his or her membership of a kinship system, not from work.

Two qualities are essential if a kinship group is to remain intact: loyalty to fellow members and a willingness to share one's goods and services with members of one's kinship group. The latter quality is governed by norms of reciprocity particular to each group. Reciprocity is that principle of behavior wherein every service received, solicited or not, demands a return, the nature and proportion of the return determined by the relative statuses of the parties involved and the kind of exchange at issue.[8]

---

[5] See Simon Roberts, *Order and Dispute* (Harmondsworth: Pelican, 1979) 59–60.

[6] Robert H. Lowie, *Social Organization* (New York: Holt, Rinehart and Winston, 1948) 57.

[7] See Rodney Needham, *Rethinking Kinship and Marriage* (London: Tavistock, 1971) 184.

[8] See Mary R. Hollnsteiner, "Reciprocity as a Filipino Value," *Society, Culture and the Filipino*, ed. Mary R. Hollnsteiner (Manila: Ateneo de Manila University Press, 1979) 38.

Example: Fiji

In Fiji's kinship system a *kerekere* is a request for something accompanied by an implicit obligation on the part of the requestor to reciprocate should the potential giver desire at some point to *kerekere* in return. *Kerekere* can be used repeatedly to cause a movement of goods from the better-off to those who are *leqa*, "in need." At the same time, the ritual of *kerekere* socially elevates the giver over the receiver, so that repeated giving can bring a person general social prestige.[9]

Robert Winthrop's definition of the family is sufficiently broad to cover types of families in most cultures: "a core group of closely related, co-operating kin, encompassing two or more generations."[10] The extended family system and ideology are at the heart of premodern cultures. This type is a combination of several nuclear families, with an older couple maintaining a residence in which several other generations related by blood, marriage, or adoption may live.

In Asia, as in most parts of Africa and the South Pacific, the ideology of the extended family commonly reigns supreme. One could well describe the Philippines as "an anarchy of families" and the same description could be made of almost any Asian or African nation—what best serves my family is the moral measure of most things. Few family members would dare to go against this unwritten norm.

The extended family system is in contrast to two other types, namely, the *nuclear* family and the *detached* nuclear family. The nuclear family is sometimes referred to as the "immediate," "primary," "simple" family, and is generally considered to be universal in all societies, although in many cultures various significant additions are made to it. This type of family is two-generational, that is, it consists of father/mother and children. In the *detached* nuclear family the nuclear family is not connected by obligation to any other kin groups outside itself, the obligations of members to one another are often legally short-lived or fragile, e.g., parents are not responsible for their children beyond a certain age,

[9] See Marshall D. Sahlins, *Moala: Culture and Nature on a Fijian Island* (Ann Arbor: University of Michigan Press, 1962) 145–6.
[10] Robert H. Winthrop, *Dictionary of Concepts in Cultural Anthropology* (New York: Greenwood Press, 1991) 114.

the bond between husband and wife is increasingly easy to legally break through divorce.

Potential for Exploitation

Where extended kinship obligations conflict with the demands of a modern economy and loyalty to a wider society, the potential for abusing individuals is obvious. The following case studies further illustrate this dynamic.

Examples: New Zealand

Anthropologist Joan Metge notes that Maori kinsfolk in New Zealand are in danger of abusing traditional loyalties and obligations to share goods with relatives. In the city particularly it is easy for the less scrupulous "to trade on the dutiful feelings of kin, staying indefinitely in their homes, and demanding assistance they have neither means nor intention of repaying."[11] It is difficult to recruit Maoris for the police force simply because they would feel obliged not to arrest members of their extended family.[12]

Fiji Islands

In the 1960s, while researching the development of Credit Unions (i.e., small, self-run savings and loans societies) in Fijian villages, I found frequent cases of individuals who felt bullied by chiefs and extended family members into giving them money even though the laws of Credit Unions forbade it. They felt abused and intimidated by such demands, but felt powerless to stop giving lest they be ostracized by their relatives.[13] To give evidence of thrift or miserliness is to sin against tradition. A government report condemned the practice with little success: "An

continued on next page

---

[11] Joan Metge, *The Maoris of New Zealand* (London: Routledge and Kegan Paul, 1976) 126.

[12] Ibid., 125.

[13] See also Ray F. Watters, *Koro: Economic Development and Social Change in Fiji* (Oxford: Clarendon Press, 1969) 259–62.

> energetic and progressive man can be completely ruined by his predatory relatives."[14]

In brief, an extended family system is traditionally a source of identity and support for its members, but it may also be a cause of conflict for people trying to adjust to contemporary economic life.

Jesus Christ Critiques Extended Kinship Mythology

The extended family was for the Jewish people at the time of Christ the foundation of society, so, when Jesus openly and strongly criticized it, his listeners would have been deeply offended. Yet he insisted that justice, compassion, mercy, must be shown not just to family members but to all peoples, no matter what culture they belonged to (Luke 10:29-37).

On one occasion his relatives, including with his mother, "were standing outside and were anxious to have a word with him" (Matt 12:46) and they sent a messenger to tell him this. By Jewish custom he should have immediately stopped his preaching, and obeyed, leaving the crowds behind, but he used the incident to explain that the ultimate mark of family loyalty is one's commitment to justice and love, and these virtues must extend beyond family demands (Matt 12:47-50). Whoever is in need is a family member, and God is the Father of all (Matt 6:9-15; 19:29; Luke 14:26). The family of Jesus is those who do his father's will (Matt 12:50; Luke 2:48-9).[15]

Patriarchy: Subjugation of Women

The term *patriarchal* is commonly used of societies in which power lies without question with men. It has been defined as any system in

[14] *The Burns Commission Report*, Fiji Council Paper, no. 1 (1960) par. 66; see Gerald A. Arbuckle, "Economic and Social Development in the Fiji Islands through Credit Unions," *Credit Unions in the South Pacific*, ed. Neil Runcie (London: University of London Press, 1969) 90–108.

[15] See Bruce J. Malina and Richard L. Rohrbaugh, *Social-Science Commentary on the Synoptic Gospels* (Minneapolis: Fortress Press, 1992) 99–101.

which men achieve and maintain social, cultural, and economic dominance over females and younger males.[16] Differences of power, privilege, and prestige entrench and continue patriarchy in cultures and helps to explain ongoing violence against women.

Anthropologists Edwin Ardener and Sherry Ortner argue that in premodern cultures pregnancy and birth are processes that appear dark, mysterious, and dangerous, and yet are envied by men. Men are able to arrange or exchange legal rights over women's offspring, but the ability to create life is beyond them. Because men lack this power, they assign women to the wild world of nature, in contrast to the men's world of control and order. Women become, therefore, in a sense outside the order of the good world of the culture; they are symbolically marginal or liminal, individuals restricted to only the reproduction of life.[17]

View: Patriarchy—Oldest Form of Domination

Sexual oppression, springing from deep anti-female prejudice, may not only be the oldest form of human domination, but it is possibly also, says Rosemary Radford Ruether, the most entrenched type of prejudice/discrimination: "the domination of women is the most fundamental form of domination in society, and all other forms of domination, whether of race, class, or ethnic group draw upon the fantasies of sexual domination."[18] Male dominance is achieved through educational processes, e.g., boys are taught to be strong, uncommunicative, competitive, and in control, but girls are raised to be compliant, other-oriented, and not to express their anger directly.[19]

---

[16] *Dictionary of Sociology*, eds. David Jary and Julia Jary (Glasgow: HarperCollins, 1991) 457.

[17] See Edwin Ardener, *The Voice of Prophecy* (Oxford: Basil Blackwell, 1989) 72–85 and "Belief and the Problem of Women," *The Interpretation of Ritual*, ed. Jean Fontaine (Cambridge: Cambridge University Press, 1972) passim; see also Fiona Bowie, *The Anthropology of Religion* (Oxford: Blackwell, 2000) 182–3; Sherry Ortner, "Is Female to Male As Nature Is to Culture?" *Women, Culture and Society*, ed. Michelle Rosaldo and Louise Lamphere (Stanford: Stanford University Press, 1974) 67–88; Henrietta L. Moore, *Feminism and Anthropology* (Oxford: Polity, 1988).

[18] Rosemary R. Ruether, "Women's Liberation in Historical and Theological Perspective," *Soundings*, vol. 53 (1970) 363.

[19] See David A. Wolfe and others, "Interrupting the Cycle of Violence," *Child Abuse*, ed. David A. Wolfe and others (London: Sage, 1997) 106.

Male Initiation: Rites of Violence

Education to instill male superiority is clearly emphasized in pre-modern cultures. Male initiation rites, particularly in parts of Africa and the South Pacific, include an important stage of separation from the mother and women in general. Often this separation is marked symbolically by dramatic and physically hurtful actions: the message is that men cannot be true men until they have learned to stand together and suffer physical pain without any show of fear. The violence against the initiates and the fear[20] that the ritual evokes in them, aim to test them and to instruct them that they are to be stronger than women and keep a distance from them to avoid being polluted, and that they are their superiors. Integral to these initiation rites is the insistence that true men must uphold the traditions of the tribe or clan, including male dominance.[21]

Mamphela Ramphele in her study of contemporary urban African children in a township in Cape Town discovered that similar definition of "manhood" still runs through all stages of the development of boys' identity. The boy is still repeatedly told that as a man he is to be a fighter, warrior, protector, hero, provider, and initiator, reinforced at every stage by particular strategies. Those willing and able to succeed in showing their "manhood," be it in gang warfare or courtship and capture of the trophy called woman, are celebrated. The weak are seen as "mere women."[22]

Western Experience

Until well into the nineteenth century, notes Karen Cerulo, "violence provided American husbands and fathers with a legitimate means for maintaining control over their domiciles. The 'rule of thumb,' based on English common law, allowed husbands to physically control or

---

[20] See Harvey Whitehouse, "Rites of Terror: Emotion, Metaphor and Memory in Melanesian Initiation Cults," *Journal of the Royal Anthropological Institute*, vol. 2, no. 4 (1996) 703–15.

[21] See Kenneth E. Read, "Nama Cult of the Central Highlands," *Oceania* 23, 11; Harvey Whitehouse, "Rites of Terror: Emotion, Metaphor and Memory in Melanesian Initiation Cults," *Journal of the Royal Anthropological Institute*, vol. 2, no. 4 (1996) 703–15.

[22] Mamphela Ramphele, "Teach Me How to Be a Man," *Violence and Subjectivity*, ed. Veena Das and others (Berkeley: University of California Press, 2000) 102–19.

punish their wives within 'reasonable limits.'"[23] While legal support for violence against women may have ended in the West, premodern views about masculinity are maintained, for example, through mass media which encourages youth to be violent, coercive, and sexist in relationships.

Australia: Sport as a Male Initiation Rite

In Australia the mass media constantly reiterates the message of gender domination through their coverage of sporting events. Women's sport occupies only 8 percent of the total space devoted to reporting sports' results. Participation by boys in sport has become a kind of initiation ritual into manhood. They must be tough, show no pain, bond with one another. Coaches are known to berate unsuccessful teams as "playing like a pack of girls." Betsy Wearing concludes: "Because women are deemed to be inferior at sport, by inference they are less capable in other areas of life."[24]

When "masculinity" is portrayed as synonymous with physical strength and power to dominate women, for a man to be called "effeminate" is an insult of considerable proportions.[25] In most sports men are associated with physical power and contact, but when they enter graceful activities like figure skating, the pejorative label "feminine" is common. Hence, these sports are considered of less importance, not "manly enough."[26]

Anthropologist John M. Coggeshall studied sexual relations among male inmates of an American prison. He writes that prison provides, "a social microcosm of the consequences of gender inequality in American culture. . . . By a complicated process, certain inmates are

[23] Karen A. Cerulo, *Deciphering Violence: The Cognitive Structure of Right and Wrong* (London: Routledge, 1998) 15–6.

[24] See Betsy Wearing, *Gender: The Pain and Pleasure of Difference* (Melbourne: Longman, 1996) 87.

[25] See Roland Bleiker, *Popular Dissent, Human Agency and Global Politics* (Cambridge: Cambridge University Press, 2000) 151–2.

[26] See Kendall Blanchard and Alyce Cheska, *The Anthropology of Sport* (South Hadley: Bergin & Garvey, 1985) 243.

redefined as women . . . and this allows males engaging in homoerotic behavior to retain a heterosexual identity, and it also justifies the brutalization of these inmates who have been redefined as females."[27] Exploiters gain power and self-esteem by subjugating fellow prisoners they class as women. In effect, prison culture offers a caricature of patterns that are easily identifiable in the wider society.

Case Study: Jesus Confronts Culture-Based Sexism

At the time of Christ women were second-class Jews, excluded from the worship and teaching of God, with status scarcely above the slaves. Therefore, the actions of Jesus toward women were revolutionary. He expressed concern for their welfare, but in ways that were not condescending or prejudiced; he healed sick women, and forgave sinners among them. He ignored the requirements of ritual impurity (Mark 5:25-34, 35-43). He gave them equal rank with men as daughters of Abraham (Luke 13:10-17) and the highest respect as persons (Matt 5:28). Women were members of his intimate circle of friends (Luke 8:1-3). He appeared to Mary Magdalene before he revealed himself to his apostles, and she is charged to carry the news of the resurrection to the disciples (John 20:11-18).[28]

Cosmology: The Bullying Power of Spirits

By "cosmology" is meant "a theory or conception of the nature of the universe and its workings, and of the place of human beings and other creatures within that order."[29] In the cosmology of the premodern culture there is a hierarchy of transcendent gods/spirits intimately concerned with the well-being of the group and its stability. There are intermediary and more approachable spirits helping people to relate to

[27] John M Coggeshall, "Those Who Surrender Are Female: Prisoner Gender Identities as Cultural Mirror," *Customs and Conflict: The Anthropology of a Changing World*, ed. Frank Manning and others (Peterborough: Broadview Press, 1990) 153–4.

[28] See Elizabeth Achtemeier, "Women," *The Oxford Companion to the Bible*, ed. Bruce M. Metzger and Michael D. Coogan (New York: Oxford University Press, 1993) 807.

[29] Bowie, *The Anthropology of Religion*, 119.

the higher, more remote gods/spirits. Harmony is maintained by the gods/spirits, who keep evil forces under control, but people can allow these forces to enter their lives through "sin."

Sin and Sickness

Sin is not a personal affront to gods/spirits, but simply the breaking of rules and the predictability of social order. Things must be put right, not by an interior change of heart, but by formal rituals appeasing the spirits.[30]

The potential for bullying by using gods/spirits is considerable. Although people with premodern beliefs may recognize that there are immediate and rational causes for misfortune, for example, that cancer causes death, the fundamental question, "Why have *I* got cancer?" requires a different response. The *ultimate* cause of evil in the form of sickness or death is commonly that ancestors are punishing the living for not showing them respect or for breaking tribal taboos.

The living can also harm others through intentional or unconscious use of magical forces such as sorcery and witchcraft. Sorcery is the deliberate use of magic to harm some person or group, witchcraft is seen as a malign quality innate in a person. Witches, unlike sorcerers, are generally unaware that they have this quality or are exercising it. For many peoples, for example, the aboriginal Yolngu community in Australia, a death is generally believed to be the result of sorcery, usually by enemies or rivals.[31]

Case Study: Death without Physical Causes

A Maori man in New Zealand had been sentenced to a lengthy jail term. After a short time he called his Maori friends together and told them he would die shortly, even though he was physically very fit. He believed his offense would be punished by sorcerers at the instigation of the relatives of the man he had killed.

continued on next page

---

[30] See Mary Douglas, *Natural Symbols: Explorations in Cosmology* (New York: Pantheon Books, 1970) 102.

[31] See Janice Reid, *Sorcerers and Healing Spirits* (Sydney: Australian National University Press, 1983) 152.

Within a week he had died, but it was impossible to find any medical cause of the death and his friends said he had died from *mate Maori* ("Maori sickness").

The premodern cultural religious world can be one of fear of being intimidated by evil spirits and manipulative sorcerers, and people seek to defend themselves through rituals. There is a variety of specialists (e.g., shamans, diviners) and processes to discern precisely which spirit or person is causing the illness or the failure to succeed, the reasons, and the necessary remedies. Once people are persuaded of the source of the evil, then the challenge is to get the right ritual to neutralize the power of the malignant force. If there is no success, it is because the correct ritual has not been used or the words or action wrongly applied.[32]

Case Study: Jesus Confronts Cultural Bullying

The culture that Jesus belonged to was premodern, so the disciples accepted without question a causal link between sickness and the breaking of a cultural norm. When they "saw a man who had been blind from birth" they asked Jesus: "Rabbi, who sinned, this man or his parents, that he should have been born blind?" Jesus refused to accept the causal link, replying: "Neither he nor his parents sinned" (John 9:1-3). People such as lepers and the blind were defined by the community as dangerous to society, and marginalized from community relationships. They would have felt desperately alone, bullied into isolation by the cultural pressures, their self-image gravely affected. Jesus refused to accept the culturally assigned cause of sickness and concentrated on the physical and social healing of the sick by restoring them to community life.

For centuries in the Western world illness was believed to be caused by God as a punishment for people's immorality or their breaking cultural taboos. God was seen as harsh and punitive, a "big bully"

---

[32] See M. J. Meggitt, *Gods, Ghosts and Men in Melanesia*, ed. P. Lawrence and M. J. Meggitt (London: Oxford University Press, 1965).

contrary to Gospel revelation. Cholera, of epidemic proportions in the nineteenth century, was often thought to result from a life of sin. This belief still lurks in the background and can emerge quite suddenly depending on the nature of a disease or calamity. For example, in the early stages of the epidemic of HIV/AIDS (1982–85) a moral panic erupted, with fear evident in society and the mass media that people succumbed to the disease because God was punishing them for an immoral lifestyle.

Family Secrets, Rituals, and Power

People in premodern cultures cherish and fear secrets.[33] Many rituals are kept secret because they are about controlling or manipulating evil spirits to one's advantage, for example, through sorcery. Ritual specialists can dominate people's lives in violent ways because of the power they are assumed to possess. People will also hide incidents of breaking customs lest members of other clans hear and publicly ridicule them or make them targets of sorcery. Clan enemies will do all in their power to find out the secret rituals of their rivals, as well as their cultural infractions.

Fictive Kinship Systems

Biological kinship can be used as a metaphor. When people relate to one another as though they were members of a biological kinship group this extension of the idiom of kinship is termed "fictive." Ethnicity and ethnicity-based nationalism are normally modeled as extensions of the mythology of common biological descent (see chapter 9). A wide range of organizations, e.g., trade unions and various welfare organizations, also follow the same pattern using family terminology to describe how members should relate to one another. As in extended family relationships, considerable potential for violence also exists in fictive kinship as the following examples will illustrate.

---

[33] For example, see Kenelm Burridge, *Mambo: A Melanesian Millennium* (London: Methuen, 1960) xvi.

Patronage, Cronyism, and Corruption

1. Patronage Systems

Patronage is a way for someone without power to cope with the impersonal and often hostile requirements of government or bureaucratic agencies.[34] The assumption of the patron-client relationship is that the patron has and controls access to political, economic, or cultural resources that the client needs. The client obtains resources not through access to formal bureaucracies, which are openly accountable to the public, but by the manipulation of personal relationships of reciprocity.

The explicit or implicit language of these relationships is the metaphor of the family. The "father" patron gives to the dependent "family" but expects back from the "family" total filial-like support and loyalty.[35] While patronage can assist clients in need, it has oppressive qualities, both from the point of view of the clients and of those excluded from such protection: people are compelled to become subservient to another human being because of their powerlessness. In Italy patronage still drives politics and public life nationwide and is the source of much corruption and oppression of the powerless.[36]

A less institutionalized form of patronage can pervade economically and democratically advanced societies at both the corporate and political levels. For example, in the United States political patronage significantly developed from the mid-nineteenth century through to the late 1920s, due to the rapid rise of urbanization, increased immigration, and economic inequalities.[37]

2. Cronyism

"Cronyism" is a less-structured form of the patron-client relationship. In cronyism a person with political and economic power appoints

---

[34] See A. H. Galt, "Rethinking Patron-Client Relationships," *Anthropological Quarterly*, vol. 58 (1985) 47–62; S. N. Eisenstadt and L. Roniger, *Patrons, Clients and Friends: Interpersonal Relations and the Structure of Trust in Society* (Cambridge: Cambridge University Press, 1984) 48–50.

[35] See Jon P. Mitchell, "Patrons and Clients," *Encyclopedia of Social and Cultural Anthropology*, ed. Alana Barnard and Jonathan Spencer (London: Routledge, 1966) 416–7.

[36] See *The Economist* (7 July 2001) 18.

[37] See S. N. Eisenstadt and L. Roniger, *Patrons, Clients and Friends: Interpersonal Relations and the Structure of Trust in Society* (Cambridge: Cambridge University Press, 1984) 191–5.

without any public accountability biological family members and friends (who become honorary family members) to, for example, key financial positions. The bonds between the person who appoints and the beneficiaries, however, are far weaker than those in a patronage system.

The people who particularly suffer under cronyism (and patronage), therefore, are those who have no access to the system, so a nation's poor especially are the most intimidated. Innocent people suffer and lack the political and legal structures to seek redress for the injustices they experience.

Examples of cronyism abound in history. Ferdinand Marcos, while president of the Philippines, concentrated financial power in the hands of a few personal friends and their corporations; his introduction of martial law in 1972 was inter alia an attempt to avoid public accountability in order to protect the crony system.[38] President Suharto fostered a similar "family-oriented" political economy in Indonesia.[39] Likewise it was so in Pakistan, mainland China, the Philippines under President Joseph Estrada, and Georgia under President Edward Shevardnadze.[40] The fundamental cause of Kenya's economic disaster is to be found in the presidential cronies who systematically undermine government institutions to their own advantage.[41]

Mafia and Triads

The mafia is any hidden criminal organization providing protective services that amounts to a substitute government administering its own law and justice. Originating in Sicily,[42] this type of organization spread to North America and now to many parts of the former Soviet Union. In some bilateral instances a government and the mafia share the protection racket and may have overlapping membership.[43] Chinese "triads" have organization and purpose similar to the mafia

[38] See Bernardo Villegas, "The Economic Crisis," *Crisis in the Philippines* (Princeton: Princeton University Press, 1986) 163–4.

[39] See Susan Rose-Ackerman, *Corruption and Government: Causes, Consequences and Reform* (Cambridge: Cambridge University Press, 1999) 32.

[40] See *The Economist* (15 July 2000) 32.

[41] See *The Economist* (1 July 2000) 48.

[42] Ibid., 18.

[43] See Diego Gambetta, *The Sicilian Mafia* (Cambridge, Mass.: Harvard University Press, 1993).

and operate wherever there are significant numbers of Chinese. With the collapse of the Communist government in the Soviet Union, there was no official substitute immediately in place. Professional mafia-style patronage organizations rapidly developed and spread to most areas of business life, including even shops and street stalls.[44]

Family ideology is the foundation of the mafia organization. Membership of a "family" is not based on blood ties but on residence in a particular territory. As in other premodern groups members are expected to be totally loyal to the "family," and betrayal can mean death. In return, members can expect not only financial return but also protection from outsiders, including government agencies. The initiation rituals are demanding; for example, candidates may have to prove themselves by committing murder.[45]

The Olympic "Family"

The mythology of an extended family has molded the culture of the Olympic movement. When the founder of the modern Games, Baron Pierre de Courbertin, established the International Olympic Committee (IOC) he wanted a family-like organization with "no silly democracy or accountability."[46] Consequently, it became what *The New York Times* called "an undemocratic, secretive, unaccountable organization"[47] noted for its cronyism, secrecy, male-domination, limited external accountability.

Business Firm as "Family"

The Japanese place a high value on *maihoimushuge* which means "love of family life"; literally, "my-home-ism."[48] "My-home-ism," however, in practice refers not just to one's immediate family, but to one's school peer group and employment. One's sense of belonging and

[44] See Richard Clutterbuck, *Drugs, Crime and Corruption* (London: Macmillan, 1955) 138–47.

[45] Ibid., 131–7; Rose-Ackerman, *Corruption and Government: Causes, Consequences and Reform*, 121–4.

[46] See Andrew Jennings, *The Great Olympic Swindle* (London: Simon & Schuster, 2000) 98.

[47] See editorial, *The New York Times* (17 July 2001) A18.

[48] See Takeshu Ishida, *Japanese Society* (New York: Random House, 1971) 50; Chie Nakane, *Japanese Society* (Harmondsworth: Penguin, 1970) 132–3.

identity is dependent on being accepted into such groups that become fictive, extended families.

This extension of family belongingness to employment and other groups is at considerable cost to nuclear families; employers demand long hours of work from their employees, so much so that fathers commonly only see their children asleep—they leave home for work before the children are awake and return when they are asleep. This is an example of corporate cultural bullying.

"Family" Groups Under Siege

When the identity or existence of cultures or subcultures is threatened people commonly bond more closely in an effort to defend themselves against the perceived "evil" (see axiom 1, chapter 1). Failings on the part of the "we" group will be disguised lest they be used to destroy the "brotherhood." Initiation into "we" groups, e.g., elite army corps or militia, can be extremely demanding, often taking the form of "boot camp" methods, the aim being to instill the qualities of total obedience and family-like loyalty. The following are examples of groups under siege and how they relate to violence.

1. Nations Conceal Torture[49]

John Conroy reinvestigated three case studies of torture that had already been published in the mass media—by police in the United States, and the army in Israel and Northern Ireland. He concluded that "torturers are rarely punished, and when they are, the punishment rarely corresponds to the severity of the crime."[50] Why? The public as a whole show "rampant indifference"[51] in most societies in the face of revelations of torture. A simple reason is: the nation is a fictive family "under siege" by international scrutiny. Officials, including politicians in democratic societies, deliberately seek to conceal what happens in

---

[49] Torture is "any act by which severe pain or suffering, whether physical or mental, is intentionally inflicted by or at the instigation of a public official on a person for such purposes as obtaining from them or a third person information or confession, punishing them for an act they have committed, or intimidating them or other persons. . . . " United Nations, as cited by John Conroy, *Corruption and Government: Causes, Consequences and Reform* (London: Vision, 2001) 36.

[50] Ibid., 228.

[51] Conroy, *Corruption and Government: Causes, Consequences and Reform*, 233.

order to preserve the honor of the nation through a mixture of denial and doublespeak.

2. Police "Brotherhood"

Police forces are customarily organized according to a military model, with uniforms, formal lines of command, long-established disciplinary rules, and formal training. However, the more emphasis there is on discipline, the more stress is given to rules and regulations. Police forces are apt to develop a siege mentality—"they" (i.e., the criminals, mass media) are "out to get us" and "we" must protect ourselves from attack.

The combined need to maintain a strong group identity and the fear of "them" has two serious consequences: first, police can become far more concerned about preserving the system of rules and regulations than about their methods of relating to the public; secondly, police are tempted to hide mistakes and corrupt practices in order to maintain the loyalty of "the brotherhood"[52] and public goodwill. If an officer informs on a colleague he is attacking the "brotherhood," the source of his own identity and support. Similarly, if an officer has himself been guilty of corruption, he hesitates to inform on others lest his own shady operations are revealed.[53]

Examples: New York and Los Angeles

The Mollen Commission Report on the New York Police Department found that leaders of a police department contributed to the culture of corruption by their particular reactions to organizational crises. They had become "paranoid over bad press"; they were so worried about the damage to the public image of the department through negative publicity that they neglected the problem of police corruption.[54]

continued on next page

---

[52] See John Kleinig, "Police Violence and the Loyal Code of Silence," *Violence and Police Culture,* ed. Tony Coady and others (Melbourne: Melbourne University Press, 2000) 219–34.

[53] See John Skolnick and John Fyfe, *Above the Law: Police and the Excessive Use of Force* (New York: Free Press, 1994) 80.

[54] See *Commission Report (Mollen Report): Commission to Investigate Allegations of Police Corruption and the Anti-Corruption Procedures of the Police Department* (The City

In a report on why police officers sought to protect colleagues who applied excessive force against Rodney King, a black citizen in Los Angeles, it was noted inter alia that the identities of individual officers were so dependent on the group that to betray the group would be equivalent to betraying themselves and destroying their own identities: "They live in a world of desperately conflicting imperatives, where norms of loyalty wash up against the standards of law and order. . . . So . . . they see, hear, and speak no evil."[55]

3. The "Old Boys' Club"

In an "old boys' club" or network power is tightly controlled by an "in" group; those excluded will be: women, members of minority groups, and those who have not attended the "right" schools. Those on the "outer" will be bullied into accepting the status quo. Sometimes, in order to give the correct political impression, the "in" group will invite a few members of the excluded group(s) to join the organization. This will be mere tokenism as there is no intention to change the system of the "brotherhood." Professional bodies can easily fall into the trap of so protecting their "turf" that they become exclusive clubs.

Example: The Medical Profession

Feminist studies critique the patriarchal power in the medical profession. In Britain, in the healthcare service, for example, women still suffer from inequality of job opportunity, low status positions, and poor pay.[56] In Australia women as specialists are

continued on next page

---

of New York, 1994) 3; Janet B. Chan, *Changing Police Culture: Policing in a Multicultural Society* (Cambridge: Cambridge University Press, 1997) 90–1.

[55] Jerome H. Skolnick and James J. Fyfe, "Rodney King and Use of Excessive Force: Police Work and Organizational Culture," *Corporate and Governmental Deviance*, ed. M. David Ermann and Richard Lundman (New York: Oxford University Press, 1996) 250.

[56] See Sheila Hillier and Graham Scambler, "Women as Patients and Providers," *Sociology As Applied to Medicine*, ed. Graham Scambler (London: W. B. Saunders, 1997) 126–33.

confined to certain areas considered to be "women's work," that
is, areas of medicine of relatively low status, such as gynecology,
pediatrics, or plastic surgery.

When traditionally all-male organizations, e.g., the armed forces, are
opened to female recruits, men can sometimes marginalize the women
in bullying ways. The perpetrators and their superiors conceal such
behavior on the assumption that men have a right to do this. If women
want to join their organizations they should become tough like men
and take it without complaining.[57]

4. Youth Gangs

A gang is a peer association of mainly adolescent and early adult
males, bound together by a family-like loyalty and particular territory,
hierarchically structured around a gang leader, and commonly engaged in various deviant activities.[58] Women may be associated with
gangs, but have second-class status. The more cohesive groups have
ritualized initiation ceremonies, sometimes involving an act of criminal
violence on the part of the novice. Loyalty to other members is a fundamental requirement of gang life.

Gangs provide a substitute family in which members achieve com-
panionship, protection, status, respect, and a sense of identity as men
that the wider society denies them. Gangs also offer members the opportunity to exercise power over others in ways that can be violent. In
fact, gangs may actually seek violence, not only as a method of initiation for members, but as the "normal" way to express their frustration.
Access to firearms reinforces the centrality of violence in many contemporary gang cultures. Territoriality is used by gangs as a way of artifi-
cially forming disputes, and it is the means, but not the cause, of many
conflicts and violent activities.[59] Scott Decker and Barrik Van Winkle in
their study of gangs in the United States emphasize the interconnection
between violence and fear in the rise and maintenance of gangs:

[57] See example in Australia, "Navy Lessons Poorly Learned," editorial, *The Australian* (28 March 2000) 12.

[58] See Nicholas Abercrombie and others, *The Penguin Dictionary of Sociology* (London:
Penguin, 2000) 147–8; New Zealand Government Committee on Gangs, *Report of the
Committee on Gangs* (Wellington, 1981) 4.

[59] *Report of the Committee on Gangs*, ibid., 7.

From entrance to exit, violence is ever present in the form of threat
—threat from rival gangs and the threat created by gang members
themselves. . . . [It] compels individuals to join their gang, increases their level of activity and commitment to the gang. . . .
Threat causes [them] to . . . look toward the objective circumstances of life under threat of violence, the need to affiliate with a
gang for protection and the resulting isolation from social institutions.[60]

Summary

- The elements most marked in premodern cultural mythology are:
the ideology of the extended family, patriarchy, conformity to tradition, and systems to maintain the status quo.

- Significant value is placed upon loyalty to the extended family, and the
individual can be subjected to considerable, even violent, pressure to
conform; transgressions of customs are concealed in case outsiders
find out and use them to threaten the well-being of the whole family.

- The mythology of premodernity assigns women an inferior status
and provides men with structural approval to assert themselves
physically at the expense of women.[61]

- Sickness is not so much a biomedical matter as a social one. It is primarily attributed to social, not physical, causes: cultural norms have
been broken and the spirit world is punishing the victim.

- "Fictive" kinship systems, e.g., the mafia, gangs, police forces, are
groups in which members relate to one another according to the
norms of biologically defined families, e.g., group loyalty and the
code of silence.

- The following chapter describes the adoption of premodern cultural
structures by the Church and the ways in which these can become instruments of undue coercion of members.

---

[60] Scott H. Decker and Barrik Van Winkle, *Life in the Gang: Family, Friends, and Vio-
lence* (Cambridge: Cambridge University Press, 1996) 280; see also Elijah Anderson,
Code of the Street: Decency, Violence and the Moral Life of the Inner City (New York:
W. W. Norton, 2000) 69–71.

[61] See Stephen Jones, *Understanding Violent Crime* (Buckingham: Open University
Press, 2000) 86–101.

Discussion Questions

1. "Violence in our homes, schools and streets . . . is destroying the lives, dignity and hopes of millions. Hostility, hatred, despair, and indifference are at the heart of a growing culture of violence" (United States Bishops, 1994). Am I contributing at least unconsciously to violence by my speech and actions? Are there families in my neighborhood that are being destroyed by the culture of violence? If so, is there some way I can help them?

2. Jesus expected his apostles to give him "an account of all that they had done" (Luke 9:10). Why did Jesus have the right to do this? Are there agencies in my city, village, parish, that are unnecessarily secretive? How can I network with others to ask that they be accountable to the community for their actions?

Chapter 3

Premodernity: Impact on the Church

> We know well that even in this Holy See, until recently, abominable things have happened. . . . We intend to use all diligence to reform the Roman Curia. (Pope Adrian VI,[1] 1523)

This chapter explains:

- how the Church took on premodern imperial structures of power and organization and how the entire Church became identified with the local church of Rome;

- how Gospel values were acculturated to premodern controlling values such as patriarchy, fictive kinship;

- why the Church reacted in a retreatist manner as the values of the Enlightenment spread, with consequences for theological reflection and clerical/religious life formation;

- the impact on local churches of the development of centralized powers by the Roman Curia.

The Church's culture developed through the centuries a number of premodern customs such as its monarchical and patriarchal structures of government. As a human institution, as well as being of divine origin, it is not surprising that the Church's culture began to reflect the premodern world that surrounded it. This chapter and the next one briefly explain these customs and how this situation developed.

---

[1] Cited by Luigi Accattoli, *When a Pope Asks Forgiveness* (New York: Alba House, 1998) 7.

There has long existed in the mythology of the Church's culture a fundamental tension between the complementary polar opposites Papal Rome and local churches. The tendency has been for the first pole in the tension, Rome, to become increasingly the dominant partner in the relationship and a process of theological and cultural splitting has occurred (see axiom 7, chapter 1). Local churches have at times been seen by Rome as threats to its survival, and their powers have been severely curtailed or removed.

The early Church began with local churches, each of which was led by a bishop and in each of which the one Church of God was believed to be present.[2] A local church was understood not as a province or a department of the universal Church; it was rather the universal Church in that particular place.[3] The Church of Rome was seen as one local church and not the universal Church, but its authority as the first among episcopal sees was never questioned.[4] Over time, however, the local church of Rome claimed that it was the universal Church and other churches were but departments or provinces dependent on it. Consequently, Rome over the centuries increasingly dominated other local churches, preventing them from developing their rightful autonomy.

Sometimes Rome's intervention was justifiable; for example, during the Middle Ages secular and ecclesiastical Europe was on the brink of anarchy and papal authority alone saved it from disintegration.[5] But Rome rarely retreated when its involvement was no longer required. Whenever Rome intervened without justification it acted in a theologically and administratively intimidating manner to the detriment of collegiality.

Rome made its dominant position historically more powerful by the gradual adoption of the model of authority prevailing in the contemporary secular world, namely, an imperial and centralized structure. From time to time since the fourth century the imbalance in favor of the center has been theologically questioned, but after the fifteenth century opposition to Rome's centralizing authority weakened. The Vatican II Council (1963–65) tried to restore the balance between the central and

---

[2] See "The Church," *The Documents of Vatican II*, ed. Walter Abbott (London: Geoffrey Chapman, 1966) par. 26.

[3] See Walter Kasper, "On the Church," *The Tablet* (23 June 2001) 927.

[4] Ibid.

[5] See Yves Congar, *Power and Poverty in the Church* (London: Geoffrey Chapman, 1965) 104–10.

local authority, but Rome has since sought to reestablish its supremacy over local churches (see chapter 8).

The evolution of papal Rome's coercive hold over local churches is explained in more detail in the following section.

The Church Develops Monarchical Customs

With the Peace of Constantine in 313 C.E., the political atmosphere became favorable for the Church's leadership and it uncritically acculturated itself to the courtly and hierarchical ways of the imperial system. Bishops now used the power symbols of royalty, e.g., in dress, titles; priests accepted authority over people and downplayed the role as servants within a community of believers.[6] Worship left the home and entered the basilica.[7] Negative aspects of Roman legalism began to have a deep impact on Christian institutions. Sin, for example, which had earlier been thought of as breaking a relationship with the person of Christ and members of the community, was now seen in legal terms as fracturing a divine or ecclesiastical law.

Fr. Yves Congar, the Dominican ecclesiologist, describes the absolutist centralizing movement from the time of Emperor Constantine (d. 337) in this way: "There existed an imperialism which tended to confuse unity and uniformity, to impose everywhere the Roman customs and rites, in a word, considering the universal Church as a simple extension of the Church of Rome. . . . We find in Pope Siricius in 385, in Innocent I in 416 . . . the astounding affirmation that no one can truly have the faith of Peter unless he observes the customs and rites of Peter, that is, of Rome."[8] However, there was also a movement to respect local church authority and customs; for example, Pope Gregory the Great (590–604) at the same time declared: "If there is unity of faith, a difference of custom does no damage to the holy Church."[9]

[6] Ibid., 112–27.

[7] See Anscar J. Chupungco, "Liturgy and Inculturation," *East Asian Pastoral Review*, vol. 18, no. 3 (1981) 264; Gerald A. Arbuckle, *Earthing the Gospel: An Inculturation Handbook for Pastoral Workers* (London: Geoffrey Chapman, 1990) 11–2; Frank C. Senn, *Christian Liturgy: Catholic and Evangelical* (Minneapolis: Fortress, 1997) 163–6.

[8] Yves Congar, "Christianity as Faith and as Culture," *East Asian Pastoral Review*, vol. 18, no. 4 (1981) 310.

[9] Gregory I cited by Yves Congar, *Diversity and Communion* (Mystic, Conn.: Twenty-Third Publications, 1985) 25.

Throughout the Middle Ages the subordination of episcopal government to papal control quickened as a way to prevent or weaken lay
involvement in ecclesiastical affairs; legates from the pope became
more common in the courts of Europe.[10] Pope Gregory VII (1021–85)
stated the theory of an absolutist, monarchical view of the papacy:

> [The] pope can be judged by no one; the Roman church has never
> erred and never will err. . . . [The] Roman church was founded by
> Christ alone; the pope alone can depose and restore bishops; he
> alone can make new laws . . . he alone can revise his judgments;
> his legates . . . have precedence over all bishops; . . . a duly
> ordained pope is undoubtedly made a saint by the merits of
> St. Peter.[11]

By the time of Pope Innocent III (1198–1215), the title Vicar of Christ
had been exclusively applied to the pope, though earlier it had been
used for both kings and bishops. The idea was that the pope alone
represented Christ, but the other bishops were simply vicars of the
apostles.[12]

Rome attempted to take firm leadership in liturgical matters though
with little initial success. Gregory VII commanded that dioceses in the
Western Church should adopt the liturgical customs of the Roman see
exclusively and unquestioningly accept its liturgical laws.[13] For him the
principle was that whoever believes in the faith of the Roman church
must also practice its liturgy.[14] It is from this period also that the role of
the laity in liturgy declined, as Theodor Klauser notes: "[The] liturgy,
which was once and always should be the common act of priest and
people, became now exclusively a priestly duty. The people were still
present, but they devoted themselves during the sacred action to non-
liturgical, subjective, pious exercises."[15] The earlier retention of Latin as

[10] See Richard W. Southern, *Western Society and the Church in the Middle Ages* (Harmondsworth: Penguin, 1970) 212.

[11] Cited by Bokenkotter, *A Concise History of the Catholic Church*, 112; for an over-
view of the development of papal monarchical theory see Terence L. Nichols, *That
All May Be One: Hierarchy and Participation in the Church* (Collegeville: The Liturgical
Press, 1997) 133–70.

[12] See Nichols, *That All May Be One*, 146.

[13] See Theodor Klauser, *A Short History of the Western Liturgy* (Oxford: Oxford University Press, 1979) 95.

[14] See Congar, *Diversity and Communion*, 31–2.

[15] Klauser, *A Short History of the Western Liturgy*, 97.

the liturgical language in the West had reinforced the perception that the liturgy was reserved for the clergy only.[16]

After the Reformation papal authority over the universal Church intensified further weakening the powers of the local churches and the collegial powers of bishops. The Council of Trent (1545–63) reaffirmed papal supremacy, further strengthening the hold of the pope over the Church as a whole. The council gave to the Curia (the papal bureaucracy) exclusive jurisdiction in liturgical issues. The Roman liturgy was made mandatory in all dioceses except those which had had their own particular liturgy for over two hundred years.[17] The council reasserted the rights of bishops to control their dioceses, subject to the papal authority. Lay involvement in the Church's administration was proscribed. As historian Thomas Bokenkotter comments: "[Trent] left no room for participation of the laity in the administration of the Church. In sum, they bequeathed to modern Catholics a highly authoritarian, centralized structure that was still basically medieval."[18] This model of papal authority, together with a claim to supremacy over civil society as a whole, has been termed "one of the grandest, most integrated, and best-developed systems that has ever been devised for the conduct of human life."[19] In brief, after Trent the Church was governed more and more in an autocratic way.

Example: Matteo Ricci's Inculturation Attempt Condemned

The power of the Rome-centered movement is tragically evident in the condemnation in 1704 and 1715 of Matteo Ricci's approach to evangelization in China. Ricci (1552–1610), a Jesuit with pastoral insight and cultural sensitivity, had attempted with growing success to enter into a dialogue with the Chinese culture; he and his companions had used Chinese words to express Christian ideas. They also had given permission to their converts to perform under certain conditions rites in honor of Confucius and their ancestors. They were condemned by the Roman authorities for

continued on next page

---

[16] See Senn, *Christian Liturgy*, 187–8.

[17] See Klauser, *A Short History of the Western Liturgy*, 118–9.

[18] Thomas Bokenkotter, *A Concise History of the Catholic Church* (New York: Doubleday, 1979) 217.

[19] See Southern, *Western Society and the Church in the Middle Ages*, 102.

encouraging what the latter wrongly thought was idolatry. In reality the Jesuits had refused to impose on the Chinese a uniform Roman ritual and a faith imbued with European cultural values and customs.[20] The evangelizing thrust of the Church in China and elsewhere would suffer for centuries to come.

Control Increases

Papal power over the Church had further increased by the end of the eighteenth century as a consequence of the Reformation, the French Revolution, and the Enlightenment. The French Revolution helped to destroy the stable sociopolitical order with which the Church had been allied for centuries. Napoleon wanted the Church to be directly under the control of the state, and thus to establish a new pattern for the rest of Europe of state-Church relationship; this the Church could not theologically and administratively accept. The life of the Church was further threatened by the Enlightenment and the Industrial Revolution with their values of naturalism, rationalism, liberalism, democracy, and their emphasis on the empirical sciences and historical research methods.

The more the Church's leadership resisted the revolutionary insights and values emerging in the Western world, the more it withdrew the Church from what was taking place in history and in people's lives. The Church as a culture became increasingly closed and inward-looking, defensive and protective of its members and its customs. It became a Church under siege.

The centralizing process within the Church gathered considerable momentum under Pius IX (1792–1878). Two broad groups of Catholics emerged in the Church: the Ultramontanes, who fervently believed that Church and civilization would survive only if all power to rule the Church was centered in Rome; and the Gallicans, who disagreed with this policy. The ultramontane position prevailed, notably with the declaration of papal infallibility at Vatican I in 1870. Cardinal Newman, with others, was distressed over the curial intrigues and intimidating tactics that preceded the infallibility decree: "whatever is decided eventually about the definition of the present Council, the scandals which

---

[20] See G. Minamiki, *The Chinese Rites Controversy from Its Beginning to Modern Times* (Chicago: Loyola University Press, 1985).

have accompanied it will remain, and the guilt of those who perpetrated them."[21]

Power of the Curia Increases

Under Pope Pius IX, the Curia, which had been modeled on the bureaucracies of secular monarchical governments,[22] became an extension of the pope's power. By the end of his pontificate, bishops had been reduced to papal servants, "field managers who work only under instructions from central authority."[23] Newman's assessment of the excessive centralizing efforts by Pius to control all Church affairs from Rome was strong:

> We have come to a climax of tyranny. It is not good for a Pope to live 20 years. It is an anomaly and bears no good fruit; he becomes a god, has no one to contradict him, does not know facts, and does cruel things without meaning to.[24]

Following the definition of papal infallibility at Vatican I, the reverential mystique surrounding the person of the pope increased, so much so that few would be bold enough to criticize his decisions and those of the curial offices.[25] Loyalty to Rome in all things was required. At the same time as Pius was solidifying his hold over bishops, he was also increasingly isolating the Church from the modern secular world. Earlier, in 1864, Pius had condemned in the document *Syllabus of Errors* a number of contemporary movements such as rationalism and liberalism. He anathematized all who demanded that the Roman Pontiff can and should reconcile and adapt himself to progress, liberalism, and modern civilization.[26]

Following Pius IX, the fears of "modernism," that is, the movement that sought to bring the tradition of Catholic belief into closer relation

[21] John Henry Newman cited by Garry Wills, *Papal Sin* (New York: Doubleday, 2000) 268.

[22] See Thomas J. Reese, *Inside the Vatican* (Cambridge, Mass.: Harvard University Press, 1996) 157.

[23] John R. Quinn, *The Reform of the Papacy* (New York: Crossroad, 1999) 154.

[24] Newman cited by Wills, *Papal Sin*, 269.

[25] See Quinn, *The Reform of the Papacy*, 51.

[26] See, *Rome Has Spoken*, ed. Maureen Fiedler and Linda Rabben (New York: Crossroad, 1998) 29.

with the modern world, continued, even intensified, in Rome. Pius X "pursued a policy of internal surveillance, punishment, and retaliation unprecedented in its effectiveness," writes historian Fr. John O'Malley, S.J. The Holy Office of the Inquisition functioned with a vigor it had not known since it was instituted in the sixteenth century. Subsequent popes until Vatican II were less severe, but "an ecclesiastical style, not altogether dissimilar in certain particulars to the style of modern totalitarian states, prevailed."[27] Pope Pius X commanded that secret vigilance committees be established in every diocese worldwide to report suspected modernists to Rome.[28]

Such heresy-hunting caused pain to thinkers like Jacques Maritain who wrote privately in the 1930s that "the Church defends a truth by blockading it with ways of thinking that simple human experience has left way behind. . . . It is not I alone who will be the target of their attack, it is all sorts of germinations of life and of good movements . . . which will be ruined."[29]

The Church: A Premodern Culture

The purpose of this section is to highlight further premodern aspects of the Church's pre-Vatican II culture. It was in many respects a culture of intimidation and control, though it would rarely have been perceived as such because this way of acting was taken for granted.

A Fictive Family System

The Catholic Church was one huge family, under the fatherhood of God and Christ's Vicar on earth—the Holy Father. Fictive kinship terminology became the metaphor for describing the tightness of bonding that should exist within parishes, dioceses, and the Church at large. As kinsfolk baptized into the one true Church, we were encouraged to look after our own first. To protect itself against all the evils surrounding it,

---

[27] John W. O'Malley, "Interpreting Vatican II: A Break from the Past," *Commonweal* (9 March 2001) 21.

[28] See David G. Schultenover, *A View from Rome: On the Eve of the Modernist Crisis* (New York: Fordham University Press, 1993) 1.

[29] Jacques Maritain cited by Bernard Doering, "Silent Dissenter: Jacques Maritain," *Commonweal* (18 May 2001) 18–9.

the Church became in many countries a powerful, inward-looking subculture of the wider nation, with its own school system, sodalities, clubs, hospitals, and status systems.[30] Even canonically approved mixed denomination marriages were so discouraged that they had to be celebrated in rectories or sacristies not in the parish church. The symbolism was clear: the Catholic partner had become exposed to the contaminating forces of the "impure" and needed to be reminded of the dangers.

This critique of the Church's premodern culture is not to denigrate the remarkable service the Church gave to people through education and other services. Without these services, millions of people, especially the poor, would never have been educated or medically assisted.

Clerical Formation: Loyalty to the Status Quo

The initiation of men into the clerical state mirrored in significant ways male initiation rituals of premodern societies; seclusion and fear were used to inculcate the clerical mythology of the Church. In a monastic atmosphere of unchanging order, candidates were taught that the world was evil and to be avoided. Information was handed down from above to be received without question. Conformity to a theological, ecclesiastical, and pastoral status quo was the most esteemed value in a candidate, and testimony to the success of the training program. The fear of punishment, for even the innocent infringement of regulations, was an effective method of instilling conformity in candidates.

The stress on keeping even minute rules, under threat of disproportionate punishment, gave candidates a false sense of what was truly sinful. Issues of sexuality and personal development were considered unimportant for the externally conforming clerics. The training encouraged candidates to hide mistakes and to protect the system at all costs.

Clerical teachers were chosen chiefly for their known ability to accept and maintain the status quo. Teaching abilities were not necessary because all that was needed was to provide candidates with information already set out in manuals and then to check that it had been adequately received. Lecturers did not encourage students, in fact, they actively discouraged them from examining their intellectual and

---

[30] For an excellent overview of the pre-Vatican Church in the United States, see Mark S. Massa, *Catholics and American Culture* (New York: Crossroad, 1999).

emotional responses to the material given them.[31] Since the Church was seen as the perfect society, it was assumed to have all the answers. Creative theologians fared poorly in this system, as Yves Congar (later a cardinal) found to his sadness:

> The present pope [Pius XII] has . . . developed almost to the point of obsession a paternalistic regime consisting of this: that he and he alone should say to the world what it has to think and what it must do. He wishes to reduce theologians to commenting on his statements and not daring to think something or undertake something beyond mere commentary. . . . [The] whole history of Rome is about insisting on its own authority and the destruction of everything that cannot be reduced to submission.[32]

Ritual Control

Ritual in the pre-Vatican II centuries had become increasingly formal and concerned with the exact performance of detailed rules and regulations, a characteristic of premodern cultures. Laity attended Mass simply as passive observers; they could recite the rosary at the same time because priests as ritual experts would be interceding for them before God in a language that the laity did not need to understand.

Officials of the Church also held power over people's devotional lives outside Mass. The pope, through his control over indulgences, could decree how many days one could "escape" purgatory by reciting certain prayers so many times or in particular shrines. It was assumed that the institutional Church was the only intermediary between the distant God and people. St. Teresa of Avila, in the sixteenth century, was suspected by the Inquisition of being a heretic because she claimed in her writings that there could be an exclusive relationship between God and the soul without the mediation of the Church. The freedom that one could discover in prayer was for her and her followers the secret weapon of her reform.[33] It was a danger to the tight boundaries of the premodern Church culture.

---

[31] See Gerald A. Arbuckle, *From Chaos to Mission: Refounding Religious Life Formation* (London: Geoffrey Chapman, 1996) 103–4.

[32] Yves Congar, "Silenced for Saying Things," *National Catholic Reporter* (2 June 2000) 20.

[33] See Cathleen Medwick, *Teresa of Avila: The Progress of a Soul* (New York: Alfred A. Knopf, 1999) 247, 216.

Interdenominational Communication

The Church decreed with whom one could pray. To pray with non-Catholics would endanger one's faith. If one did so, one would be ritually declared impure, a danger not just to oneself but also to others. One could not formally discuss one's faith with outsiders without permission, as the Code of Canon Law in 1917 forbade "Catholics from participating in disputations or discussions with non-Catholics without the permission of the Holy See" (Canon 1325 §3). The fact that the Holy See alone and not the local bishop could give this permission illustrates the grave nature of the issue.

Theology: Mirrors Culture

In a premodern culture the status of gods or spirits mirrors the hierarchical structures of the culture itself. This was the situation in the Church. God the Father was theologically represented as someone remote and fear-evoking, a God of the Old Testament, and Jesus as a Judge recording in detail one's sins and imperfections. The Holy Spirit, the comforter and the abiding presence of God challenging one to create new ways to pray and to teach the healing message of Christ, was rarely referred to. The Mother of God and the saints were presented as approachable, compassionate, and understanding intercessory beings having particular cultic significance in various needs, in contrast to the stern and remote God the Father and the sacrificing, judging Jesus Christ.

Example: Acculturation of Marian Theology

The theologian Elizabeth A. Johnson[34] traces how the biblical role of Mary changed under the Church's emerging premodern culture. She describes two models of devotion to Mary—the patronage and the companion models. The first model depicts Mary as a distant regal-like figure. The second model views Mary as a companion on our journey, one whose example of mothering God

continued on next page

---

[34] See Elizabeth A. Johnson, "Mary of Nazareth: Friend of God and Prophet," *America* (17 June 2000) 7–13; see also Eamon Duffy, "True and False Madonnas," *The Tablet* (6 February 1999) 169–71.

to bring God to birth in the world of her time encourages us to do the same today. Mary is our partner in this difficult task; she has gone before us, embraced suffering in order to help others. Her prophetic voice, evident in the *Magnificat*, energizes us down through the centuries.

This accompanying and prophetic role of Mary was lost sight of as the premodern culture of the Church affected people's understanding of her. Mary became instead the quiet retiring mother at Nazareth and a particularly powerful intercessor for our needs before the throne of her Son. In the hierarchy of saints she held the top position. Johnson describes this intercessory role of Mary as the patronage model, a model that is not to be found in the New Testament or in the early Christian era. The patron-client relationship developed in the Church's devotional Marian practices under the influence of the secular patronage system of the late Roman Empire. This is an example of acculturation, not inculturation. It is an uncritical acceptance of secular customs into the life of the Church. Naturally, the prophetic role of Mary had no place in this patron-client relationship.

In brief, the primary theological stress, particularly in reaction to the Reformation, moved away from community evangelization to the salvation of the individual soul. In the early centuries evangelization had been directed to the individual, but in and through the community or congregation of believers. The overall goal of evangelization became the implantation of the Church as an institution, a monarchical and hierarchical entity, the sole instrument of individual salvation and welfare. The strongly clerical Church was depicted as the visible vehicle of salvation—a boat that ferries its members across the turbulent seas of life, or as a cable car that lifts them over the abyss into which they otherwise would fall.[35]

The industrial revolution had created hardship and injustices for working-class people, but the institutional Church until Leo XIII, with the exception of some prophetic leaders within local churches, had failed to become involved. In 1891 Leo XIII's encyclical *Rerum Novarum* sought to move the Church to confront the most significant social prob-

---

[35] See Avery Dulles, *Models of the Church* (New York: Image Books, 1978) 39–50.

lem of his day—the need to alleviate the plight of workers through organized action and social reform. It argued that workers have the rights to organize and to earn a living wage. The profit motive should not be the primary measure of economic activity.[36] It was a positive move, but decades overdue. It would not be until the encyclical *Pacem in Terris* of John XXIII in 1963 that the Church would formally articulate a list of human rights.

Patriarchy and the Church

The institutional Church became patriarchal in both its thinking and structures. Consider the remarkable example of St. Teresa of Avila (1515–82), Doctor of the Church, who astounded the male-dominated Church with her extraordinary gifts and insights. This was possible, it was said in the papal bull of her canonization, because she had overcome "her female nature,"[37] that is, she had become the equivalent of a man. Women could not do great things without the gifts of masculinity. Fundamentally, little has changed, even after the reforms of Vatican II.[38] Recall axiom 3 from chapter 1, namely, that cultures have inbuilt resistance to change, and the Church's tardiness to modify its patriarchal ways merely exemplifies this.

Why did the Church become so patriarchal in its mythology? The following is a brief descriptive explanation.

1. Gender Equality: Biblical Background[39]

In the New Testament there are two traditions represented. The first appears in writings attributed to Paul, mirroring values of the wider secular society, and affirms patriarchal values and women's inferiority as accepted in the wider secular culture (1 Cor 11:5-10; Eph 5:22; 1 Cor 14:34-35). The second tradition that is in other writings of Paul was overlooked; here, an egalitarian gender emphasis is evident (Gal 3:28;

---

[36] See Marvin L. Krier Mich, *Catholic Social Teaching and Movements* (Mystic, Conn.: Twenty-Third Publications, 2000) 20–8.

[37] Quoted by Medwick, *Teresa of Avila: The Progress of a Soul*, 248.

[38] See *Woman and Man: One in Christ: Report on the Participation of Women in the Catholic Church in Australia*, ed. Marie Macdonald and others (Sydney: Harper-Collins, 1999) viii.

[39] See Maureen Fiedler, "Gender Equality: Theory and Practice," Fiedler and Rabben, *Rome Has Spoken*, 120–1.

Rom 16:1-6).[40] In the Gospels Jesus also strongly stresses the egalitarian approach of love and ministerial service in words and actions, not the culture of patriarchy (John 20:11-18; Luke 18:1-8).[41]

2. Acculturation to the Patriarchal Culture

An egalitarian emphasis in ministry was common in early Christian communities. In pre-Pauline and Pauline Christian communities, women appear to have acted in almost identical ways to men.[42] As Maureen Fiedler records, "Women led eucharistic worship in house churches, preached the gospel, went on missionary journeys, and filled leadership functions in early Christian communities."[43]

But with the Peace of Constantine the Church's leadership embraced the patriarchal structures of contemporary Roman culture. In Roman law a woman was under the control of the father before marriage and under the husband's authority following marriage. A woman had no legal protection; her status was that of physical and mental weakness. From the fourth century restrictions on women ministering in the Church intensified.[44] Several early Church Fathers spoke of women as dangerous to men. "You are the devil's gateway," declared Tertullian as early as the third century, "You are the unsealer of that [forbidden] tree; you are the deserter of the divine law."[45] Because women were seen as in some way impure—a characteristic of premodern cultures—they had to be excluded from direct involvement in liturgies. The Synod of Laodicea in the fourth century declared: "Women are not allowed to approach the altar."[46] The Synod of Paris in 829 bluntly told women not to press around the altar or touch the sacred vessels.[47]

Pope St. Gregory I, in his instructions to the English bishop Augustine in the early seventh century, explained why women were to be considered inferior and dangerous: "When a woman has given birth . . . she

[40] See Elizabeth Schüssler Fiorenza, *In Memory of Her: A Feminist Reconstruction of Christian Origins* (London: SCM Press, 1983) 205–41.

[41] See Francis J. Moloney, *"A Hard Saying": The Gospel and Culture* (Collegeville: The Liturgical Press, 2001) 3–34.

[42] See Valerie Abrahamsen, "Women," *Oxford Companion to the Bible*, ed. Bruce M. Metzger and Michael D. Coogan (New York: Oxford University Press, 1993) 816.

[43] See Fiedler, "Gender Equality," 1121–2; Fiorenza, *In Memory of Her*, passim.

[44] See Abrahamsen, "Women," 816.

[45] Tertullian quoted by Fiedler and Rabben, *Rome Has Spoken*, 114.

[46] Synod of Laodicea, in ibid., 115.

[47] Synod of Paris, in ibid., 116.

should abstain [from entering a church] for thirty-three days if she had a boy, sixty-six if she had a girl. . . . During the time she is menstruating she should not be hurried to enter a church."[48] This fear of women explains the ritual of "churching," whereby a woman was purified following childbirth. Canonists and theologians bought into this patriarchal culture without question, e.g., Gratian, an influential canon lawyer writing in the twelfth century, asserted that "women should be subject to men. . . . [Women are] not made in God's image."[49] Fra Cherubino's influential *Rules of Marriage*, written in the fifteenth century, gave husbands the following guidance: "scold [your wife] sharply, bully and terrify her. And if that . . . doesn't work, take up a stick and beat her soundly, for it is better to punish the body and correct the soul than to damage the soul and spare the body."[50]

3. Women and Religious Life

There is evidence of communities of consecrated virgins even before the time of St. Benedict (ca. 480–547). Some argue that they were formed as a protest against the exclusion of women from the increasing patriarchy in the Church.[51]

However, after the time of St. Benedict, women's religious congregations emerged as counterparts to the men's orders and were dependent on them in various ways, for example, liturgically, and in a number of instances for supervision. The patriarchal premodern culture of the Church and society effectively stifled efforts by women to act alone in devising new forms of religious life. Female orders were usually far more enclosed than their male counterparts, a practice reinforced by society's beliefs that unmarried and unenclosed women would be in danger of exploitation and of threatening male-oriented structures and ministries.[52]

As the centuries passed the enclosure of religious sisters became stricter, and their habits and veils more copious, lest "in appearing to the world they either made others desire them, or saw things which

[48] Pope St. Gregory I, in ibid., 115.

[49] Gratian quoted by Terry Davidson, *Conjugal Crime: Understanding and Changing the Wife-Beating Pattern* (New York: Hawthorn, 1978) 99.

[50] Fra Cherubino quoted by Davidson, *Conjugal Crime*, 99.

[51] See J. Simpson, "Women and Asceticism in the Fourth Century: A Question of Interpretation," *The Journal of Religious History* (Sydney), vol. 15, no. 1 (1988) 53.

[52] See Edward A. Wynne, *Traditional Catholic Religious Orders: Living in Community* (New Brunswick: Transaction Books, 1988) 136–7.

they themselves desired."[53] Women like St. Angela Merici (1474–1540), the founder of the Ursulines, and Mary Ward (1586–1646), attempted to dispense with the cloister and habit and become involved directly in ministry to people, but without success. Religious women without solemn vows, habit, cloister, and dependency on male congregations could not be imagined in a patriarchal Church.[54]

Rome and Religious Life

The nineteenth century was a period of intense growth in the number of religious congregations: about six hundred new communities were formed worldwide during that time. Most opted for the apostolic model developed by St. Ignatius Loyola. However, Rome insisted that unsuitable monastic and conventual customs had to be integrated into the constitutions of these congregations. The dynamic founding energy of the communities was quickly suffocated by, for example, the wearing of ill-designed habits and the maintenance of at least a semicloister that hindered members from being actively involved in frontline ministry. A process of myth substitution occurred (see chapter 1): in an effort to control apostolic religious congregations Rome imposed on them a founding myth of conformity to the premodern culture of the Church that was radically opposed to the prophetic nature of apostolic congregations.[55] Their ability to critique the world and the Church became severely restricted. For this reason, it is correct to say that many apostolic communities in these centuries were never founded; that is, they became from their beginning what their founders did not want, namely, highly structured, rule-oriented communities ill-equipped for apostolic mobility and creativity.

Summary

- Over the centuries the Church absorbed or developed, to the detriment of collegiality, the spirit and customs of premodern secular cultures, and significant elements continue to exist, e.g., a monarchical

---

[53] See Southern, *Western Society and the Church in the Middle Ages*, 311.

[54] See Gerald A. Arbuckle, *From Chaos to Mission*, 26–7.

[55] See Gerald A. Arbuckle, *Out of Chaos: Refounding Religious Congregations* (London: Geoffrey Chapman, 1988) 65–77.

structure of government, a centralized bureaucracy, and patriarchal values. The Curia, while accountable to the pope, came to be seen as superior to the college of bishops.

- Prophetic people, e.g., St. Bernard of Clairvaux (d. 1153), St. Francis of Assisi (d. 1226), and Bl. John XXIII (d. 1963), through the centuries have challenged the Church's imitation of the secular feudal and monarchical governmental structures and values, but with limited success. St. Bernard censured Pope Eugenius III for looking "more like Constantine's successor than St. Peter's."[56]

- As the Enlightenment and democratic movements unfolded, the Church withdrew from dialogue with the world, developing a ghetto-like culture of protection. Clerical and religious life formation were structured to maintain this culture.

- The next chapter focuses on the relationship of gossip, shame, and humor to violence in premodernity. It will be seen that the Church continues to use gossip and shaming as ways to control and punish suspected dissidents.

Discussion Questions

1. The Church "is an institution of men and women on earth" (Vatican II). John Paul II has offered many apologies for human frailties in the history of the Church. What should I ask God to forgive in the Church today?

2. Our forebears, through their self-sacrifice, provided through the Church educational and healthcare aid to millions of migrants. What motivated such self-sacrifice? What can we learn from our ancestors who held on to their faith, even in difficult times?

3. Read the account of Jesus in dialogue with a Samaritan woman at the well (John 4:1-42). Are women being treated with respect in my parish? If not, what can I do about it?

---

[56] St. Bernard of Clairvaux quoted by Yves Congar, *Power and Poverty in the Church*, 125.

Chapter 4

Premodernity: Violence through Gossip, Shame, and Humor

Backbiters do kill, more men with a word,
Then souldiers in field,
destroyes with their sword.
(Thomas Churchyard,[1] 1594)

This chapter explains:

- that gossip can be used to coerce people;

- the importance of honor and shame in premodern cultures and their potential to foster a violent environment;

- that Jesus introduced a new system of honor and shame to counter the abuse of power in cultures;

- the fear of gossip and shaming help to ensure theological and organizational orthodoxy;

- that the fear of shaming the Church has contributed to the concealment of the sexual abuse by clergy and religious.

During the Cuban missile crisis in 1962, one of the most perilous moments in recent history, the fear of shame was uppermost in the minds of significant Soviet military leaders. Nikita Khrushchev, the Soviet dictator, later reported that his military advisers were especially

---

[1] Thomas Churchyard, "The Manners of Men" (1594), quoted by Patricia M. Spacks, *Gossip* (Chicago: University of Chicago Press, 1986) 27.

concerned that the Chinese or the Albanians would accuse them of weakness if they gave into the demand of President Kennedy to withdraw the missiles. They were more worried about what people would gossip about them than anything else.

This incident highlights two powerful human emotions that are the concern of the first part of this chapter: the fear of being gossiped about and mocked behind one's back and the fear of being shamed. These two fears are complex and highly efficient informal controllers of behavior, especially in premodern culture, and may be the cause of violence against innocent people. The second part of the chapter explains ways in which the institutional Church has used gossip and shaming to maintain theological and organizational conformity.

The Dynamics of Gossip

Definition

Gossip is here defined as the intimate exchange of prejudicial information about people who normally are not present. As James C. Scott notes, gossip is a familiar and elementary form of disguised violence,[2] that is, the use of information for violent purposes. Gossips may preface their comment with "You know, I do not wish him or her any harm, but . . ." (after which gossips proceed to do precisely what they have said they will not do). Gossip that does not have a violent purpose is better referred to as tittle-tattle and is not our concern here.

Gossip: An Act of Violence

In all gossip at least three people or groups are involved: the gossip, the listener(s) gossiped to, and the person or group gossiped about. The gossip, motivated by revenge, envy, or rage over other people's successes or failures, achieves at the moment of gossiping a sense of power over the person gossiped about. The person receiving the information not only shares this sense of power, but also feels flattered that they are trusted to hear the news. The gossip and the receiver of the information at least temporarily feel the satisfaction of disempowering the person or group gossiped about.

---

[2] See James C. Scott, *Domination and the Arts of Resistance: Hidden Transcripts* (New Haven, Conn.: Yale University Press, 1990) 28.

The satisfaction and intimate alliance that come from being trusted to pass on gossip and to receive it are very fragile. Because gossip is an expression of a response to a narcissistic need for power over others, gossips know deep down that they in turn can readily become objects of gossip spread by the very persons with whom they gossip.

Gossip is a safe form of power manipulation or aggression for its perpetrators for two reasons: the gossip claims to be merely passing on information and so refuses to take responsibility for it; and it is done in an atmosphere of trustful secrecy. Violence is done without anyone being called to testify to the information's accuracy. Sociologist Samuel Heilman speaks of gossip as "surreptitious aggression which enables one to wrest power, manipulate, and strike out at another without the other's being able to strike back."[3]

Case Study: FBI Gossips about Martin Luther King Jr.

J. Edgar Hoover deliberately passed falsified information to Robert Kennedy, Attorney General, branding King a communist, and spread malicious rumors about King's personal life among Church leaders, in an effort to stop civil rights activism.[4]

Gossip as business has reached massive proportions. Scandal or gossip magazines, purporting to "tell all" about the rich, powerful, and famous, lock-in on people's deep-seated need to experience power over others. In the secrecy of their rooms, readers can feel at once envious of and superior to the rich and powerful ("they may be rich and powerful, but I know all about them"). The reader experiences a passing satisfaction at having inside knowledge of, and thus a sense of power over, others.[5]

Gossip: Inclusion and Exclusion

Gossip is about clarifying social boundaries; it is a process of including or excluding people from social relations and identification with a

---

[3] Quoted by Spacks, *Gossip*, 30.

[4] See Fred Powell, *Free at Last? The Civil Rights Movement and the People Who Made It* (Boston: Little Brown Press, 1991) 610.

[5] See Patricia Mellencamp, *High Anxiety: Catastrophe, Scandal, Age and Comedy* (Bloomington: Indiana University Press, 1992) 194–229.

particular group.[6] The process of exclusion is commonly an act of silent violence toward those who are the targets of the gossip.

Case Studies in Control

Sociologist Chie Nakane, writing on the way Japanese individuals are controlled by the fear of gossip within the group, notes: "The feelings that 'I must do this because A and B also do it' or 'they will laugh at me unless I do such-and-such' rules the life of the individual with greater force than any other consideration and thus have a deep effect on decision-making."[7] This has an immense potential for an insidious form of violence against people. As Nakane says "the power at the top, always a dominant group and never an individual, always succeeds in imposing its aims, with even the law powerless to offer any check."[8] An example of this is the traditional custom of *murahachibu* (social ostracism), which is a form of "silent" gossip. When surplus labor is to be shed, a company's personnel department may encourage workers to ostracize those targeted for dismissal. A middle manager, for example, who has worked for the company for years fails to receive his cup of green tea from the office lady; a week later he is not invited to the regular morning meeting. Then the phone is disconnected, followed by the computer. Finally, the desk is removed. It finally dawns on the victim that he is being collectively mocked by his work colleagues, and when it becomes unbearable he leaves. This form of ostracism is common in the Japanese corporate world.[9]

Gossip in Scripture

Examples of gossip abound in the Scriptures, frequently as a device to obtain power over people. The serpent with evil intent gossips with Eve about God: "No! You will not die! God knows in fact that the day

---

[6] See Max Gluckman, "Gossip and Scandal," *Current Anthropology*, vol. 4., no. 4 (1963) 309.

[7] Chie Nakane, *Japanese Society* (Harmondsworth: Pelican, 1973) 155–6.

[8] Ibid., 156.

[9] See *The Economist* (14 November 1999) 76.

you eat, your eyes will be opened and you will be like gods, knowing good and evil" (Gen 3:5). The brothers of Joseph gossip about him, even planning to kill him (Gen 37:18-20). Herod, for his own cruel ends, seeks to engage the wise men in gossip, but they break its spell by being warned in a dream not to cooperate further (Matt 2:7-12). In the account of the temptation of Jesus in the desert, the devil calculatingly seeks to involve Jesus in gossip about God. Jesus will have none of it: "Away with you, Satan! The Lord your God is the one to whom you must do homage" (Matt 4:10). Jesus later condemns his critics for gossiping maliciously behind his back.

On another occasion Jesus identifies a whispering campaign against him and upbraids those responsible for it: "Stop complaining to each other" (John 6:43). They had scorned his teaching: "Surely this is Jesus, son of Joseph, whose father and mother we know" (John 6:42). In this incident the people feel that Jesus is trying to get honor for himself that he does not deserve; Jesus must conform to the code of honor expected of his status as a mere carpenter's son.

Shaming, Gossip, and Violence

In this section the relationship between shame and violence is examined.

Definitions

- "To have a sense of shame" is to respect the expectations of society and to conform to them. Shame in this sense can be put to good use. Indeed, without a sense of shame we would find it difficult to restrain dangerous or unacceptable tendencies. However, "having a sense of shame" can encourage people to tolerate violence against them.

Example: Shame and Domestic Violence

In cases of domestic violence it has been found that fear of public shaming can prevent the violated from revealing abuse. For example, the violated may feel too shamed to let others know that he or she is not loved by their spouse, or unable to protect

continued on next page

themselves and their children from an abuser and their physical and financial powerlessness.[10]

- "Shaming" refers to all social actions, including ridicule or gossiping, that express "disapproval [and] have the intention or effect of invoking remorse in the person being shamed and/or condemnation by others who become aware of the shaming."[11] Shaming can be good, for example, when people feel coerced to act justly, but it can also be bad when people are unjustly affected. In this chapter shaming is being used in this second sense.

- "To feel shame" means that the mocking or disapproval has hit home. It is that piercing feeling of humiliation that public exposure causes,[12] something far worse than feeling embarrassed, which is a short-lived experience of discomfort because some social norm has been ignored. Shame occurs when a person or a group feels they are negatively evaluated by others (and even by themselves as measured by their personal standards), and manifests itself through behavior such as speech disruption, lowered or averted gaze, blushing, or barely audible speech, the desire to hide.[13]

Example: Feeling Shamed

Anthropologist Maori Marsden describes the meaning of "being shamed" for Maori people. *Whakamaa* (shamed) is the experience of being looked down upon by others. People show they are *whakamaa* in external behavior that ranges from limited responsiveness and monosyllabic answers, through withdrawal

continued on next page

---

[10] See Alexander C. McFarlane and Bessel A. Van der Kolk, "Trauma and Its Challenge to Society," *Traumatic Stress,* ed. Bessel A. Van der Kolk and others (New York: Guilford Press, 1996) 31–2.

[11] John Braithwaite, *Crime, Shame and Reintegration* (Cambridge: Cambridge University Press, 1989) 100.

[12] See James D. Whitehead and Evelyn E. Whitehead, *Shadows of the Heart: A Spirituality of the Negative Emotions* (New York: Crossroad, 1995) 103.

[13] See Thomas J. Scheff, "Shame and Conformity: The Difference-Emotion System," *American Sociological Review,* no. 53 (1988) 395–405.

into the self while physically present, to actual running away from the threatening situation. They are exterior expressions of inward disintegration or overall loss of self-worth because "you know you are not what you should be within your group. . . . You have a certain place in society, and anything that takes you off your base in cultural terms causes *whakamaa*."[14]

St. Thomas Aquinas, following Aristotle, argued that the desire to act violently is the result of having been shamed; people feel justified in getting revenge for having been treated with contempt and disrespect.[15] Criminologist James Gilligan supports this view from his research. He concludes that the basic psychological motive, or cause, of violent behavior is the desire to prevent or eliminate the feeling of being shamed and replace it with its opposite, the feeling of self-worth.[16]

Shame and Guilt

Shame is about our status as a person or *who we are;* it is about identity. A violator aims to destroy the victim's sense of social/personal self-worth. Once, when I was researching socioeconomic effects of credit unions in rural Fiji, I asked a group of Fijians what it was like to be in the presence of British colonial officials. One informant replied: "When I approach a white official I suddenly feel inferior all over. I have done nothing wrong, but he tells me by the way he looks that I am worth nothing. My knees shake and my heart beats hard." The haughty behavior of the official reflected the colonial racist culture of his day.

Shame emerges from the public uncovering of vulnerability, but guilt is something private that follows a sense of failing to maintain private and internal standards.[17] Guilt is the inner experience of having broken a moral norm: shame is the inner feeling of being looked down upon by the social group. Guilt is something that can be expiated, e.g., a

---

[14] Maori Marsden quoted by Joan Metge, *In and Out of Touch: Whakamaa in Cross-Cultural Context* (Wellington: Victoria University Press, 1986) 77.

[15] See Thomas Aquinas, *Summa Theologiae* I–II Q. 47, II–II Q. 41.

[16] See James Gillian, *Preventing Violence* (London: Thames and Hudson, 2001) 29.

[17] See Lenore Terr, *Too Scared to Cry: Psychic Trauma in Childhood* (Grand Rapids: Harper & Row, 1990) 113–4.

person goes to prison for a set period following conviction for a crime, but the shame of being an ex-prisoner is impossible to erase.[18]

Shaming can lead to a false sense of guilt in the victim. Thus victims of abuse are often made to feel that they, not the violators, are the guilty party. In instances of sexual abuse the victim can be judged by the community to be the guilty one. This is common in cases of sexual abuse by the clergy: people assume a priori that the minister or priest could not be at fault because of the moral authority of the culture to which they belong, so the victim is branded as the perpetrator. The victim is made to feel guilt, in addition to shame—a twice-bitter experience of being violated.[19]

Stigmatizing and Reintegrative Shaming

John Braithwaite, a criminologist, argues that contemporary Western justice systems are weighted in favor of stigmatizing shaming, not reintegrative shaming. Stigmatizing shaming occurs when young offenders on apprehension by the authorities are ritually degraded and humiliated as individuals, then subjected to additional degradation rituals, e.g., courts, jailing, that further convey to them that they are deviant. The individual becomes stigmatized in the eyes of the community as an outcast, a social nonperson. Shame is intensified through the whole legal process. The logical outcome is that the person becomes increasingly angry, vindictive, and alienated from the community.[20] Stigmatizing shaming is a form of violence. Reintegrative shaming, on the other hand, is a process of involving the community and the offender in the latter's personal and social integration, thus avoiding stigmatizing shame.[21]

---

[18] See Robert Atkins, "Pauline Theology and Shame Affect," *Listening: Journal of Religion and Culture*, vol. 31, no. 2 (1996) 140.

[19] See Elisabeth A. Horst, *Recovering the Lost Self: Shame-Healing for Victims of Clergy Sexual Abuse* (Collegeville: The Liturgical Press, 1998) 21.

[20] See Braithwaite, *Crime, Shame and Reintegration*, 12–3.

[21] See examples in Pat Howley, *Breaking Spears and Mending Hearts: Peacemakers and Restorative Justice in Bougainville* (London: Zed Books, 2002) 119–44.

Shame and Honor

The complementary value of shame is honor. Honor is a person's or group's sense of self-worth and the public, social acceptance of that assessment. Honor is the foundation of one's reputation, of one's social status in the community.[22] The earlier example of the Cuban crisis illustrates that honor can be subject to frequent challenges by outsiders. The acquired honor of the Western world was challenged by the Soviets in the person of the president of the United States, threatening the peace of the world. It was a dangerous period and ended only when Khrushchev yielded. His followers never forgave him for the shaming or loss of honor that the Soviet Union had experienced in the eyes of the nation and its satellites, and he was deposed in punishment for this national humiliation.[23]

Claiming Honor

There are various ways people claim or maintain honor in their community, and each may involve violence or abuse of power.

1. Revenge Violence

People resort to violence when they see no other way to revenge or prevent shame except by humiliating others. Hitler gained power with the promise to avenge the shame of Versailles. The allies had met at Versailles in 1918 to impose heavy penalties on Germany for causing the First World War.[24]

2. Lying/Doublespeak

Deceit can be a culturally acceptable ritual to maintain honor in premodern culture. Anthropologist Juliet du Boulay, in a study of rural Greece, identified at least eight different types of lies, and found that

---

[22] See Bruce J. Malina and Jerome H. Neyrey, "Honor and Shame in Luke-Acts: Pivotal Values of the Mediterranean," *The Social World of Luke-Acts*, ed. Jerome H. Neyrey (Peabody, Mass.: Hendrickson, 1991) 44; Julian Pitt-Rivers, *The Fate of Shechem: Essays in the Anthropology of the Mediterranean* (Cambridge: Cambridge University Press, 1977) 1.

[23] See Martin Gilbert, *A History of the 20th Century: 1952–1999* (London: Harper-Collins, 1999) 315.

[24] See Gillian, *Preventing Violence*, 53.

some forms of lying are not only implicitly accepted, but almost expected, if a person's or family's honor is at stake.[25]

Watergate Cover-Up

Richard Nixon, in an effort to hide the Watergate break-in scandal, instructed his staff to cover-up what had happened to protect the honor of the presidency.[26] For him the end justified the means. Even when he sacrificed some of his closest aides, he still claimed that this was necessary in order to maintain the status of the presidency.

In totalitarian societies governments will attempt to rewrite history so that atrocities and oppression are ignored or concealed. In more democratic societies people will defend their honor through skillful "diplomatic" or doublespeak language that is a form of lying. It is language that avoids or shifts responsibility, conceals or prevents thought.[27] Doublespeak can take several forms; for example, flattery without foundation,[28] professional jargon or spin-doctoring, tendentious leaks to the press, language that is gobbledygook or bureaucratese. Terms like "friendly fire" or "collateral damage" are subtle attempts to conceal official and tragic mistakes. The term "downsizing" is currently popular in industry to describe a method of revitalizing a project, but it is also a form of professional jargon to hide violence done to employees who are dismissed from their work, that is, "sacked."

3. Display and Conspicuous Consumption

Generosity and public display of one's wealth and power are ways to claim and maintain one's honor. For example, in Japan giving help, gift-giving, or entertaining guests is commonly thought to be a necessary way to maintain or upgrade one's honor.[29]

---

[25] See Juliet du Boulay, "Lies, Mockery and Family Integrity," *Mediterranean Family Structures*, ed. J. G. Peristiany (Cambridge: Cambridge University Press, 1976) 405–6.

[26] Cited by Gilbert, *Challenge to Civilization*, 473.

[27] See William Lutz, *Doublespeak* (New York: HarperCollins, 1990) 1.

[28] For example, see the explanation by Takie Sugiyama Lebra, *Japanese Patterns of Behavior* (Honolulu: University of Hawaii Press, 1976) 125–6.

[29] See Lebra, ibid., 126–7.

Example: "Potlatch" and Honor

Among some Indian tribes of North America the *potlatch* is a lavish, carefully arranged feast in which much property is given to others and at times even openly destroyed. The ritual occurs on such occasions as weddings, funerals, or claims by a chief to establish an heir. The best potlatchers distribute so many items that people feel they could never repay the "generosity." Sometimes the rituals are accompanied by boastful speeches extolling the honorable status of the host and mocking the poverty and inferiority of the receivers. Somewhat similar rituals are practiced in parts of contemporary Melanesia.[30] In the Western world the ritual of *potlatch* occurs, for example, when nations compete with one another in struggling to maintain national airlines, despite their economic unprofitability. Parishes can do this by building a bigger church than the neighboring parish church. Politicians practice it at election times by making excessively generous promises.

---

4. Self-Praise

Self-praise as a way to reaffirm one's honor is common in most societies. For example, in the West, the ritual begins with, "This may sound like boasting, but . . ." The Pharisee at prayer in the Temple asserts his honorable status before God by self-praise: "'I am not grasping, unjust, adulterous like everyone else, and particularly I am not like this tax collector here'" (Luke 18:11). Jesus, of course, uses the incident to declare that the criteria of the truly honorable person are not those set by the Pharisees (Luke 18:14).

5. Arrogance

Arrogant behavior can be a ritual to dominate others through a display of power; for example, politicians in Australia achieve honor through making arrogant speeches that include the humiliation of their opponents. However, in Japan, an arrogant person is described in terms such as "overbearing," "making fun of others," "playing the big shot," and will lose honor.[31]

[30] See Victor Barnouw, *Anthropology* (Homewood, Ill: Dorsey, 1979) 226–7.
[31] See Lebra, *Japanese Patterns of Behavior*, 128.

6. Show Trials

The rituals of show trials, generally held when a regime feels under threat, are a particularly unpleasant method of asserting honor. For example, in the public trials of dissidents in Soviet Russia the aim of the regime was to so shame the victims that they became nonpersons. Even when guiltless, victims were expected to make elaborate confessions of treacherous acts; they were charged by anonymous accusers, generally tortured, and "represented" by a corrupt counsel. The ritual was meant to reinforce the honor and stability of the regime in the eyes of the people. The papal system of Inquisition initiated in the thirteenth century was also a method of shaming victims and enhancing the honor of the papacy in times of theological and political confusion. Its victims were subjected to anonymous denunciations, were not permitted defense counsel or supporting witnesses, and were often forced to "confess" through the use of torture.[32]

Honor and Shame in Sacred Scriptures

It is impossible to understand the Scriptures without a knowledge of the dynamic interaction between honor and shame.[33] For example:

- In the Old Testament, Israel's claim to honor is its intimate relationship to Yahweh (Ps 8:5). As long as Yahweh maintains protective care, Israel experiences honor, but when the people are crushed by enemies it is a sign to them that the special relationship has ceased and they experience deep shame (Jer 46:12). The prophets proclaim that Israel is shamed because of the people's sins (Jer 3:25).

- In the New Testament, Christ is out to show that his definition of honor is radically different from that of his listeners. In brief, Jesus aims through a process of myth substitution to establish a new

[32] See Thomas Bokenkotter, *A Concise History of the Catholic Church* (New York: Image, 1990) 118–9; John Paul II has publicly apologized for the violence of the Inquisition. See Luigi Accattoli, *When a Pope Asks Forgiveness* (New York: Alba House, 1998) 171–5.

[33] See *Biblical Values and Their Meaning*, ed. John J. Pilch and Bruce J. Malina (Peabody: Hendrickson, 1993) 95–104; Saul M. Olyan, "Honor, Shame, and Covenant Relations in Ancient Israel," *Journal of Biblical Literature*, vol. 115, no. 2 (1996) 201–18.

mythological foundation for all human cultures. For example, a person with authority at the time of Christ was expected for the sake of honor to dominate and demean others such as servants or citizens. Jesus insists verbally and in action that his followers must adopt different behavior (Mark 10:42-43).

- Jesus had to submit to a series of show trials: before the Sanhedrin council (a court made up of local elite frightened that their prestige with the people was threatened [Luke 22:66-71]); before Pilate (Luke 23:13-25); and before Herod (Luke 23:8-12). All aimed to shame Jesus publicly in the eyes of the people, and successfully to reestablish the honor of the accusers. The shaming of Jesus so that he became a nonperson continued with mocking, flogging, and the humiliating carrying of the cross.[34]

- According to Jewish culture, Jesus should have felt terribly shamed because he submitted to death and worse, death by crucifixion. Death by crucifixion was considered to be the cruelest and most shameful capital punishment. He was mocked as a king, onlookers ridiculed him, and his friends left him. Jesus was no longer a man of honor according to the local cultural code,[35] yet, in this action, Jesus establishes a new code of honor: sacrifice of oneself for others out of love. The true Christian is one who is prepared to be reviled, even to die, that others may live. The Beatitudes turn the contemporary culture's code of honor upside down. "Blessed" means "how honorable"; thus, "How honorable are you when people hate you . . . on account of the Son of Man" (Luke 6:22).[36] Likewise, whoever loves their enemies is truly honorable; not to love them is shameful (Luke 6:27).

Gossip and Shaming in the Church

Rituals characteristic of premodern cultures are used to ensure that theologians in the Church remain orthodox. In Germany no professors

---

[34] Bruce J. Malina and Richard L. Rohrbaugh, *Social-Science Commentary on the Synoptic Gospels* (Minneapolis: Fortress Press, 1992) 406–8.

[35] See John J. Pilch, "Death with Honor: The Mediterranean Style Death of Jesus in Mark," *Biblical Theology Bulletin*, vol. 25, no. 2 (1995) 65–70.

[36] See Malina and Rohrbaugh, *Social-Science Commentary on the Synoptic Gospels*, 322–33.

can be appointed to Catholic faculties of theology in universities without the permission of the responsible bishop *and* the appropriate congregation in Rome.[37] The person rejected by Rome has no access to the documentation that formed the congregation's decision. Nor are they told the names of the people who condemn them. The late Redemptorist moral theologian Fr. Bernard Häring wrote that the Roman congregations that decide theologians' fates encourage an undercover world of prejudicial gossip by nameless informers.[38]

Similarly, the assessment of the writings of theologians in other parts of the world is carried out without the theologians being notified; they know only after the Congregation for the Doctrine of the Faith has declared that a theologian is in error. The theologian is informed indirectly through his or her superior general or bishop, and asked to recant or face severe consequences, as the following case study explains.

Case Study

Recently Cardinal Franz Konig publicly complained that a well-known and respected Jesuit theologian and lecturer, Father Jacques Dupuis, S.J., had not been told *directly* that his writings were being investigated. He had been notified via his superior general. The Congregation for the Doctrine of the Faith stated that the investigation at that stage was not official, but merely a preliminary step in a process. However, the request to Fr. Dupuis to answer a number of questions relating to his writing could scarcely be called preliminary. Cardinal Konig condemned the Congregation's damaging use of gossip against the theologian: "The case in hand . . . is surely a sign, an indication, that mistrust, suspicion and disapproval are being prematurely spread about the author. . . . We are concerned here with the spreading of a general suspicion, in and outside the Church, that will be difficult to dispel."[39]

---

[37] See Wolfgang Seibel, "Filling Theological Chairs," *America* (7 October 2000) 12–3.

[38] See Bernard Häring, "The Church I Want," *The Tablet* (28 July 1990) 944.

[39] Cardinal Franz Konig, "In Defence of Fr. Dupuis," *The Tablet* (16 January 1999) 76.

Theological creativity is extremely difficult in an environment of distrust, gossip, and suspicion.[40] Great theologians have suffered this environment of congregational gossip in the past; for example, Frs. John Courtenay Murray, S.J., Henri de Lubac, S.J., Yves Congar, O.P., and Teilhard de Chardin, S.J.

Bishops frequently complain that Rome encourages anonymous people to report their actions and those of their priests. The late Archbishop Derek Worlock of Liverpool, who had experienced this problem some time before, wrote to a friend that "It is rather sickening to know that such denunciations continue."[41]

"Doublespeak rituals" making the bad seem good have been used in the past to avoid the need for such admissions and for reform. Pope Gregory XVI in 1832, for example, declared it was wrong "to infer that the Church could be subject to any defect or diminution or any other imperfection of a similar kind."[42] Pope Leo XIII in 1888 spoke glowingly of the Church's battles against slavery over the centuries, claiming the support of many of his predecessors, yet in fact popes had condemned only "unjust slavery."[43] Pope John XXIII asserted that "The Church does not identify herself with any particular culture, not even European and Western culture,"[44] but the Church's history contradicts this. Here mythology diverges from the facts (see chapter 1, above).

Vatican II emphasized the need for collegiality among bishops, for dialogue with people inside and outside the Church, and that the Curia's task was to faithfully serve the council's decrees. John Paul II has reiterated his belief that, "Much has been done . . . for the reform of the Roman Curia, the organizations of Synods and the functioning of Episcopal Conferences."[45] But as noted significant problems remain. There are still frequent public complaints from bishops that they are

[40] See Richard O'Brien, "Muzzling the Theologians," *The Tablet* (20 March 1999) 397.

[41] Derek Worlock, cited by Clifford Longley, "Licence for Vatican Sneaks," *The Tablet* (28 August 1999) 1154.

[42] Gregory XVI, Encyclical Letter *Mirari Vos* (1832), cited by Accattoli, *When a Pope Asks Forgiveness*, 7.

[43] See *Rome Has Spoken: A Guide to Forgotten Papal Statements*, ed. Maureen Fiedler and Linda Rabben (New York: Crossroad, 1998) 85.

[44] John XXIII, Encyclical Letter, *Princeps Pastorum* (1959), *Modern Missionary Documents and Africa*, ed. R. Hickey (Dublin: Dominican Publications, 1982) 143.

[45] John Paul II, Encyclical Letter, *Novo Millennio Ineunte* (2001) (Sydney: St. Paul Publications, 2001) par. 45.

not being consulted by the Roman Curia on matters that relate to their dioceses.[46] In fairness, however, as explained earlier (chapter 1), cultural change is slow and hesitant and that has certainly been the case in the Curia since the council. Episcopal conferences need to pressure the Curia to be more accountable for their actions. Uncritical loyalty is a quality of a premodern Church; it is shameful to criticize the "family" culture. Vatican II asserts this is a false shame and inimical to the mission of the Church in the modern world and to the ongoing reform of the Curia.

Honor and Shame: Some Dynamics

The code of family honor in premodernity demands unquestioning obedience and loyalty of members to patriarchal leaders. The relationship between the family head and the members is that of the patron to clients; people maintain status in the family circle to the extent that they are loyal to the leader. In premodern societies, such as in some Mediterranean countries, manliness is commonly the key to maintaining honor,[47] that is, the ability to protect the family or group's name and prestige when they are threatened. For women, however, the primary mark of honor is a sense of shame; that is, a woman has honor as long as she is totally submissive to her husband or guardian, and dresses and deports herself in ways that avoid drawing attention to her physical attributes. The honorable man insists that women behave in this way. Not to do so is to lack honor and experience shame. In fact, if the woman "misbehaves," the man, in order to redeem his honor, may at times kill her, as is the case today in some Muslim countries.

Jesuit historian Fr. David Schultenover argues that Rome became trapped in the Mediterranean model of honor, shame, and patronage, and that theological issues became of secondary importance.[48] The Church developed within the Mediterranean culture and so is affected by its strengths and weaknesses. Since in the Mediterranean family,

---

[46] For example, see "Submission of Bishops' Conference of England and Wales to the 1985 Bishops' Synod," *The Tablet* (3 August 1985) 816; Bishop Peter Cullinane, "A Time to Speak Out," *The Tablet* (28 November 1998) 1589.

[47] For example, see Julian Pitt-Rivers, "Honour and Social Status," ed. J. G. Peristiany, *Honour and Shame: The Values of Mediterranean Society* (London: Weidenfeld and Nicolson, 1965) passim.

[48] See David G. Schultenover, *A View from Rome: On the Eve of the Modernist Crisis* (New York: Fordham University Press, 1993).

"the father's authority is divinely ordained and virtually absolute, we have here a virtual identification of the papacy and the hierarchy with God. With that identification comes divine sanction of hierarchical action and divine condemnation of any contrary action."[49] He illustrates his analysis with the way Rome acted to condemn theologians it considered modernist. Rome's relationship to women in the Church further illustrates the thesis. While the institutional Church has encouraged the energy and gifts of women in building and staffing schools and hospitals and now as parish assistants, it is reluctant to allow them any real authority in the Church. Women are expected to remain submissive in a patriarchal cultural Church. Those who fail to do so are considered to lack any sense of shame.

Fr. Hans Küng believes that bishops are selected "according to two tried and trusted principles of sound moral standards, and the uncritical loyalty to Rome which is called 'obedience.'"[50] These are understandable requirements as long as the Church's culture remains fundamentally premodern. The one who has uncritical loyalty will not shame the "family" culture by questioning what is happening in the Church.[51] The same loyalty is expected of National Conferences of Bishops and other diocesan or interdiocesan gatherings.

Sexual Abuse: Honor, Shame, and Cover-Up

The revelations in the 1980s and 1990s of sexual abuse by clergy and religious were at first generally denied by Church authorities. It became clear that such abuse had often been dealt with by bishops and religious superiors knowingly reassigning violators to other parishes and communities where sexual misconduct was repeated. Questions began to be asked: Has there been a conspiracy among bishops, clergy, and religious to conceal this abuse in the past? Is there something in the Church's culture that has encouraged a cover-up for so long? It is important in seeking answers to these questions that we do not confine

[49] Schultenover, "The Church as a Mediterranean Family," *America* (8 October 1994) 13.

[50] Hans Küng quoted by Peter Hebblethwaite, *In the Vatican* (Oxford: Oxford University Press, 1986) 96.

[51] See Tim Unsworth, "Submissiveness Now a Cardinal Virtue," *National Catholic Reporter* (30 October 1998) 19; Thomas J. Reese, *Inside the Vatican* (Cambridge, Mass.: Harvard University Press, 1996) 242.

ourselves to cases of sexual abuse.[52] Until recent times, for example, authoritarian behavior and the alcoholism of clergy and religious have also been repeatedly hushed up. These aberrations are not unique to the Catholic ministers. In fact, argues Philip Jenkins, "Catholic clergy are not necessarily represented in the sexual abuse phenomenon at a rate higher than or even equal to their numbers in the clerical profession as a whole."[53] Why then the dramatic spotlight on the Catholic Church? A significant factor is the past attempts at concealment. In the case of sexual abuse, the actual acts "have been magnified for the victims by the extent to which the brotherhood of priests and bishops has closed ranks in denial, cover-up, and protection for the offenders."[54] Two explanations for the cover-up can be presented.

1. Psychological Explanation

A helpful way to consider these questions is to apply the psychological insights of dysfunctionality, addiction, and codependency within family systems to the Church. Virginia Curran Hoffman describes the dishonesty at the institutional level of the Church to be equivalent to delusion, that is, people are so immersed in their lies that they can no longer detect the difference between reality and what they say.[55] She claims that officials assume that they alone have the power to make decisions and are answerable only to God. Whatever they do to protect "God's special people," the Church, from public ridicule or condemnation is right and just. These people are addicted to power and its maintenance, and others in the Church become codependents when they do not question this abuse.

Codependence is an unhealthy way of relating founded "on low self-esteem and on the belief that one's worth depends on attachment to, or the approval of, some other person or group."[56] So, Catholic traffic offi-

---

[52] See Jason Berry, *Lead Us Not into Temptation: Catholic Priests and the Sexual Abuse of Children* (Urbana: University of Illinois Press, 2000) 5–168.

[53] Philip Jenkins, *Pedophiles and Priests: Anatomy of a Contemporary Crisis* (Oxford: Oxford University Press, 1996) 8.

[54] Joanna Manning, *Take Back the Truth: Confronting Papal Power and the Religious Right* (New York: Crossroad, 2002) 126–7. See also William J. Bausch, *Breaking Trust: A Priest Looks at the Scandal of Sexual Abuse* (Mystic, Conn.: Twenty-Third Publications, 2002) 11–8.

[55] See Virginia Curran Hoffman, *The Codependent Church* (New York: Crossroad, 1991).

[56] Ibid., 15.

cers will not give a ticket to a speeding priest, a policeman will not charge a clerical or religious pedophile, religious and clerics will conceal the sexual crimes and other misbehaviors of their colleagues to protect the public image of the Church and/or congregation. People who cover-up such actions are reminded by those in power that they are doing the right thing in protecting the Church's reputation and will receive approval from the Church and God. Whenever they assent to this they become codependents, unable to think or act according to the norms of objective reality.

2. Cultural Explanation

The cultural approach emphasizes the dynamic of shame and honor. The Church is traditionally seen as male and clerical, and it is the honorable thing for clerics to rule alone in order to protect "Mother Church" from being publicly shamed. Since public disclosure of sexual abuse would set the clergy up for ridicule and weaken public esteem for the power structures, concealment is the honorable action.

Humor as Violence

Humor, especially in the form of ridicule, can serve as a vehicle for violence because it can convey prejudicial information that is demeaning, arrogant, taunting, sneering, scornful, and malicious.[57] The example of Christ on the cross tragically illustrates how this can happen.

Example: Jesus Is Mocked

The passersby sneeringly laugh among themselves at the crucifixion of Jesus: "'He is the king of Israel; let him come down from the cross now, and we will believe in him'" (Matt 27:42). It is true that Jesus is present when this is happening, but he is totally unable to defend himself, and the cruel gossips knew this. Even the bandits crucified beside him scoff at him (Matt 27:44). The gossip is like a vicious slap on the face. Karl-Josef Kuschel comments that in "no comparable text of the great religions does one find

continued on next page

---

[57] See Conrad Hyers, *The Comic Vision and the Christian Faith* (New York: Pilgrim Press, 1981) 26–8.

such a combination of mockery . . . and laughter."[58] Nothing can equal the pathos of such mockery—Jesus Christ, the suffering God, is gossiped about by the very people he is dying for!

Sexist, ethnic, or racial jokes are culturally based, so that their full meaning depends upon knowledge of the cultures from which they emerge. Male joke-tellers in a patriarchal culture may use sexist jokes, even when women are not present, as a way to reinforce their gender dominance. Their jokes may not just be verbal, but erotic calendars openly displayed can have the same "joking" effect.[59] The often hidden object of ethnic jokes is to "put down," demean, or shame members of other cultures and reinforce the superiority of the culture from which the joke-teller comes.[60] Ethnic jokes are painful and degrading to members of minority groups, who, if they are present when the jokes are told, are expected to laugh submissively and accept the ascribed expressions of inferiority. When minority members retell ethnic jokes about themselves, it is frequently to deprive the jokes of their emotional and bullying power and to build up an immunity to the prejudices inherent in them, thus curbing their anger toward members of the dominant culture.[61]

Case Study: One Ethnic Joke Too Many

In Australia English people are sometimes pejoratively referred to as "poms." One English migrant comments on his experience: "I was an electrician's assistant in a large hospital. I do not think I am overly sensitive to being laughed at, but after several months

continued on next page

[58] Karl-Josep Kuschel, *Laughter: A Theological Reflection* (London: SCM Press, 1994) 82; see also Michael A. Screech, *Laughter at the Foot of the Cross* (London: Penguin Press, 1997) 17–8.

[59] See Peter Randall, *Adult Bullying: Perpetrators and Victims* (London: Routledge) 64–8; Angela Ishmael, *Harassment, Bullying and Violence at Work* (London: The Industrial Society, 1999) 4–7.

[60] See Alan Dundes, *Cracking Jokes: Studies of Sick Humor Cycles and Stereotypes* (Berkeley: Ten Speed Press, 1987) 115–42.

[61] See Mahadev L. Apte, *Humor and Laughter: An Anthropological Approach* (Ithaca: Cornell University Press, 1985) 140–6.

of being the butt of jokes about 'silly poms,' I felt I could not take it much longer. When they joked it was as though they thought I was not present in the room. I decided to object to what was being said, but this fired up several of my mates even more. And this got to me—it was day-after-day torture. Finally I decided to go home to England."

Whistleblowers: Targets of Violence

Given that loyalty is the preeminent virtue in premodern family-like groups, people daring to break the code of secrecy and silence are in danger of automatic expulsion or, of what happens in the mafia, death. The pressure to maintain silence is considerable. For example, doctors rarely publicize the incompetence of their colleagues, even though the frequency of medical malpractice decisions indicates it must come to their notice. College athletes do not commonly speak about under-the-table payments to colleagues who become superstars. If they do, they are branded with such "dishonorable" titles as "rat," "squealer," "whistleblower,"[62] "rebels," "deviants," "traitors to tradition."[63] The idiom "blowing the whistle" is too trite to describe either the agonies behind this form of identifying and reporting the wrongdoing of others or its dramatic consequences.

The Prophets as Cultural Whistleblowers

The fate of whistleblowers is starkly evident in the lives of biblical prophets. Their task was to identify and name the cultural and individual violence of the world in which they lived and to offer people an alternative model of life based on love, justice, and compassion.[64]

---

[62] For an example from the Australian police force see Janet B. L. Chan, *Changing Police Culture: Policing in a Multicultural Society* (Cambridge: Cambridge University Press, 1997) 80.

[63] See Myron P. Glazer, "Ten Whistleblowers," *Corporate and Governmental Deviance*, ed. M. David Erman and Richard J. Lundman (New York: Oxford University Press, 1996) 257–77.

[64] See Walter Brueggemann, *The Prophetic Imagination* (Philadelphia: Fortress Press, 1978) 13.

Violators were not dissuaded; they wanted the prophets to collude in their oppression of the poor: "To the seers they say, 'See nothing!' To the prophets, 'Do not prophesy the truth to us; tell us flattering things; have illusory visions; turn aside from the path, rid us of the Holy One of Israel'" (Isa 30:10-11). If the prophets refused to comply they were punished by ostracism, imprisonment, or death.

The bully King Ahab condemned Elijah as "you troubler of Israel" (1 Kings 18:17) because Elijah had castigated the king for maintaining his oppression of the poor and had called for an alternative system in favor of the marginalized. The prophet Amos, facing banishment for the same reason (Amos 7:10-17), was labeled a "conspirator." Amos had been reported to the king for naming reality: "the country cannot tolerate his speeches" (Amos 7:10). Jeremiah was branded with the word "treason" (Jer 38:4) for daring to challenge the unjust status quo. Of Hosea the people cry: "The prophet is a fool. This man of the spirit is crazy" (Hos 9:7). Jesus was called "blasphemous" (Mark 2:7) for daring to name the bullies publicly in the society of his time. The book of Wisdom succinctly summarizes the rage and violence of people who see the prophets as traitors: "Let us lie in wait for the virtuous ones, since they annoy us and oppose our way of life. . . . Before us they stand, a reproof to our way of thinking; the very sight of them weighs our spirit down. . . . Let us test them with cruelty and with torture" (Wis 2:12, 14, 19).

Yet the prophets did not fail God, because they were converted to God's service in faith and prayer; they were "trapped" or "seduced" (Jer 20:7) by the friendship they shared with Yahweh (Ps 25:14). Through faith in Yahweh and the truth of their message, they obtain a new identity, a new source of honor: "On God rests my deliverance and my honor; my mighty rock, my refuge is in God" (Ps 62:7). They are Yahweh's friends and this is now the source of their honor, not membership in a corrupt and oppressive culture.

Whistleblowers in the Church

Pope Pius XII in 1950 recognized the urgency for the Church to be open to responsible and principled dissent. Speaking first in general terms about organizations, he said that "when there is no expression of public opinion, above all, where it has been ascertained that no public opinion exists, then one is obliged to say that there is a fault, a weakness, a sickness in the social life of that [group]." He then applied this to the Church: "For she too is a living body, and there would be something missing from her life if there were no public opinion within her, a defect for which pastors as well as the faithful would be responsible."[65] Thirteen years earlier the same Pope had spoken sympathetically of dissidents: "we must be solicitous for them and ceaselessly concerned ever to understand them better . . . we must beware of too hastily attributing perverseness to them."[66] John Paul II has also spoken out in favor of principled "nonconformists": "a loyal opposition is a necessity in any community."[67]

Despite the imperative need for contemporary prophets in the Church, they are rarely able to function with any ease.[68] Loyal dissenters are people who identify the contradictions between the use of power in the Church and the Gospel: they are prophetic whistleblowers; like their biblical ancestors they imaginatively point to what should be done to use power in the service of the Gospel, but the Church's culture like other cultures inevitably resists change (see chapter 1, axiom 5). Signs of the authenticity of prophets are:

1. Gifts of the Holy Spirit

"What the Spirit brings," says St. Paul, "is . . . love, joy, peace, patience, kindness, goodness, trustfulness, gentleness and self-control" (Gal 5:22-23).

2. Union with Christ Suffering

They experience the "rigors of the narrow way," tested by personal suffering, often of an intense kind. The sense of abandonment by friends, even by God, will be theirs, just as Christ himself experienced in his own passion and death. An example is the suffering of Cardinal Newman, often caused by the authoritarian behavior of ecclesiastical officials, which he recorded in his private journal:

---

[65] Pius XII cited by Karl Rahner, *Free Speech in the Church* (London: Sheed and Ward, 1959) 5.

[66] Pius XII to bishops of France, December 1957, cited by Yves Congar, *Lay People in the Church* (London: Bloomsbury, 1957) 444.

[67] John Paul II cited by Leonard Swidler, "Democracy, Dissent, and Dialogue," ed. Hans Küng and Leonard Swidler, *The Church in Anguish* (San Francisco: Harper and Row, 1987) 312.

[68] See Robert McClory, *Faithful Dissenters: Stories of Men and Women Who Loved and Changed the Church* (Maryknoll: Orbis Books, 2000).

I have no friend in Rome. I have laboured in England, to be mis-
represented, backbitten, and scorned. I have laboured in Ireland,
with a door even shut in my face. I seem to have had many failures,
and what I did well was not understood. I do not think I am saying
this in any bitterness.[69]

The key comment is in the last sentence: rejection without bitterness.
St. Teresa of Avila, frequently the object of intimidating attacks by
ecclesiastics and her religious sisters, on one occasion was physically
prevented from entering one of her convents. Finally allowed in she
spoke courageously but sensitively to the sisters: "[T]he Lord . . . will
see to it that gradually our deeds become commensurate with our desires and intentions."[70] She could remain calm and on task because she
had allowed herself to be purified in the suffering of Christ.

3. Constructive Love of the Church

The prophet can sense how the mission of the Church should be realized at a particular time, but others come to this intuition only slowly, if
at all. The authentic prophet avoids taking ideological positions that
would lead to avoidable polarizations within the ecclesial community.

4. A Sense of Humor

Good humor is the kindly contemplation of the incongruities of life.
When prophets put too much trust in their own powers they are able to
recognize the incongruity of the situation and laugh at themselves.
Bernard Häring, who suffered much painful intimidation at the hands
of officials in the Church, never took himself too seriously. He wrote:

[The prophet in the Church] never treats principles as rigid issues,
never misuses them to justify automatic, impersonal and even
heartless behavior. [The prophet] probes for the values expressed
by the principles and is guided by them . . . [and] takes God and
his work with the utmost seriousness . . . but never takes himself
(sic) too seriously. . . . Protest and confrontation so often degenerate into violence because of the lack of a sense of humor on one
side or the other.[71]

[69] John Henry Newman, *John Henry Newman: Autobiographical Writings*, ed.
H. Tristam (London: Sheed and Ward, 1956) 251.

[70] Teresa of Avila cited by E. A. Peers, *St. Teresa of Jesus* (London: Faber & Faber,
n.d.) 22.

[71] Bernard Häring, *A Theology of Protest* (Toronto: Doubleday, 1970) 68, 75.

Summary

- Gossip as an act of violence is designed to ruin an individual's or a group's reputation. It gratifies the envious and revengeful feelings gossips feel toward others by denigrating the victims' achievements; it provides gossips with a temporary sense of power over people and a feeling of bonding with their listeners.

- Gossip in many forms, e.g., whispering campaigns, flourishes in premodern cultures as an informal method of maintaining loyalty and conformity to the group.

- Shaming refers to social actions, such as gossiping, which aim to make the victim feel demeaned, worthless, or socially a nonperson.

- Honor is a person's or group's sense of self-worth and the public, social acceptance of that assessment. There are various ways people claim or maintain honor in their community, and each may involve violence or abuse of power, e.g., doublespeak or show trials. Cultures of families, government bureaucracies, armies, police, professional associations, and religions all have their own particular ways of covering-up and lying about their expressions of violence in order to protect their public honor. People learn to keep silent about issues whose public exposure would threaten their group's positive self-image. Telling the truth is culturally forbidden: it is unpatriotic, whistle-blowing, disloyal, traitorous, giving support to the enemy.[72]

- Humor, especially in the form of ridicule, can be a form of violence, e.g., ethnic jokes.

- Whistleblowers, that is, people who publicly name wrongdoing in organizations, become objects of gossip and shaming. By daring to reveal organizational denial such as political corruption, corporate malpractice, and violations of professional codes, they break the "family's" code of honor and they suffer social marginalization or worse as a consequence.

- In order to ensure that orthodoxy is maintained among theologians, the Church commonly uses processes that conform to values of a premodern culture. For example, since the common good has priority

---

[72] See Stanley Cohen, *States of Denial: Knowing About Atrocities and Suffering* (Cambridge: Polity, 2001) 6, 11.

over individual rights, the names of accusers are concealed, independent counsel is forbidden, and there is no right of appeal.

• Recent popes have spoken of the need to have a prophetic opposition in the Church to guarantee that violence does not prevail in any aspect of its culture. Pope John Paul II, in particular, has expressed deep regret that the Church has in the past acted in oppressive ways to people inside and outside the Church: "How can we remain silent in the face of so many forms of violence perpetrated in the name of the faith?"[73]

• In the following chapter the mythology of modernity is examined and its potential to facilitate and legitimize particular forms of violence.

Discussion Questions

1. Read the story of the Prodigal Son (Luke 15:11-31). In what ways do you think this is a story about different views of honor and shame?

2. "The human person is entitled to the lawful protection of their rights, a protection that should be efficacious, impartial and in conformity with the true norms of justice"(John XXIII, *Pacem in Terris*). Do you know of people in the Church who feel their rights are not protected? If so, what would you advise them to do? How could you help?

---

[73] John Paul II, "Memorandum to Cardinals," (spring 1994), cited by Luigi Accattoli, *When a Pope Asks Forgiveness* (New York: Alba House, 1998) 174.

Chapter 5

Modernity, Rationality, and Violence

> We can hold our industrial and technological civilization responsible for the camps [during the Holocaust], not because any spectacular industrial measures were required to carry out the mass murders . . . but because a technological mentality invaded the human world as well. (Tzvetan Todorov[1])

> [M]ere purposive rationality unaided by such phenomena as art, religion, dream, and the like, is necessarily pathogenic and destructive of life. (Gregory Bateson[2])

This chapter explains:

- the founding myth of modernity and the ways in which it differs from premodernity;

- the difference between the public and the operative myths of modernity;

- that the myth of modernity has the potential to foster extensive and brutal violence such as wars, racist oppression, depersonalization of work, and lack of bureaucratic accountability;

- that modernity has had significant indirect influence on the Church's administrative structures and theology.

The above comment by Tzvetan Todorov may sound overly dramatic, but the purpose of this chapter is to show that the mythology of

---

[1] Tzvetan Todorov, *Facing the Extremes: Moral Life in the Concentration Camps* (London: Phoenix, 1999) 290.
[2] Cited by John Brockman, *About Bateson* (New York: Dutton, 1977) 92.

modernity contains within itself the potential for types of violence, including genocide, never previously imagined.

Since about the sixteenth century, reinforced by the writings of the Enlightenment period in the eighteenth and nineteenth centuries, a pivotal symbol of modern culture has been the *self*, not the group as in premodern culture. As Daniel Bell writes: "The fundamental assumption of modernity, the thread that has run through Western civilization since the sixteenth century, is that the social unit of society is not the group, the guild, the tribe or the city, but the person. The Western ideal was the autonomous man *[sic]* who, in becoming self-determining, would have freedom."[3] Such autonomous persons through reason and the sciences attain objective knowledge of a reality and discover lasting truths about an orderly world. The founding myth of modernity asserts that the human person is perfectible through his or her own efforts; progress is open to all who try hard enough (see table 1.1, chapter 1). The preeminent position of the person and the assumption that progress is inevitable for humankind found support in the emergence of classical physics. Matter was thought to be the foundation of all life and the material world was assumed to be a huge orderly machine consisting of elementary parts. These assumptions of classical physics were adopted by scientists and Western society in general and they deeply affected the thinking of politicians, social commentators, economists, and philosophers.

René Descartes' (1596–1650) influence on the evolution of this culture model has been profound in at least two ways. First, with his famous axiom "I think, therefore I am," it was concluded that individuals must equate their identity with their rational mind. The idea of an integrated body, mind, and spirit was not considered. This encouraged people to overlook the need to use their bodies as avenues of knowing and, unlike the premodern culture model, to separate themselves from the natural environment. Living organisms were thought to be machines built from separate parts; so also cultures. The latter could be divided up and sections destroyed without any sense of guilt because machines do not feel. Such a view supported a ruthless colonialism and extreme capitalism.[4]

---

[3] See Daniel Bell, *The Cultural Contradiction of Capitalism* (New York: Basic Books, 1976) 16.

[4] See Gerald A. Arbuckle, *Healthcare Ministry: Refounding the Mission in Tumultuous Times* (Collegeville: The Liturgical Press, 2000) 20–1.

Second, given Descartes' emphasis on rationality, forms of knowledge that do not fit the norms of precise, logical thinking are considered of no value whatsoever. Hence, knowledge through symbols and myths is not considered valid. As poetry, metaphysics, and theology could not measure up to the need for clear and distinct ideas, they were considered unworthy of the authentic thinking person.

The emphasis on rationality impacted on people's views of God. To some, Isaac Newton's (1642–1727) view of the cosmos as an orderly entity pointed to God's omnipotence and wisdom. As the cosmos was so neatly ordered, so also would society be if we left things to God; the deity would reconcile conflicting interests of individuals just as the creator keeps the planets at peace with one another. This viewpoint, however, eventually gave way to the assumption that the law-like behavior of the natural world showed it did not need God. God was dispensed with. Materialism and secularism thus became acceptable in the modern culture.

National, even world order was seen to be possible if enough people come to a consensus that it is good to work together; self-fulfillment is impossible if order is lacking in society. This kind of rational thinking about the conditions necessary for achieving self-fulfillment paradoxically contributed to the emergence of the welfare state, for example, in Britain, the British Commonwealth countries, France, and to a much more limited extent, the United States.

For Max Weber (1864–1920) modernity's emphasis on rationality and order would be best realized in *bureaucratic* organizations. A bureaucracy is administration in which decision-making power is vested in offices rather than in individuals as was the case in premodernity. Weber identified the following qualities of the ideal bureaucracy:

- a hierarchical line of authority;

- decisions made on the basis of technical knowledge;

- discipline impartially enforced;

- members recruited on the basis of their abilities;

- a system of assured tenure.[5]

---

[5] See Max Weber, *The Theory of Social and Economic Organization*, trans. A. M. Henderson and Talcott Parsons (New York: Free Press, 1947) 329–41.

Modernity:
Public and Operative Myths

Jim McGuigan distinguishes two types of modernity: "intellectual" and "historical,"[6] but the following terms as explained in chapter 1 are preferable, namely: "public" and "operative" myths of modernity. A public myth is a set of stated ideals that people openly claim bind them together. Modernity's public myth, as explained above, has come to be synonymous with unbounded progress, capitalism, technology, industrialization, urbanization, and other institutional and ideological features that separate the modern Western world from premodern societies. The public myth connotes positive values—optimism, perfectibility, progress.

An operative myth is what in reality gives people their felt sense of identity and this can differ dramatically from the public myth. The public myth about the positive effects of modernity is often contradicted by the operative myth, that is, its actual practice. There is no doubt about the positive impact of modernity, e.g., health, employment, etc. Yet modernity's record for violence over the last two centuries is appalling, in shocking contrast to its widely proclaimed trust in human reason and progress.

Modernity: Operative Myth—Roots of Violence

What went wrong? In order to answer this question it is necessary to appreciate, in addition to the other forces already mentioned, the pervasive influence of Social Darwinism and of the a nineteenth-century German philosopher Friedrich Nietzsche. Colonial oppression of non-European peoples and the wars between European powers cannot be understood without reference to these influences.

- The followers of Social Darwinism believed that individuals, societies, and groups were destined by nature to compete for survival. Only the strong would continue—the weak would die; weak societies must not be helped to survive because this would hold back the strong from progress. They assumed that nation-states were fundamental units of evolutionary selection, and war was the natural way

---

[6] The distinction is made by Jim McGuigan, *Modernity and Postmodern Culture* (Buckingham: Open University Press, 1999) 37–8.

for the strong to survive this process. Not to enter a war for survival would be to bring shame and destruction to a nation.[7]

- Nietzche's philosophy was not unlike Social Darwinism. He revolted against the dominant morality in the Western world that had its roots in the Judeo-Christian tradition. Loving one's neighbor was a sign of weakness. The sign of progress for an individual was the ability to dominate others for one's own benefit: "To see others suffer does one good, to make others suffer even more . . . is a . . . principle to which even the apes might subscribe. . . . Without cruelty there is no festival."[8]

The following analysis explains particular ways in which modernity's mythology has the potential to incite people to violence (see figure 5.1).

1. Individualism/Self-Interest Foster Violence

With the "death of God," sin lost its previous meaning of a break in the relationship with God. The focus moved to the self and the imperative to concentrate on personal and national fulfillment; sin became synonymous with the failure to use opportunities to one's advantage. If minority groups became obstacles to fulfillment, they had to be destroyed and their resources used to foster an "orderly" world in favor of the individual or the nation.

Modernity:
Potential
for
Violence

1. Individualism
2. Knowledge
3. Bureaucracy
4. Medical Model
5. Machine technology
6. Male dominance
7. Male sport
8. Colonialism
9. Denial of loss

Figure 5.1

---

[7] See Jonathan Glover, *Humanity: A Moral History of the Twentieth Century* (London: Jonathan Cape, 1999) 195–9.

[8] Friedrich Nietzsche quoted by Glover, ibid., 16–7.

Impact of Modernity on Genesis Creation Myth

A myth can *drift* (see chapter 1), that is, it can change, degenerate, or disappear without any deliberate planning on the part of individuals and groups. This happened to the Genesis creation myth under the impact of modernity. Extreme capitalism, with its emphasis on individualism, displaced the original stress in the myth on humankind's responsibility to be co-creators with God in this world. Social consciousness was downplayed. Marxism substituted a living God to whom all are accountable with an authoritarian state. Remove God, and individual dignity was left unprotected. Both distortions of the Genesis story have led to widespread violence.[9]

Renunciation of violence is proclaimed by governments in the West as a value of modernity, especially after the genocidal actions of the Nazis, Communists, and Fascists. However, while governments may foster justice at home, they frequently refuse to do so beyond their own borders, for reasons of self-interest, as the following case studies illustrate.

United States: National Self-Interest

The U.S. congressional investigations have established that the CIA spent at least $13 million to thwart the democratically elected President Salvador Allende in Chile.[10] Once Allende was overthrown, the American government proceeded to support the corrupt regime of Augusto Pinochet. The United States had no direct role in the disappearances of innocent people in Chile, Argentine, and other South American nations during military dictatorship years, but its anticommunist enthusiasm certainly contributed to the ideology and practices that became the cultural preconditions

continued on next page

---

[9] See Gerald A. Arbuckle, *Earthing the Gospel: An Inculturation Handbook for Pastoral Workers* (London: Geoffrey Chapman, 1990) 40–1; Thomas Fawcett, *The Symbolic Language of Religion* (Minneapolis: Augsburg, 1971) 277.

[10] See Penny Lernoux, *Cry of the People* (Harmondsworth: Penguin, 1980) 222–3, 297.

for mass killing. Defense Secretary Robert McNamara told Congress: "The primary aim . . . is to aid . . . the continual growth of the military and paramilitary forces. . . ."[11]

Congo: Legacy of Greed

When Congo became independent in 1960 under Mobutu Sese Seko, one of the more tyrannical rulers in independent Africa, America and Europe supported him because he was anti-communist, even though he, like King Leopold II of Belgium before him, considered the country his personal possession. He is gone, but the nation is in a bloody civil war, with, reports *The Economist*, Western governments aiding one side or the other in the hope of financial gain from Congo's rich mineral resources.[12]

Australia: Collusion with a Bully

The Australian government secretly encouraged the Indonesian invasion in 1975 of East Timor that involved ultimately "perhaps 100,000 unnatural deaths in [East Timor's] population of about 650,000."[13] Publicly it condemned the invasion. The Australian Ambassador in Jakarta cabled his government: "I am recommending a pragmatic rather than a principled stand but that is what national interest and foreign policy is all about."[14]

2. Knowledge: Power to Dominate

In modernity, knowledge is proclaimed to be synonymous with liberation because it allows people to control their lives. This is now

[11] Robert McNamara quoted by Ervin Staub, *The Roots of Evil: The Origins of Genocide and Other Group Violence* (Cambridge: Cambridge University Press, 1989) 230.

[12] See Hamish Hamilton, "In the Heart of Darkness," *The Economist* (9 December 2000) 25–8.

[13] Hamish Hamilton, "Politics of Betrayal," *Sydney Morning Herald* (13 September 2000) 11.

[14] Cited by Desmond Ball and Hamish McDonald, *Death in Balibo: Lies in Canberra* (Sydney: Allen and Unwin, 2000) 160.

questioned by those who perceive that knowledge can be a form of violence, as the following critiques explain.

Examples: Critiques of Knowledge

Michel Foucault (1926–84) challenges modernity's assumption that knowledge leads to liberation; on the contrary, knowledge is often a way to acquire domination over people (see chapter 1).[15] For example, Foucault criticizes the authoritarian nature of medical knowledge: "[Medicine] set itself up as the supreme authority in matters of hygienic necessity. . . . [It] claimed to ensure the physical vigour and the moral cleanliness of the social body; it promised to eliminate defective individuals, degenerate and bastardized populations."[16]

Ivan Illich's (1926–) basic thesis is that uncritical dependence on knowledge is enslavement to need, not liberation from want. In his analysis of medical domination he speaks of "cultural iatro-genesis," that is, doctors have made the natural experiences of pain and death forbidden topics for others. By encouraging us to deny these experiences, doctors hinder us from fully and naturally living: "The medicalisation of society has brought the epoch of natural death to an end. Western man has lost the right to preside at his act of dying. Health, or the autonomous power to cope, has been expropriated down to the last breath."[17]

---

3. Bureaucracies and Domination

Max Weber, having described the ideal type of bureaucracy, warns against its potential to dominate people's lives.[18] The following are interconnected negative qualities of bureaucracies that Weber and other observers have identified, each one generating its own particular brand of organizational subjugation:

---

[15] See, for example, Michel Foucault, *Madness and Civilization: The History of Insanity in the Age of Reason* (New York: Random House, 1965) and *The Birth of the Clinic: An Archaeology of Medical Perception* (New York: Vintage Books, 1975).

[16] Michel Foucault, *An Introduction: The History of Sexuality–Vol. 1* (London: Penguin, 1979) 23.

[17] Ibid., 210.

[18] See Gareth Morgan, *Images of Organization* (London: Sage, 1986) 277–8.

• *Bureaucratic Detachment: Holocaust*

Zygmunt Bauman[19] asserts that modernity's pursuit of rationality in organization endangers the future of the world, and by way of example he analyses the causes of the Holocaust. German bureaucrats, some at the drafting board, others organizing the imprisonment and transport of Jews, others at the doors of the gas chambers, all shared in this horrific action of mass murdering. Each act was done according to a routine and each departmental level was committed to implementing its own functions without questioning the overall purpose of the operation. This is the tragic perfection of bureaucracy!

Why could people do this without apparent guilt or going mad? In bureaucratic rationality the most important quality is *instrumental* reason, that is, *how* to do something rather than *why* to do it. The bureaucrat becomes detached from values and people and concerned for practical implementation. The culture allows separation of ethics from instrumental rationality.[20] Integral to modernism is the possibility that rational means will displace moral ends. The use of doublespeak also helps to hide the reality of violence from bureaucrats; for example, under the Nazis no mention was to be made, even in secret correspondence, of killings or killing installations, but instead euphemisms like "special treatment" or "evacuations" were used.[21]

Case Study

Hannah Arendt, an outstanding political philosopher of the last century, drew attention to one of the most frightening qualities of violence, namely, the often sheer ordinariness of its perpetrators. She calls this the "banality of evil." In her description of Adolf Eichmann's trial for mass murder during the Holocaust, she pointed to the plainness of his life and his views of the world, while everyone around him claimed he was the quintessence of evil. True, the racist rantings of Hitler's writings were shockingly

continued on next page

---

[19] See Zygmunt Bauman, *Modernity and the Holocaust* (Cambridge: Polity Press, 1989).

[20] Ibid., 206.

[21] See Raul Hilberg, "The Nazi Holocaust: Using Bureaucracies, Overcoming Psychological Barriers to Genocide," *Corporate and Governmental Deviance*, ed. M. David Ermann and Richard J. Lundum (New York: Oxford University Press, 1996) 158–79.

violent, but Eichmann along with so many thousands of people like him, was an ordinary, sane, unreflective bureaucrat. He was not mentally ill. As Arendt concludes, Eichmann's actions were shockingly violent, but as a person he was thoroughly ordinary, apparently not motivated by evil intentions but rationally committed to achieving personal fulfillment through a bureaucratic career.[22]

• *Lack of Personal Accountability*

Organizationally, the overall task of a bureaucracy is divided among different offices, each of which has responsibility for a small section. It is not for people at each level to question their seniors. Their task is to do what is asked of them, an argument advanced by soldiers explaining their collaboration in atrocities or failed projects of any kind.[23]

Example: My Lai Massacre

During the My Lai massacre that occurred in Vietnam in March 1968, dozens of innocent Vietnamese were slaughtered in cold blood by U.S. troops. Their leader, Lieutenant Calley, in his defense claimed that every soldier must carry out orders given by superiors without question.[24] Similar defenses had been used much earlier by Hitler's subordinates.

• *Facts over Feelings*

This is not unrelated to the previous point. To the bureaucrat, the world is a world of facts to be treated in accordance with preestablished rules: impersonally, without emotional or personal attachment to clients or fellow workers. People are recruited for the ability to be detached and for specialized knowledge.[25] Dennis Gioia, Ford's Field

---

[22] See Hannah Arendt, *Eichmann in Jerusalem: A Report on the Banality of Evil* (New York: Penguin Books, 1964) 276.

[23] See Todorov, *Facing the Extremes*, 141–57.

[24] See Herbert C. Kelman and V. Lee Hamilton, "The My Lai Massacre," *Corporate and Governmental Deviance*, ed. Ermann and Lundman (New York: Oxford University Press, 1978) 180–206.

[25] See Charles W. Mills, *The Sociological Imagination* (New York: Oxford University Press, 1959) 117.

Recall Coordinator in the early 1970s, admits that although he *felt* something was seriously wrong with a new model car, emotion had no place in the bureaucratic chain of command and consequently the car was sold with a serious fuel tank safety problem unresolved.[26]

• *Abuse of Information*

Bureaucrats are expected to implement policies made by the people in authority, but their control of the implementation gives them the opportunity to reinterpret the material of the policies, as well as to delay or even obstruct its introduction.[27]

• *Self-Perpetuating Succession*

A bureaucracy takes on a life of its own. The danger is that it will do anything to keep perpetuating itself, so people are recruited who will maintain the status quo.[28] Recall the axioms in chapter 1: people aim to maintain the cultural status and destroy whatever threatens it. The dynamics of bureaucracies can exemplify this form of coercion.

4. Medical Model

Modernity gave rise to the medical model of healthcare. The human body is likened to a machine that can be restored to health through correct scientific detection of disease and treatment. While the benefits of this model are not denied, enthusiasm for it has far exceeded its accomplishments.[29] An overemphasis on technical responses to diagnosis and curing of disease has produced a healthcare culture that can demean the dignity of people in the following ways:

• neglect of holistic healthcare, that is, denial of the interaction of body, soul, and spirit in maintaining health;

• an excessive concentration on acute hospital services to the detriment of primary care, and reduced attention to the socioeconomic causes of disease;

[26] See Dennis A. Gioia, "Why I Didn't Recognize Pinto Fire Hazards," *Corporate and Governmental Deviance*, ed. Ermann and Lundman, 153.

[27] See Andrew Heywood, *Politics* (London: Macmillan, 1997) 351.

[28] See Robert Michels, *Political Parties* (New York: Free Press, 1949); McGuigan, *Modernity and Postmodern Culture*, 45–6.

[29] See David Locker, "Social Causes of Diseases," *Sociology As Applied to Medicine*, ed. Graham Scrambler (London: W. B. Saunders, 1997) 30.

- focusing resources on patients who are attractive from a technical perspective, while the handicapped, elderly, and mentally ill are often in inappropriate conditions;

- monopoly by doctors in determining the allocation of resources.[30]

5. Domination by the Machine and the Company

A. THE ASSEMBLY LINE

In the twentieth century, workers became affected by industrialization in ways unforeseen in the previous century. A new form of cultural violence emerged—the unskilled worker's subjugation to the machine. Henry Ford recognized that his methods of assembly-line production were dehumanizing and saw no need to soften them, commenting: "A great business is really too big to be human."[31] Anthony Sampson believes that Fordism "marked the extreme of the command system, the industrial counterpart to political dictatorships in Germany and Russia, providing cheap, efficient products by dictating to both the worker and the consumer."[32]

B. THE "COMPANY MEN"

New forms of cultural exploitation developed affecting no longer only the average worker but skilled people as well. Ownership slipped from identifiable individuals or families to anonymous large or small groups of shareholders. The latter especially became subject to the intimidating tactics of high-powered company directors who could stage-manage annual shareholders' meetings. A new breed of organizational bureaucrats emerged—managers, or, as they became termed, "Company Men" (women long remained excluded from this function). These managers were expected to give their entire lives to the company, no matter the cost to their families or health. Workaholism became an esteemed virtue, provided it served the well-being of the company.[33]

---

[30] See Arbuckle, *Healthcare Ministry*, 20–7.

[31] Henry Ford quoted by Anthony Sampson, *Company Man: The Rise and Fall of Corporate Life* (London: HarperCollins, 1995) 44–5.

[32] Ibid., 45.

[33] See Morgan, *Images of Organization*, 279–80.

6. Male Dominance: Coercive Entitlement

A leading exponent of liberalism in the nineteenth century, John S. Mill, believed that women should be educated in order to be able to maintain the social norms as established by men. A poorly educated wife would weaken a man's ability to keep society's standards at the right level.[34] Modern culture's standards of the "real man" are: one who is self-possessed; is rational, never walks away from a fight; he is tough and strong, not given to expressing his feelings, and never fails. Varda Burstyn, in her study of men's violence, speaks of the mythology of "coercive entitlement" in modernity, expressed in phrases like "might equals right," "survival of the fittest," "rugged individualism," "winner take all." She claims men are culturally encouraged to accept "coercive entitlement," that is, men are stronger than women, might is on their side, and women must submit to this even if it means being subjected to violence.[35] It is common, for example, for men to be portrayed in movies and television as dominating women even in violent ways; "the woman who is beaten or raped may be seen as somehow deserving it."[36]

7. Ritualized Violence: Men's Sport

Initiation into manhood by way of violence is not the only function of major men's sports and sport culture, but it is one of the most important. The similarities between big-time sport and war are a common culture of combat and competitive placement of force and violence; war terminology is regularly applied to sports, e.g., "battleground," "combatants," "enemy." Praise of ritualized violence is taken for granted in commercial sports journalism: there is admiration for the victors when they have been able to wound the "enemy" such as in boxing and wrestling. As a result, when pressures build up in domestic or other relationships, men feel venting them by violent methods is legitimized by society.

---

[34] See Moira Galens, *Feminism and Philosophy* (Bloomington: Indian University Press, 1999) 176.

[35] See Varda Burstyn, *The Rites of Men: Manhood, Politics, and the Culture of Sport* (Toronto: University of Toronto Press, 1999) 162.

[36] See Daniel J. Sonkin and Michael Durphy, *Learning to Live without Violence* (Los Angeles: Volcano, 1982) 15.

Relationship between Sports and Violence:
Controversial Views

There is some suggestion that sport culture can foster physical and sexual violence against women. In the United States it was found that rapes by team athletes on college campuses are taking place at a statistically higher rate than in the student population.[37] Anthropologist Richard Sipes[38] investigated the catharsis theory of violent sports for the spectators and participants: that sports are healthy ways of releasing accumulated tension that can be controlled by society, that they are a means of stopping aggression boiling over into war or other forms of violence. He concludes that the negative effects are greater than the benefits: such violent sports lower the threshold of repugnance in society toward violence in general; that war and combative sports are seen to overlap and reinforce one another, and not as substitutes for one another.

---

8. Colonialism and Violence

Since the egalitarian ideal of intellectual modernity did not operatively extend beyond white Europe and the masculine world, other peoples were liable to exploitation and subjugation. Social Darwinism gave colonial officials philosophical support for their violence toward non-European peoples.

Example: Oppression of Aborigines, Australia

When British settlers first arrived in Australia in 1788, they concluded that the country was *terra nullius*, a land without a people, that it was theirs for the taking. If the Aborigines contested this assumption, they were killed or further pushed back into inhospitable parts of the country. Many died, if not from violent causes, then from new diseases to which they had no resistance. For much of the twentieth century, politicians, bureaucrats, and Church

continued on next page

---

[37] Cited by Burstyn, *The Rites of Men*, 169.

[38] See Richard G. Sipes, "War, Sports and Aggression: An Empirical Test of Two Rival Theories," *American Anthropologist*, no. 75 (1973) 64–86.

> people would remove children of mixed parentage from their Aboriginal mothers to bring them up in institutions; the hope was that over a few generations "the color would be bred out of them." Under this policy an estimated 20,000–25,000 children were effectively orphaned between 1900 and 1970.[39] Not surprisingly, Aborigines were not granted citizenship in their own country until 1967.[40]

9. Violence through Denial of Loss

> Give sorrow words: the grief that does not speak
> Whispers the o'er-fraught heart, and bids it break.
> (Shakespeare, *Macbeth*, IV, iii, 209)

Success is integral to the mythology of modernity—any failure or expression of grief over loss is a sign of weakness. This is evident in the way modernity encourages denial even of physical death. Anthropologist Geoffrey Gorer concludes: "[Grieving in the West] is treated as if it were a weakness, a self-indulgence, a reprehensible bad habit, instead of a psychological necessity."[41] Philippe Aries, an authority on the topic, writes of modernity's denial of death: "It is above all essential that society . . . notice to the least possible degree that death has occurred. . . . If a ceremony still marks the departure, it must remain discreet and must avoid emotion."[42]

Loss-denying modernity oppresses or degrades individuals and cultures because it is a human cultural imperative to admit loss; not to do so is to be consumed by sadness and depression. The Latin poet Ovid said: "Suppressed grief suffocates."[43] Emphasis is on looking, feeling, and acting young. One dare not look old, for then one would have to

---

[39] See Robert Manne, "Right and Wrong," *The Sydney Morning Herald* (31 March 2001) 11; for background see Human Rights and Equal Opportunity Commission Australia, *Bringing Them Home: National Inquiry into the Separation of Aboriginal and Torres Strait Islander Children from Their Families* (Sydney: Sterling, 1997).

[40] See *The Economist* (9 November 2000) 12; Henry Reynolds, *This Whispering in Our Hearts* (Sydney: Allen and Unwin, 1998).

[41] Geoffrey Gorer, *Death, Grief and Mourning in Contemporary Britain* (New York: Doubleday, 1965) 85.

[42] Philippe Aries, *Western Attitudes Towards Death: From the Middle Ages to the Present* (London: Johns Hopkins University Press, 1974) 90.

[43] Ovid, *Tristia*, Book V, ele. 1, line 63.

face the reality of death. The dying are isolated from the living and reduced to the level of a technological problem. The denial of loss is tragic, for the experience of significant loss should mean not only an end but a transition to a new period of creative action: "both terror and liberation, both something violent and something maturing from within, something happening to us but also something we ourselves perform."[44]

Case Study: Vietnam War

Not only individuals, but entire nations are negatively affected by the denial of loss. The United States failed in the wars in Korea and Vietnam, but successive governments have been reluctant to acknowledge this; therefore, people have not been given public permission to grieve the tragic loss of thousands of lives. (The "Vietnam Wall" memorial was built by private initiative and funding.) As long as the government refuses to admit the defeats, the nation remains trapped in a false belief that the war was a success, fulfilling the American dream. Important lessons for the nation's future will be not be learned and thousands of veterans and their families must continue to sorrow privately, their inner pain and the truth of the nation's failure ignored.

Modernity, Governments, and Violence

As was explained in chapter 1, there are commonly binary opposi-tions in myths.[45] In the mythology of modernity there is a tension between two symbols or polarities: equality and freedom, that is, be-tween the rights of common good and the rights of the individual. However, as in all great myths no detailed instructions are given on how the tensions between symbols are to be reconciled in practical terms; in practice, one pole will be stressed to the detriment of the other. Countries have sought to reconcile this fundamental tension in the mythology of modernity in different ways, sometimes at consider-able cost to the freedom of individuals or the common good.

---

[44]Josef Pieper, *Death and Immortality* (London: Burns and Oates, 1969) 30–1.
[45]See Claude Lévi-Strauss, *Structural Anthropology*, vol. 1 (New York: Basic Books, 1963) 202–7.

1. "Pro-Individual" States: Democracies

Some democracies such as the United States give far more emphasis than others to the rights of the individual over the common good. In others such as Britain, Canada, Australia, and New Zealand, the emphasis shifted in the late nineteenth and early twentieth centuries in favor of the common good, that is, the egalitarian pole in the tension. State intervention is accepted to a degree unheard of in the United States. Significant state involvement in the provision of healthcare has occurred, together with considerable assistance to marginal peoples, the unemployed, and the aged.

Case Study: United States—Structural Violence

In America's founding myth there is the belief that Americans are called to build a new land of peace, plenty, and justice—a land where, unlike the Europe the Founding Fathers had left, no person or group (especially a government) will suppress the rights of the individual. The rights of the individual, not the well-being of the community, have priority.[46] Individuals have the unqualified right to own guns despite the violent consequences to the community. It is a world made for capitalism—unrestrained competition, not collaboration for the common good. Marginalized people, such as minority groups and the poor, must solve their own problems, and many become trapped in an oppressive culture of poverty. There are about forty-three million Americans without medical insurance, including millions of poor people who do not qualify for Medicare or Medicaid. Many live in fear of sudden and expensive illnesses and feel devalued as persons because the nation classes them as beggars dependent on the goodwill and charity of hospitals.[47] They are victims of structural violence, that is, political, economic, and social institutions coerce the poor into remaining poor.[48]

---

[46] See Robert N. Bellah and others, *Habits of the Heart: Individualism and Commitment in American Life* (San Francisco: Harper and Row, 1985) 275–96.

[47] See Thomas S. Bodenheimer and Kevin Grumbach, *Understanding Health Policy: A Clinical Approach* (Stamford, Conn.: Appleton and Lange, 1995) 22, 26.

[48] See Arbuckle, *Healthcare Ministry*, 65–6.

2. "Pro-State" States: State Terrorism

Some states restrict the rights of the individual to an extreme degree; terror regimes are created in order to maintain control over the population.

• *Fascism*

Fascism is an authoritarian, nationalistic political movement that arises out of particular experiences of social and economic chaos. Examples are: Italy under Benito Mussolini between 1922 and 1945; German Nazism; the Spanish Falange; Chile under General Pinochet; and Iraq under Saddam Hussein.

Fascism: Mythic Foundations

Historian Roger Griffin argues that the distinctive element common to fascist movements is to be found in a common mythic core from the Enlightenment: "the vision of the (perceived) crisis of the nation as betokening the birth-pangs of a new order."[49] The nation that has been corrupted through the rationalism of modernity can be regenerated provided citizens are prepared to give themselves totally to the state; if necessary, they must sacrifice their individual existence to the struggle against the forces of degeneration that have brought the nation to disaster. At the heart of the state, however, is the cult of the male leader, the all-powerful leader to whom all must submit. He will lead the nation to a new youthfulness. Of all fascist leaders, Hitler best articulated this mythic vision: "National Socialism . . . is more even than a religion: it is the will to create mankind anew."[50]

Hitler's mythic vision was based on the beliefs of Nietzsche: the rejection of Judeo-Christian morality and the obligation to exterminate the weak. The Holocaust was a consequence of Hitler's acceptance of Nietzsche's amoral philosophy.

---

[49] Roger Griffin, *Fascism* (Oxford: Oxford University Press, 1995) 3.
[50] Hitler quoted by Glover, *Humanity: A Moral History of the Twentieth Century*, 315.

• *Marxism*

Marxist mythology originated in reaction to the violence of industrialism in Europe and promised people an egalitarian utopia. It offered a coherent belief system based on the Enlightenment's assumption of human perfectibility and the pseudo-science of economic determinism. Marxists, like Nazis, rejected Judeo-Christian morality. Marxism showed the tragic implications of carrying out the Enlightenment myth of redesigning society on a rational foundation without human or moral controls.

Marxism and Violence

Marxism has caused untold violence. Forty-two million Soviet citizens alone perished in the forced collectivization of the Ukraine between 1928 and 1930 and in the nationwide purges from 1935 to 1952.[51] Likewise in China there has been Chairman Mao's killing of a million landlords, the Anti-Rightist Campaign against China's intellectuals, the disaster of the Great Leap Forward that produced the world's most destructive famine, the violent turmoil of the Cultural Revolution, and Deng's Tiananmen Massacre.[52] Add to this the genocide by Pol Pot in Cambodia. The human mind has difficulty in grasping the immensity of the Marxist-inspired violence.

Modernity and the Catholic Church

The Catholic Church's reaction to the rise of modernity was largely defensive and negative. . . . The result was a divorce of secular culture from the Church and the stage of siege mentality that characterized modern Catholicism down to our day. (Thomas Bokenkotter[53])

---

[51] See Martin Gilbert, *Challenge to Civilization: A History of the 20th Century* (London: HarperCollins, 1999) 722.

[52] See Arthur Kleinman, "The Violences of Everyday Life," *Violence and Subjectivity*, ed. Veena Das and others (Berkeley: University of California Press, 2000) 233.

[53] Thomas Bokenkotter, *A Concise History of the Catholic Church* (New York: Doubleday, 1990) 231.

As explained in chapter 3, the Church after the Reformation and the Enlightenment withdrew into a fortress-like culture. It appeared to remain untouched by modernity, unlike its Protestant counterparts. However, the Church in fact became deeply but indirectly affected by modernity's emphasis on rationality and order. It was an unacceptable syncretism that few theologians or ecclesiastics were able to challenge until Vatican II.[54]

1. Impact on Theology

The Church encouraged a theology condensed into orderly theological manuals far removed from the world of experience and feeling in order to defend itself against the logical and rational arguments of Protestants. Scripture was primarily used to support preset theological positions. It was a theology that could not equip Catholics to relate to the pastoral realities of the modern world, as the following examples illustrate.

United States

By late 1954 in the United States, when support for the degrading witch-hunts of innocent people by Senator Joseph McCarthy had begun to decline, a Gallup poll showed that 40 percent of Catholics surveyed still approved of the senator and his methods, as opposed to 23 percent of Protestants surveyed.[55] A significant number of Catholics had found his fascist methods of condemning the innocent repulsive, but many fell uncritically for his fundamentalism. While there were many reasons for this, it did point to the failure of the local church in the United States to develop an appropriate pastoral response to the violent extremes of McCarthyism. Papal documents against communism were accepted with little reflective attempt to relate them appropriately to the particular conditions of American society.

---

[54] See Gerald A. Arbuckle, *From Chaos to Mission: Refounding Religious Life Formation* (London: Geoffrey Chapman, 1996) 49.

[55] See Marks S. Massa, *Catholics and American Culture* (New York: Crossroad, 1999) 77.

Australia

A similar, but less vitriolic, anti-Communist movement occurred in Australia in the early 1950s under the direction of a layman and fundamentalist ideological thinker, B. A. Santamaria, and significant bishops supported it.[56] The Movement, as it was popularly called, tore the political fabric of Australian society apart and the effects still linger. A historian, Bruce Duncan, concluded that, "Many of the bishops were extraordinarily naïve and ill-informed about basic issues of economics and politics. . . . The theological colleges . . . were small, clerical and isolated. . . . The Movement crisis starkly exposed the intellectual shallowness of this expanding and highly devotional Church."[57]

2. The Curia

The present structure of the Curia dates from the sixteenth century and reflects the centralizing policies of successive popes (see chapter 3); it developed many predictable weaknesses of modern bureaucracies listed earlier in this chapter such as resistance to change, lack of accountability, membership based on like-minded thinking, and "creeping infallibility" in administrative decisions.

The Curia was strongly criticized during the early stages of Vatican Council II for two reasons: its bureaucratic intimidation of bishops in the past, and its attempt to manipulate the council to maintain the theologically conservative status quo.[58] The bishops refused to be bullied. The Curia, on the first working day of the council, put forward 180 names for membership of the commission that would oversee the council's deliberations. The council refused to accept this interference and elected its own members.[59] In 1967 Pope Paul VI tried to reform the

---

[56] See Gerard Henderson, *Mr. Santamaria and the Bishops* (Sydney: Southwood Press, 1982) 174–5.

[57] Bruce Duncan, *Crusade or Conspiracy? Catholics and the Anti-Communist Struggle in Australia* (Sydney: UMSW Press, 2001) 388–9.

[58] See Bokenkotter, *A Concise History of the Catholic Church*, 356–9; Ladislas Orsy, "The Papacy for an Ecumenical Age," *America* (21 October 2000) 14.

[59] See Peter Hebblethwaite, *John XXIII Pope of the Council* (London: Geoffrey Chapman, 1984) 439.

Curia in line with the documents of the council, but with minimal success.[60]

3. Impact on Local Church Leadership

The historian Richard H. Tawney summarizes the major reason why the Anglican Church lost the working class during the industrial revolution in Britain in the nineteenth century: "Traditional social doctrines had nothing specific to offer, and were merely repeated, when, in order to be effective, they should have been thought out again from the beginning and formulated in new and living terms."[61]

Exactly the same could be said of the Catholic Church over the four centuries prior to the council. The bishops had become servants of the papacy, so that their ability to lead their people creatively in times of political and social crises was severely restricted; and, given the unreflective state of the theology, it was almost impossible for the Church to relate to the social challenges of modernity. The Church's social teaching and principles, which only began to take shape in the late nineteenth century, remained too broad or irrelevant to what was happening locally.[62]

Case Study: Nazi Germany

John Wilkins, editor of *The Tablet*, argues that few Catholics protested against the tyranny of Hitler because the future Pius XII, Eugenio Pacelli, as Secretary of State for the Holy See, "did not stand aside and facilitate the local Church." He believed that "the way to confront tyranny was through law and the Holy See."[63] Michael Phayer, professor of history at Marquette University, agrees: "While the pope could speak against racism, as Pius XI demonstrated, German bishops believed they could not. Ever

continued on next page

---

[60] See Peter Hebblethwaite, *Paul VI: The First Modern Pope* (New York: Paulist, 1993) 491–2.

[61] Richard H. Tawney, *Religion and the Rise of Capitalism* (New York: New American Library, 1958) 156.

[62] See John Langan, "Issues in Catholic Social Thought," *Origins*, vol. 30, no. 3 (2000) 46–7.

[63] John Wilkins, "Reformed Church, Unreformed Papacy," *The Papacy and the People of God*, ed. Gary MacEoin (Maryknoll: Orbis, 1998) 122.

since Germany and the Vatican signed the Concordat[64] at the beginning of the Hitler era, Catholic leaders had accommodated themselves again and again to the new regime,"[65] which contributed to the disastrous withdrawal of German Catholics from social and political involvement, the closure of Catholic newspapers, and the disbanding of Catholic groups.[66] As Phayer concludes: "Because church authorities left Catholics in moral ambiguity by not speaking out, the great majority remained bystanders."[67]

Case Study: Third World—Political Independence

Local churches in colonial territories were generally ill-prepared to relate to modernity and its challenges or to the emergence of independence movements. Rarely did they have locally born priests, religious, and laity in positions to lead during these tumultuous times, as they had become dependent on missionaries from the West.

Summary

- Though modernity is an elusive set of complexities that defies particular definition, its mythology has become synonymous with individualism, rationality, unbounded progress, capitalism, technology, industrialization, bureaucracy, urbanization, and other institutional and ideological features that separate the modern Western world from premodern societies.

- While modernity fostered the improvement of living standards and the reduction of disease, it has also resulted in considerable violence

[64] The Concordat between Germany and the Holy See was negotiated by Eugenio Pacelli, the future Pius XII, as secretary of state, in 1933.

[65] Michael Phayer, *The Catholic Church and the Holocaust, 1930–1965* (Bloomington: Indiana University Press, 2000) 17–8.

[66] See Wilkins, "Reformed Church, Unreformed Papacy," 122–3.

[67] Phayer, *The Catholic Church and the Holocaust, 1930–1965*, 132.

through colonialism, oppression of minorities, failure to acknowledge the spiritual aspects of the human person, and bureaucratic lack of accountability.

- The Church resisted interacting with modernity until Vatican II, but modernity did have an impact indirectly; the Roman Curia developed negative qualities typical of bureaucracies in modern cultures, such as resistance to change and authoritarianism in relationships; theology became a static discipline, highly defensive and unreflective.

- With the administrative centralization of the Church and the unreflective nature of its theology, the leadership of local churches was ill-prepared to act proactively on issues deeply affecting them such as industrialization, secularism, the rise of Nazism, Communism, and independence movements in colonial territories.

- In the next chapter jealousy, envy, and scapegoating are defined and examined with particular reference to their potential to cause violence in modern cultures.

Discussion Questions

1. "The West gives the impression of abandoning itself to forms of growing and selfish isolation . . . [and] ignores . . . its duty to cooperate in the task of alleviating human misery" (John Paul II, *On Social Concerns*). In what ways is your country ignoring its obligations to its own poor and those in foreign countries? Why is this wrong? What can you do about it?

2. Jesus taught us to pray that God's will be done on earth (Matt 6:7-15). Could you arrange with friends to pray regularly together that justice and peace may reign in the hearts and lives of people?

Chapter 6

Destructive Envy, Jealousy, and Scapegoating in Modernity

The life of the body is a tranquil heart, but envy is a cancer in the bones. (Prov 14:30)

Envy is, I believe, a pan-human phenomenon . . . a particularly dangerous emotion, since it implies hostility, which leads to aggression and violence capable of destroying societies. (George M. Foster[1])

This chapter explains:

- the meaning of envy and jealousy and their destructive potential;[2]

- that envy and jealousy are common to all peoples but cultures control or foster these emotions in different ways;

- that modernity, with its capitalist roots, particularly encourages envy;

- the nature and violent potential of scapegoating and its relation to envy and jealousy;

---

[1] George M. Foster, "The Anatomy of Envy: A Study in Symbolic Behavior," *Current Anthropology*, vol. 13, no. 2 (1972) 165.

[2] This chapter is a development of an article by the author, "Obstacles to Pastoral Creativity," *Human Development*, vol. 16, no. 1 (1995) 15–20.

- the origins of "moral panics" and their intimidating impact on people's lives;
- how the Church has scapegoated particular groups in society, e.g., the poor, lepers, Jews, women.

Envy and jealousy are almost taboo subjects in conversation and literature even though they have bedeviled humankind from the beginning.[3] Yet they are commonly causes of the misuse of power in gossip, scapegoating, and other violence. Perhaps these human experiences are so primitive that to admit to them is to damage one's sense of personal and social worth. Since even social scientists have been hesitant to write about them, possibly because they are such unpalatable topics for writers and readers,[4] this chapter concentrates on the violent dynamics of envy, jealousy, and scapegoating with particular reference to their role in modernity.

The capitalist world of modernity seductively uses envy and jealousy in particular ways. The rituals of the advertising industry, for example, commonly exalt a world of glamour, that is, the pleasure of being envied; it wants to make us envy others and to be envied by others. They slyly seek to undermine our self-worth and substitute it with a sense of self-worth dependent on looking a certain way or owning certain objects. These are rituals of violence because they degrade the dignity of the human person.

Definitions

Often the words *envy* and *jealousy* are used in lighthearted and unemotional ways—for instance, when a friend says to another, "I am envious and jealous of your holiday plans." This nonmalicious use of the words is not the meaning used in this book; rather, the words are used strictly to refer to strong, passionate feelings that have the potential to evoke violently destructive behavior.

---

[3] Foster, "The Anatomy of Envy," 23–9.
[4] See Helmut Schoeck, *Envy: A Theory of Social Behaviour* (Indianapolis: Liberty Press, 1966) 12–6.

Envy

1. Definition

• Envy is the sadness a person (or group) feels because of what someone else has and the desire or wish that the other did not possess it.
Envy is operating when another person (or group) has better gifts,
successes, or things, than oneself and this makes one feel inferior.
Envy appears when the higher gifts, successes, possessions of another
are seen as reflecting poorly on the self.

• In brief, envy is "anger at falling short of perfection, irrespective of
former successes and satisfactions."[5]

2. Fear and Destructiveness

A destructive quality is common to envy and jealousy. For example,
the jealous person has a state of mind in which pain and anger predis-
pose him or her to aggressive acts. The seventeenth-century theologian
Robert Burton wrote that "those which are jealous proceed from suspicion to hatred; from hatred to frenzie; from frenzie to injurie, murder
and despair."[6] The story of the two brothers Osiris and Seth—possibly
one of the oldest recorded myths—is about the violent quality of envy
and jealousy. The handsome god Osiris becomes king of Egypt and,
having married his attractive sister, civilizes Egypt and then the whole
world. But his evil brother Seth is envious of the abilities and achievement of Osiris; he is jealous of Osiris at the same time, because he knows
that his own wife has by trickery seduced Osiris. Enraged by these
emotions, he kills him.

Envious persons fear people will notice their inferiority; he or she
thinks that by destroying the object that causes envy the problem will
disappear. Envy, as a primitive, destructive disease, forms the foundation of many great works in English literature. In Robert Browning's
poem, "Soliloquy of the Spanish Cloister," a monk describes to himself
ways in which his entire energy focuses on the destruction of the good
Brother Lawrence. He dreams up ways to force the envied into heresy
on his deathbed, while in the meantime furtively tearing off the buds of
his melon plants. The speaker simply cannot stand Lawrence's simple

[5] David Gutmann and others, "From Envy to Desire," *Group Relations, Management, and Organization*, ed. Robert French (Oxford: Oxford University Press, 1999) 157.

[6] Robert Burton cited by Gregory White and Paul Mullen, *Jealousy: Theory, Research, and Clinical Strategies* (New York: Guildford Press, 1989) 218.

goodness. Because he cannot achieve virtue himself, he plans to destroy Lawrence:

> Gr-r-r-there go, my heart's abhorrence!
> Water your damned flower-pot, do!
> If hate killed men, Brother Lawrence,
> God's blood, would not mine kill you![7]

The First Great War had its roots in envy, with German politicians envying the power of the British. Helmut Schoeck argues that John F. Kennedy was assassinated because of envy. Lee Harvey Oswald would not have murdered him if Kennedy had been less handsome and married to an inconspicuous wife.[8]

Clarification: Envy, Coveting, and Begrudging

The psychoanalyst Melanie Klein in her study of envy diagnoses the infant's envy of the "creativity" of the good, life-giving, nourishing breast. The infant, who is dependent on it, resents that dependence and fantasizes about ingesting or destroying it.[9] It is this note of destructiveness that distinguishes envy from coveting and begrudging. To covet is to desire someone else's goods or qualities without, however, envying the owner. To begrudge is to want someone not to have the prestige or possessions that that person deserves. Unlike envy, coveting and begrudging do not connote the desire to see the envied person hurt, disgraced, or humbled.[10]

Clarification: Envy and Vandalism

Vandalism, that is, wanton or violent destruction of property can frequently be traced to envy. For example, a person who set fire to eight cars in Bridgeport (Connecticut, U.S.A.) explained his reason to the police: "I couldn't afford to own an automobile . . .

continued on next page

---

[7] Robert Browning, *Selected Poems by Robert Browning*, ed. W. T. Hutchins (London: Longmans, Green and Co., 1937) 133.

[8] See Schoeck, *Envy: A Theory of Social Behaviour*, 131.

[9] See Melanie Klein, *Envy and Gratitude and Other Works* (London: Virago, 1988) 176–235.

[10] See Gary R. Collins, *Overcoming Anxiety* (Wheaton: Key Press, 1973) 108–9.

and I didn't want anyone else to have one."[11] Likewise the destructiveness of the Indonesian militia in East Timor during the recent successful efforts to establish an independent nation would be an example of envy. If the militia could not continue to control the country, there was a perverse satisfaction in destroying everything so that the victors could not take possession. Destruction became a cleansing ritual whereby the envious party in a twisted way sought to reassert its feeling of power and superiority.

Jealousy

> O, beware, my lord, of jealousy!
> It is the green-ey'd monster, which doth mock
> The meat it feeds on.
> (Shakespeare, *Othello*, act III, scene iii)

1. Definition

- Jealousy is also a potentially destructive sadness that arises when a person either fears losing or has already lost a meaningful status or relationship with another to a rival. Jealousy assumes that what I fear losing, for example, property, prestige, I have by right; it is not caused by a feeling of inferiority, as is envy.

- The target of jealousy is what the person fears they will lose, but with envy the focus is the victim; the one who envies is not envious of the thing that is desired, but is envious of the person who is fortunate to possess it.[12]

- Jealousy is commonly cloaked beneath comments of moral indignation; for example, "Who are these people with the effrontery to take away what is rightly mine!"[13]

- Research shows that in families in which one or both partners are afflicted with jealousy, the children can become affected by its dynamic. Where violence erupts the children may be the victims of physical and emotional abuse as a consequence of the conflict between the parents.[14]

---

[11] *Fortune Magazine* (July 1952) 50, quoted by Schoeck, *Envy: A Theory of Social Behaviour*, 137.

[12] See Foster, "The Anatomy of Envy," 168.

[13] See Schoeck, *Envy: A Theory of Social Behaviour*, 115–7.

[14] See White and Mullen, *Jealousy: Theory, Research, and Clinical Strategies*, 242–6.

2. Paralyzing Emotions

Envy and jealousy are paralyzing emotions that obstruct people from making rational judgments about reality. Fueled by selfish or narcissistic desires,[15] the envious and the jealous can become so consumed by anger or rage that nothing else matters but their own world of concern. They become obsessed with gossip and scapegoating (to be explained more fully later in the chapter), the visible expressions of inner envy and jealousy. A climate of suspicion and distrust is created in which deep friendships, collaboration, and teamwork become impossible.

Biblical Insights

1. Old Testament

The Israelites had to be repeatedly warned of the primal origins and dangers of envy. Hence, the frequent reference to it throughout the book of Genesis. Adam and Eve fall because they envy God's superior knowledge and power: "You will be gods, knowing good from evil" (Gen 3:5). Cain shows all the symptoms of envy—fear, anger, sadness, and revengeful destructiveness. He could not tolerate the fact that Yahweh favored Abel and not himself. It was not in Cain's power to do anything about the assumed injustice, so, aroused by envy he seeks to even the score by killing Abel: "Cain was very angry and downcast . . . and set on his brother Abel and killed him" (Gen 4:5, 8). Even the people who attempt to build the tower of Babel are guilty of envy, not just pride and disobedience to God. Choosing to live in a great city rather than to settle in various lands as God wished and envious of God's power, they seek to build a tower of Godlike proportions, "with its top reaching heaven" (Gen 11:4). They are so consumed with envy-inspired plans that they ignore the purpose for which they were created. Their envy is self-destructive.

The account of the way in which Joseph was treated by his brothers contains all the worst elements of envy: sadness, hatred, and destructiveness. It shows how envy can bind an entire group together: "But his brothers, seeing how much more his father loved [Joseph] than all his other sons, came to hate him" (Gen 37:4). They will destroy what they cannot get themselves, namely, a favored relationship with their father,

---

[15] See Neville Symington, *Emotion and Spirit* (London: Cassell, 1994) 115–27.

and they conceal their evil deed. When they throw him down a well, the callous cruelty of their envy remains as they calmly "[sit] down to eat" (Gen 37:25).

2. New Testament

The Prodigal Son story (Luke 15:25-30) is one of jealousy, envy, and malicious gossip (see chapter 4). The young man leaves home as a brash, self-centered adolescent. Utterly destitute and alone, he accepts what is culturally one of the lowest and most shaming employments for a Jew—working among pigs. In this liminal stage of his journey, he undergoes a profound maturing experience and admits his selfishness and his need to act responsibly in relationships. The father, sensing from afar the conversion, immediately plans a celebration, because his son who had left him as an immature person now returns as an adult.

The brother of the Prodigal Son, hearing of his sibling's return, is overwhelmed not only by jealousy but also by envy of his brother. He is jealous because he fears he will lose the capital goods he thinks belong to him (Luke 15:29). He is envious because his brother now possesses what he lacks: a mature adult relationship with their father. Despite his protestations of maturity, he has not grown up to be a mature person. He wants his brother punished for his earlier adolescent selfishness, so he attempts to belittle his brother and thus destroy the joy of his father; the father will not be seduced into destroying the rich relationship that he and his son have established.

It is "out of envy that the chief priests had handed Jesus" over to Pilate to be crucified (Mark 15:10), and the reasons for their envy are many: Jesus empowers people in ways never seen before; he refuses to bribe or to be bribed; his lifestyle conforms to his teachings on poverty and humility. True to form, the envious aim to destroy Jesus, thus removing the cause of their anger. Once he is dead, Jesus' virtuous behavior will no longer be an uncomfortable reminder to the chief priests of how they themselves should be acting.

Cultures of Envy and Jealousy

There are four anthropological models of cultures in which envy and/or jealousy are especially operative and destructive. Modernity is particularly represented by models 2 and 4.

Model 1: Culture of Protection: Jealousy

Model 2: Culture of Competition: Envy

Model 3: Culture of Conformity: Envy

Model 4: Culture of Breakdown: Envy and Jealousy

Model 1: Culture of Protection: Jealousy

We have seen earlier in chapter 1 that every culture or nation tends to think that their way of doing things is right; other ways of acting are stupid, crude, uncivilized, unreasonable, evil, or superstitious. This is the social disease of ethnocentrism and it begets more jealousy than envy. People fearing that they will lose their racial, national, religious, sexual, or social superiority may act violently to protect their power.

Case Study: Ethnocentric Violence in Scriptures

Jews looked on Samaritans as racially inferior people and vice versa. When Jesus told the story of the Good Samaritan, many of his listeners must have become enraged with jealousy. Jesus had to be marginalized, they felt; otherwise, his teachings would undermine the racial and religious supremacy of the Jewish people. This rage was especially evident when Jesus formally stated that his healing mission was not to be confined to Jewish people. They wanted to kill him there and then: "When they heard this everyone in the synagogue was enraged. They sprang to their feet . . . intending to throw him off the cliff" (Luke 4:28-29).

This model can be operative in the Church, e.g., clerics may refuse to collaborate with women in ministry lest they lose their privileged power position. Religious congregational communities may object to sharing their facilities, for example, schools and hospitals, with other congregations, lest they no longer have direct control over them, and even when the only way for the apostolates to survive is through such collaboration.

Model 2: Culture of Competition: Envy

Modernity is a culture of competition because people vie with each other to get ahead and be dominant in the social and economic environment. Envy, not jealousy, is the dominant emotional force in this culture model, because it motivates people to let go of old statuses and to strive for that which makes them better than others. Jealousy encourages people to hold on to what they possess, thus inhibiting envy-inspired status climbing.

The advertising world of the mass media, using constant, subtle envy-raising techniques, proclaims that the latest is the best and that one cannot really be accepted in "correct" society if one is without it. "It" can be anything valued by the culture—cars, houses, styles of clothes, academic degrees. Mass media's envy-raising techniques are a form of subtle bullying, especially dangerous because of their often unconscious impact on people. Vance Packard in his book *The Hidden Persuaders* in 1957 first drew attention to this form of violence; advertising can be used to brainwash people to support a capitalist consumerist society. He opens his book in this way:

> Large-scale efforts are being made, often with impressive success, to channel our unthinking habits, our purchasing decisions, and our thought processes. . . . Typically these efforts take place beneath our level of awareness. . . . The use of mass psychoanalysis to guide campaigns of persuasion has become the basis of a multimillion industry.[16]

Model 3: Culture of Conformity: Envy

Conformity to tradition is a paramount in premodern societies (see chapter 2). Anthropologist George Foster writes that envy and suspicion thrive in these societies because in their worldview everything good is thought to exist in "limited" amounts; my gain (whether it be in terms of economy, prestige, or interpersonal relations) is possible only because of someone else's loss.[17] People fear they are constantly under threat from malevolent envious forces, living and dead, seeking to deprive them of their health, goods, and status. To protect them against violent forces, such as witchcraft and sorcery, they turn to various rituals:

---

[16] See Vance Packard, *The Hidden Persuaders* (Harmondsworth: Penguin, 1957) 11.

[17] See Foster, "The Anatomy of Envy," 165–202; *Cultures Under Siege: Collective Violence and Trauma*, ed. Antonius C. Robben and others (Cambridge: Cambridge University Press, 2000) 31.

• *Rituals of Praise Avoidance*

It can be very bad form to praise people for what they have done or what they possess; such praise arouses fears that those who congratulate others are envious of them and seek to destroy what they have. For example, in a New Guinea village, when I praised a father for the good health of his children and the neatness of his small house, I felt our friendly relationship suddenly change. He became distant, and the conversation ended because he saw my friendliness and interest in his family as a mask for envious intentions.

Modesty is another protective technique. The "modest" person, in replying to well-deserved praise, deflects attention with comments like "Oh, it was nothing at all. I'm really no different from you and others." Or a comment like: "Well, the honor you give me is really due to X who worked so well behind the scenes. I accept the praise on behalf of that person."

Flattery, a form of praise, on the other hand, can be a way to get what a person wants while avoiding violence. As Richard Stengel notes, "Flattery is strategic praise, praise with a purpose. . . . It is a kind of manipulation of reality that uses the enhancement of another for our own self-advantage. . . . [It] is also a kind of mask, a mask that protects and enhances the flatterer in the guise of enhancing the person being flattered."[18]

• *Rituals of Politeness*

Some people stress rules of politeness: there must be no sign of unfriendliness to others. For example, in competitive sports and politics, at least in Anglo-Saxon countries, the loser is expected to congratulate the winner, thus proclaiming the game had been fair according to the rules and that the winner deserved to win. The loser may not believe this at all, but the congratulations are a ritual and public statement that the loser is not to be envious or destructive of the winner.

• *Rituals of Creativity Avoidance*

Innovation is not encouraged, simply because any significant creative action evokes envy, as the following example illustrates.

---

[18] Richard Stengel, *You're Too Kind: A Brief History of Flattery* (London: Simon & Schuster, 2001) 14–5.

Case Study: Envy Evokes Ostracism

Soane was a young chief in Samoa. After education in New Zealand he became very critical of traditional customs of farming that encouraged laziness, poor health, and unproductive use of the land, but no one took him seriously. He gave up his title as chief and went into the forest with his family to establish a plantation of bananas and was so economically successful that he bought more property for farming. But local villagers were not impressed; they envied his success, but were unwilling to do anything for themselves. The more he succeeded the more their rage increased until they eventually decided to ostracize him and his family. First, the villagers pressured his children, then his wife, and finally Soane could take it no longer. He left the farm, paid a fine to the villagers for daring to break customs, and became absorbed into traditional, unproductive Samoan style of life.

Model 4: Culture of Breakdown: Envy and Jealousy

Culture keeps at bay what we most dread: terror-evoking chaos or the radical breakdown of order and certainties (see axiom 3, chapter 1). Among the symptoms of chaos are a sudden increase in gossip and scapegoating. The targets of envy-inspired scapegoating are often individuals or groups who are on the margins of society (a point to be explained more fully below). Jealousy also rises to new heights. For example, some people seek to escape from chaos by attempting to look back to the past in order to restore their former secure statuses and power systems. They then jealously cling to their restored positions, more fearful than ever that individuals or movements will again undermine them. Refusing to engage in dialogue with people who have different views, they defensively struggle to maintain the status quo. The following case study explains these comments.

Case Study: Australia in Crisis— Envy and Nationalism

Pauline Hanson started a new nationalistic Australian political party, "One Nation," in the 1990s, and it has had a relatively significant impact on voters. Among the reasons she gives for the

continued on next page

---

notable decline in incomes of white Australians are globalization, Asian immigration, and welfare payments to Aboriginal peoples. She skillfully draws on the unarticulated feelings of envy and jealousy that many of her followers experience. Marilyn Lake comments that Ms. Hanson "speaks to the subjectivities of (Anglo-Saxon) men—marginalised, rural, white Australian men—tapping into their pervasive sense of loss . . . mourning for lost jobs, past glories, lost power and . . . loss of national sovereignty (due to globalization)."[19] Others, e.g., migrants, city people, have moved into positions of power, but rural men have been sidelined, she claims. One commentator, in his interpretation of the rise of Hansonism, distinguishes two types of envy on the part of those Australians who feel powerless because of the economic changes in society. They experience "upward envy" of conspicuously successful urban elites and "downward envy" of conspicuous recipients of welfare services, e.g., indigenous Australians, single mothers.[20]

Scapegoating and Violence

In the previous section and in other places in this book I have referred to the process of scapegoating or witch-hunting. Because it is so intertwined with violence, the subject will now be reviewed more deeply.

Definition

• Scapegoating (or witch-hunting) is the process of passionately searching for and eliminating agents believed to be causing harm to individuals and groups. By passing the blame for their afflictions on to others, people are able to conveniently distract themselves from the real causes and the efforts they must make to remove them.

---

[19] Marilyn Lake, "Pauline Hanson: Virago in Parliament, Viagra in the Bush," *Two Nations*, ed. Robert Manne (Melbourne: Bookman Press, 1998) 118.
   [20] Ibid., 7.

- Individuals and groups displace their fears of the unknown and their aggression onto groups or individuals that are visible, relatively powerless, and already disliked or stigmatized.[21]

- The greater or more intense the chaos and consequent fear of the unknown, the more frequent and persistent is the scapegoating.

- The extent of violence involved in scapegoating depends on what the dominant culture legitimates.

Shame, envy, jealousy, and fear are among the powerful emotions behind scapegoating. For example, one who is shamed, in order to escape an inner sense of inadequacy, turns in rage on a person or group that is envied and blames them for their problems.[22]

Biblical Example

The chief priests are motivated by jealousy when they scapegoat Jesus. Their behavior is increasingly being criticized by the people and they fear they will lose their privileged social status. Rather than evaluate their own behavior, the priests prefer to make Jesus the scapegoat for their fears: "The chief priests answered [to Pilate], 'We have no king except Caesar'" (John 19:16). Self-preservation motivated this scapegoating; as Caiaphas shrewdly said: "It is better for one to die for the people" (John 18:14).

Nazi Germany

Following the First World War Adolph Hitler and other anti-Semites blamed the defeat of Germany on the machinations of international Jewry and the alleged failure of German Jews to be loyal citizens. The Allies were too powerful to be scapegoated, at least for several decades, so Hitler and his supporters turned their rage on the vulnerable Jews.[23]

---

[21] See Elliot Aronson, *The Social Animal* (San Francisco: W. H. Freeman, 1972) 189–91; Gerald A. Arbuckle, *Refounding the Church: Dissent for Leadership* (Maryknoll: Orbis, 1993) 68–72.

[22] See Stephen Pattison, *Shame: Theory, Therapy, Theology* (Cambridge: Cambridge University Press, 2000) 116, 127.

[23] See George M. Fredrickson, *Racism* (Melbourne: Scribe, 2002) 106.

Sometimes the term "stigmatization" is used as a substitute for the word "scapegoating," but there is a significant difference in meaning. Sociologically a "stigma" is a social quality that devalues an individual or a group. There are socially defined stigmas of the body (e.g., deformities), of assumed character (e.g., being gay, having a criminal record[24]), and of social collectivities (e.g., youth, the poor, a religion, tribe, nation, immigrants, race). The fact that people suffer stigmas does not mean that at this moment they are being scapegoated. It means that they are the ones most likely to be scapegoated, when the need arises, by the dominant power group for problems for which they are not responsible.[25]

René Girard: Origins of Scapegoating

René Girard (1923–) has developed a wide-ranging thesis of scapegoating. In his theory of violence he distinguishes between "constructive" and "reciprocal" violence. The former, constructive violence, contributes to the cohesion of the group, and scapegoating is a significant way to achieve this. Reciprocal violence is violence directed by an individual against another, leading ultimately to the destruction of the group.

The roots of reciprocal violence are to be found in the idea of a human self that is primarily imitative or mimetic. We come to be who we are by imitating other people. They become models for what we want to be, but a problem arises when these models become rivals and barriers to our development. They then become enemies wanting to destroy us. When tensions reach an explosive level so that society's existence is threatened, then the scapegoating dynamic becomes operative. Scapegoats are chosen and they exhaust the violence of the group, so peace is temporarily restored. Society is pure once more. The cycle is repeated whenever reciprocal violence is in danger of getting out of hand.[26] For Girard, the mimetic self and scapegoating together mold the dynamics of all religion, culture, and society. The scapegoat is sacrificed for the sake of community well-being. Through scapegoating the community

---

[24] See David Garland, *The Culture of Control: Crime and Social Order in Contemporary Society* (Chicago: University of Chicago Press, 2001) 181.

[25] See Erving Goffman, *Stigma: Notes on the Management of Spoiled Identity* (Englewood Cliffs: Prentice-Hall, 1964).

[26] See René Girard, *Violence and the Sacred* (Baltimore: Johns Hopkins University Press, 1992) 4.

protects itself from its own destructive violence, restores harmony, and reinforces social bonds.

Girard claims that, with the arrival in history of the Judeo-Christian way of life, scapegoating is no longer so effective in guaranteeing social harmony. God reveals the divine opposition to scapegoating by coming out on the side of the victim and against constructive violence. Jesus Christ, as foretold by the prophets, ends the cycle of vengeance: Christ dies asking forgiveness for his executioners who do not understand what they are doing (Luke 23:34).[27] Scapegoating is a lie invented by society to achieve an illusory feeling of peace. This is the message of Christ's life, death, and resurrection. Christ's mission is "to bear witness to the truth" (John 18:37) of the innocence of all victims of violence, and that violence in each individual and society can be controlled through God's love. Christians reject this message every time they fail to act according to the Gospel principles of nonviolence; for example, their persecution of Jews and heretics has perpetuated scapegoating down through the centuries.[28]

Scapegoating: Application of Theory

1. Domestic Violence and Scapegoating

Girard is a literary theorist rather than an anthropologist. He has been criticized for selecting examples to illustrate his theory rather than the theory emerging out of the ethnographic material.[29] However, anthropologists and other social scientists reviewing the links between sex and violence have also stressed the role of sacrificial displacement or scapegoating.

As noted earlier (see chapter 5), many consider that the power inequality between the genders and the active devaluation of females are among the fundamental causes of violence against women inside or outside the home.[30] If the man's position is threatened in the wider

---

[27] See René Girard, *Things Hidden Since the Foundation of the World* (Stanford: Stanford University Press, 1987) 219.

[28] See Robert G. Hamerton-Kelly, *Sacred Violence: Paul's Hermeneutic of the Cross* (Minneapolis: Fortress Press, 1992) 13–39; Gil Bailie, *Violence Unveiled: Humanity at the Crossroads* (New York: Crossroad, 1997).

[29] See Fiona Bowie, *The Anthropology of Religion* (Oxford: Blackwell, 2000) 179–80.

[30] See David A. Wolfe and others, "Interrupting the Cycle of Violence," *Child Abuse*, ed. David Wolfe and others (Thousand Oaks: Sage, 1997) 106.

society, he can still create or keep great power in the home through threatening violence. The female partner (or powerless child) becomes the scapegoat for the man's feelings of fear and inadequacy.[31]

2. Political Scapegoating

Tom Douglas speaks of "strategic scapegoating" in modern politics, which, he says, may be shame-driven: "The driving force behind a great deal of public scapegoating in modern times seems to be related to the possibility of exposure, a fear of being found out. . . . Hence the powerful need to dissemble, to deny with as much authority as possible, to deflect and so look for others to take the blame."[32]

Case Studies of Political Scapegoating

In recent times, farmworkers in France have been harassing McDonald's restaurants. President Jacques Chirac declared his support of this action: "I am in complete solidarity with France's farmworkers and I detest McDonald's." Why the scapegoating? The fact is that McDonald's is "very French" because it employs 30,000 workers and also buys 80 percent of its ingredients from the French market and almost all the rest from other parts of Europe. But McDonald's is doomed to be a scapegoat "for a nation painfully nostalgic for the disappearing rural idyll of *la France profonde*. France's perennial struggle against Americanisation and globalisation is as lively as ever."[33] And France's politicians for their part foster the strategic scapegoating as a way of avoiding the realities of globalization that include the commitment to freer trade between nations.

Scapegoating and "Conspiracy Culture"

In recent times the term "conspiracy culture" has become popular. It connotes a culture in which scapegoating has become a predictable way of explaining harmful or unwanted events and the explanation is termed a "conspiracy theory." The Catholic Church fosters conspiracy

---

[31] See Helen L. Conway, *Domestic Violence and the Church* (Carlisle: Paternoster Press, 1998) 76–7.

[32] Tom Douglas, *Scapegoats* (London: Routledge, 1995) 47.

[33] See *The Economist* (11 September 1999) 56.

theories whenever its decision-making processes remain secretive. For example, when Pope John Paul I died suddenly in 1978, the Vatican Press Office reported that he had been found with *The Imitation of Christ* in his hand. This was incorrect, but the story of his death was, as Peter Hebblethwaite explains, "touched up, sanitized, made more edifying for public consumption."[34] Little wonder that his death encouraged conspiracy theories.

Daniel Pipes divides conspiracy theories into *petty conspiracy* and *world conspiracy* theories; the first involve fears about people wanting to acquire local advantage, while the latter claim that evil forces are actively seeking to control global affairs.[35] The Kennedy assassination has generated an ever-increasing number of *petty* conspiracy theories that seek to explain to Americans the hidden forces that caused this tragic event. Peter Knight, an authority on conspiracy cultures, comments: "The assassination and its accompanying culture of conspiracy never seem to be far from the headlines, nor from popular culture."[36] Knight claims that a global conspiracy culture has emerged for Americans because for them their world has moved from relative stability to widespread turmoil with its accompanying uncertainties and fears. There is a breakdown of trust in governments and other agencies to control what is happening, leaving the door wide open for global conspiracy theories.[37]

"Moral Panics" and Scapegoating

The expression "moral panic" was invented by Stanley Cohen in 1972 to describe two particular qualities of contemporary scapegoating: a widespread belief that there has been a significant breakdown in social and individual morality and the ability of the mass media to highlight this "disease" with speed and in exaggerated terms. Moral panics are experiences of widespread anxiety or hysteria sparked off by apparently trivial events; social deviants must be named, bullied, and punished and then moral values will be restored to society. Moral

[34] Peter Hebblethwaite, *In the Vatican* (Oxford: Oxford University Press, 1986) 182.

[35] See Daniel Pipes, *Conspiracy: How the Paranoid Style Flourishes and Where It Comes From* (New York: Free Press, 1997).

[36] See Peter Knight, *Conspiracy Culture: From Kennedy to the X Files* (London: Routledge, 2000) 77.

[37] Ibid., 4, 242–4.

panics divert society's attention away from more serious structural and social issues that cause violence.[38]

•   Example: Britain

When British capitalism was seriously threatened in the 1970s, the authorities exaggerated the threat to law-abiding citizens from muggers and other street crime.[39] Movements such as the Teds, Skinheads, or Soccer Tribes in Britain, which are expressions of deviant youth subculture, were presented by the mass media as the "folk devils," the evil ones who undermine accepted moral values in society. They were visible reminders of what society must not become.[40] Other kinds of moral panic have developed in relation to AIDS and road rage. These events have instigated concern about the level of youth crime, violence, and drug abuse[41] and thus about education, parenting, policing, but fundamental underlying problems are covered over, e.g., unemployment and economic rationalism.

Example: Australia

In September 2001 the Australian government prevented, contrary to international law, 433 Afghanistan asylum seekers from landing in Australia after they had been rescued from drowning by a Norwegian freighter. Their decision had widespread local support. It was a good case of a moral panic. The numbers trying to land were small but many Australians felt that the refugees, if they landed, would undermine the Anglo-Saxon cultural identity of the nation.[42]

---

[38] See Eirch Goode and Nachman Ben-Yehuda, *Moral Panics: The Social Construction of Deviance* (Oxford: Blackwell, 1994).

[39] See Stuart Hall and others, *Policing the Crisis: Mugging, the State, and Law and Order* (London: Macmillan, 1978).

[40] See Stanley Cohen, *Folk Devils and Moral Panics: The Creation of the Mods and Rockers* (Oxford: Martin Robertson, 1980).

[41] See Goode and Ben-Yehuda, *Moral Panics*, 185–204.

[42] See *The Economist* (8 September 2001) 30; and James Jupp, *From White Australia to Woomera: The Story of Australian Immigration* (Cambridge: Cambridge University Press, 2002) 193–9.

Moral Panic: Physical Abuse of Children

Physical and sexual abuse of children is a tragic form of degradation and subjugation. Offenders seek to have power and control over their victims in a way that compensates for their inability to relate to adults in a mature way.[43] In recent times moral panics have broken out in reaction to well-publicized and often tragic incidents. These panics do little to encourage efforts to deal with the social roots of the problem of sexual abuse.

For example, in 2000 the British tabloid *News of the World* led a national campaign demanding that the public should be warned of the names and addresses of all those convicted of the sexual abuse of minors. This campaign, which followed a murder of a small girl, encouraged a national witch-hunt leading to rioting, beatings, and attacks on property of suspected pedophiles. Many victims were innocent people.

Why the moral panic? Clifford Longley argues that the mass hysteria had deeper roots than the tragic death of a child. Modern society is beginning to be terrified of the consequences of its own moral decay. At a deep level people have come to realize this but are too frightened to give up their own unbounded sexual freedom. Hence, they project their fears "on to those inhuman devils of popular imagination and tabloid headline, the pathetic, misguided, obsessive—and sometimes evil people we have learnt to call paedophiles."[44] Scapegoating allows the rest of us to restore the harmony of the community; the evil ones have been expelled and are unable to contaminate us again, so life can go on as usual. David Garland also argues that the inflammatory stigmatizing of child sex offenders by the mass media is a way for governments and voters to avoid having to deal with deeper problems such as child poverty, poor health care, or parental child abuse.[45]

Churches: Sexual Abuse and Moral Panic

There has been much publicity in recent times about the failure by leaders of Churches to identify and isolate sexual abusers among

---

[43] See Olive Travers, *Behind the Silhouettes* (Belfast: Blackstaff, 1999) 74.

[44] Clifford Longley, "Moral Panic over Paedophiles," *The Tablet* (12 August 2000) 1006; see comments by Harry Ferguson, "Amplifying the Deviancy of Paedophilia Can Mislead," *The Irish Times* (12 January 2001) 21.

[45] Garland, *The Culture of Control*, 136.

clergy and religious. This has generated a particular form of moral panic[46] and escapism within the Catholic Church. It is thought that once offenders are identified and punished appropriately, then moral standards in the Church will return to normal. This approach, however, avoids embarrassing questions about the cultural context of such behavior that need urgent responses, e.g.: What is being done to foster compassionate relationships between clergy? What of the authoritarian, abusive styles of leadership in the Church? Why are Vatican II's exhortations to collaborative interaction between clergy and laity not being followed?

Stigmatization and Scapegoating: Historical Comments

The qualities of the scapegoat are the same throughout history: they are people on the margins of society or those with little or no access to the power structures, e.g., the poor, women, and, at particular moments in history, Jews. We look more closely at these examples and at the Church's role in fostering scapegoating.

Demonizing the Poor

As the use of money became more general in the Middle Ages and increased with emerging modernity, the involuntary poor became more starkly socially defined by the lack of it.[47] The new rich class feared that the poor would take revenge on them for their wealth, using witchcraft and sorcery. Whenever there was a sudden downturn in an individual's or a nation's economic well-being, the poor became the targets of vicious scapegoating. To protect themselves from the machinations of the poor, the wealthy legislated to keep them at a distance.[48]

Similar scapegoating occurs in modern times, though in more subtle ways:

[46] See comments by Philip Jenkins, *Pedophiles and Priests* (Oxford: Oxford University Press, 1996) 169–71.

[47] See Robert Moore, *The Formation of a Persecuting Society: Power and Deviance in Western Europe, 900–1250* (Oxford: Basil Blackwell, 1987) 98–9.

[48] See J. Boswell, as cited by Moore, ibid. 98.

- The rich fear that the poor will nationally and internationally organize themselves to demand their share of the world's wealth. The rich are prepared to organize aid relief, but not to change structures that would allow the oppressed to take responsibility for their own lives.[49]

- Some restorationists within the Church actively discredit liberation theology (see chapter 9); this theology empowers the poor to become involved in their own liberation, but threatens the traditional clerical power base of the Church in South America.

Women as Scapegoats

Considerable witch-hunting occurred from the sixteenth to the early eighteenth centuries when Europe was experiencing rapid socio-economic changes with the development of modernity (see chapter 6). Social unrest was an inevitable consequence of these radical changes and threatened the social and religious cohesion of traditional society. The causes had to be discovered and eliminated. More than fifty thousand people were executed as witches in this period, and a similar number underwent witchcraft trials; more were acquitted or died before sentence,[50] and at least three women were accused for every one man charged.[51] Women, long thought to be threats to a patriarchal world, had little chance to upgrade their status in the midst of capitalism's speedy development. Denied access to financial resources and to decision-making roles in commerce, women were increasingly relegated to submissiveness within the home. If anything went wrong for powerful people such as sickness, death, loss of income, women must be at fault. Women were thought to bewitch people—especially "strong" men—out of revenge, envy, and jealousy or the desire for power.[52]

Witch-hunting: Involvement of the Church

The Church's history of support for witch-hunting is a sad one and no amount of apologetic arguments can remove the stain of guilt.

[49] See *The Economist* (18 August 2001) 18–20.

[50] See Keith Thomas, *Religion and the Decline of Magic* (New York: Charles Scribner's Sons, 1971) 561.

[51] See Thomas, ibid., 561, and Anne L. Barstow, *Witchcraze: A New History of the European Witch Hunts* (London: Pandora, 1994) 23–4.

[52] Barstow, *Witchcraze*, 107.

Christian society became a persecuting society in the eleventh and twelfth centuries when the clerical elites who governed both the spiritual and temporal institutions of Western Christendom entered a crisis. By the twelfth century these elites felt their power was being threatened by new power groups, e.g., urban and commercial leaders, and scapegoats had to be found and punished.[53] Heretics and Jews, like the poor, women, and lepers, had one thing in common, particularly from the eleventh century on: they had been already stigmatized by society. They became the logical targets of the threatened clerical elites in their campaigns of social, religious, and political cleansing.

The Papal Inquisition was established in the first half of the thirteenth century, and though it did not often try cases of witchcraft, it provided criteria to define heresy. In 1484 Pope Innocent VIII issued the bull *Summis Desiderantes Affectibus* which authorized two Dominican inquisitors to destroy witchcraft in Germany. They published two years later a document, *Malleus Maleficarum* ("Hammer of Witches"), that set out the ways witches were considered to act and laid down how they should be prosecuted. Claiming that witchcraft was out to destroy Christendom, the authors promoted misogyny as well as hatred of minorities and an irrational fear of conspiracies.[54] Though women were considered to be capable of receiving special spiritual powers,[55] at the same time, they were believed to be especially prone to evil and to being the agents of the devil. They are the major causes of men's problems: "all witchcraft comes from carnal lust, which is in the woman insatiable."[56] Ecclesiastical support for violence against women through the centuries found ample support in this document, though the Catholic Church was not alone in its scapegoating of women. The historian Jeffrey B. Russell comments that the Protestant Reformation stressed mistrust of women even more than did the Catholic Church: "Luther's writings writhe with fear of women."[57]

---

[53] See Moore, *The Formation of a Persecuting Society*, 27–45.

[54] See Jeffrey B. Russell, *Dissent and Order in the Middle Ages* (New York: Maxwell Macmillan, 1992) 101–2.

[55] See E. Ann Matter, "Ecclesiastical Violence: Witches and Heretics," *Concilium*, vol. 1 (1994) 84.

[56] Extract from *Malleus Maleficarum* quoted by Matter, "Ecclesiastical Violence," 85.

[57] Jeffrey B. Russell, *A History of Witchcraft: Sorcerers, Heretics and Pagans* (New York: Thames and Hudson, 1980) 116.

Anti-Semitism and the Church

Anti-Semitism is attitudes and actions against Jews based on the belief that Jews are uniquely inferior, evil, and deserving of condemnation by their very nature or by historical or supernatural dictates.[58] The long history of witch-hunting attacks on Jews by Christians is well documented, beginning with the early Church.[59]

The persecution of Jews erupted particularly whenever socioeconomic turmoil occurred and such was the case in the eleventh and twelfth centuries.[60] The Fourth Lateran Council in 1215 decreed that the Jews must wear a distinguishing badge and not appear in public at Easter time. Christians had long stigmatized Jews "as a league of sorcerers employed by Satan for the spiritual and physical ruination of Christendom,"[61] and this stereotyping justified their persecutory behavior. The Black Death plague of 1347–48, at that time Europe's greatest known disaster, had to have a cause and Jews were the logical target. By early 1348 massacres of Jews had begun in southern France. In Basle, Jews were burned to death; then in Stuttgart, Freiburg, Dresden, and many other German cities; in Strasbourg, even before the plague arrived; in Brussels, too, and then in Spain. Pope Clement VI threatened to excommunicate their persecutors, but the Christian mobs, encouraged by bizarre fundamentalist self-flagellant cults, were not listening.[62]

Anti-Semitism: Misreading of Gospels

Leo Lefebure points out that the early Christians did not see harsh language by Jesus and John the Baptist about scribes and Pharisees (e.g., see Matt 3:7; 23:13; 27:25) as an attack on Jews as a people but as a form of rhetoric which Jews used of one another at

continued on next page

---

[58] Paul E. Grosser and Edwin G. Halperin, *The Causes and Effects of Anti-Semitism* (New York: Philosophical Library, 1978) 5.

[59] For a critique of New Testament language, see Luke T. Johnson, "The New Testament Anti-Jewish Slander and the Conventions of Ancient Polemic," *Journal of Biblical Literature*, vol. 108, no. 3 (1989) 419–41; and George M. Smiga, *Pain and Polemic: Anti-Judaism in the Gospels* (New York: Paulist, 1992).

[60] See Edward Peters, *Inquisition* (Berkeley: University of California Press, 1988) 77–86.

[61] Norman Cohn, *Warrant for Genocide* (Harmondsworth: Penguin, 1970) 12.

[62] See *The Economist* (31 December 1999) 40.

> this period in their history.[63] Christians in later centuries incorrectly understood these texts to mean a denunciation of the Jewish people as a whole.

Pope John XXIII wanted the Vatican Council to make a statement on the Jews.[64] The council eventually published a Declaration on the Relationship of the Church to Non-Christians *(Nostra Aetate)* that included statements renouncing centuries of Christian anti-Semitism. The Church "deplores the hatred, persecutions, and displays of anti-Semitism directed against the Jews at any time and from any source. . . . What happened in [Christ's] passion cannot be blamed upon all the Jews then living, without distinction, nor upon the Jews of today. . . . The Jews should not be presented as repudiated or cursed by God."[65]

Pope John Paul II has frequently acknowledged the Church's role in anti-Semitism and the horrendous injustices to Jews through the centuries. On his visit to Israel in March 2000 he left a written prayer in a niche in the Western Wall, the Jewish people's most holy site, asking for forgiveness on behalf of the Church. Earlier, at the close of the European Synod in 1991 he asked for forgiveness for the indifference of Christians in the face of the Holocaust:

> Lord, our Liberator, we of the Christian communities . . . have followed worldly prudence . . . with indifference in the face of persecutions and the Holocaust of the Jews. . . . Pardon us and have mercy on us![66]

At the Pope's request, a Vatican commission published a report in 1998, *We Remember: A Reflection on the Shoah,* which acknowledged that individual Catholics collaborated in the Holocaust but asserted that the

---

[63] See Leo D. Lefebure, *Revelation, the Religions and Violence* (Maryknoll: Orbis, 2000) 71.

[64] See Michael Phayer, *The Catholic Church and the Holocaust, 1930–1965* (Bloomington: Indiana University Press, 2000) 208.

[65] Declaration on the Relationship of the Church to Non-Christian Religions *(Nostra Aetate)*, *The Documents of Vatican II*, ed. Walter M. Abbott (London: Geoffrey Chapman, 1966) par. 4.

[66] Quoted by Luigi Accattoli, *When a Pope Asks Forgiveness: The Mea Culpa's of John Paul II* (New York: Alba House, 1998) 119.

institutional Church itself incurred no responsibility.[67] The report admitted that various false interpretations of Christian teachings had contributed to centuries of prejudice and discrimination against the Jews. It distinguished between this older history, which had ended by the beginning of the nineteenth century, and a new form of anti-Semitism that developed during that century. This later anti-Semitism was based on new theories of race which were "more sociological and political than religious"[68] and culminated in the racism of National Socialism in Germany. These racial theories were contrary to the fundamental beliefs of Catholicism, and the Church had condemned them.

However, historians Michael Phayer, professor of history at Marquette University, and David Kertzer,[69] professor of Italian studies at Brown University, reject the neat distinction between the two kinds of anti-Semitism. They assert that the institutional Church did little to stop the spread of anti-Semitism right through to Vatican II. Kertzer argues that when Napoleon occupied Rome in 1798 and again in 1809, the French allowed Jews to leave the ghetto and enjoy equal rights, but one of the first actions of Pope Pius VII on his return to Rome from exile in 1814 was to force them back into the ghetto. Rome's Jews were briefly emancipated in 1848 under Garibaldi, but on the return of the exiled Pius IX to Rome in 1850 the Jews were again pushed back into the ghetto. The Church, under attack from secularism and modernity, "came to look on the Jews not as pathetic souls to be saved by conversion but as insolent masterminds plotting the destruction of all that was holy."[70] After the loss of the Papal States, the popes did little to stop the spread of anti-Semitism in Europe, except for Pius XI who became increasingly disturbed by the Nazi persecution of Jews in Germany. The ailing pope in 1938 called anti-Semitism a detestable movement that Christians could take no role in. He planned an encyclical condemning anti-Semitism but he died before it could be completed.[71]

Christian anti-Semitism, writes Phayer, "did not cause the Holocaust," but "along with modern varieties" of this racist disease "it

[67] Commission for Religious Relations with the Jews, "We Remember: A Reflection on the 'Shoah,'" *Origins*, vol. 27, no. 40 (1998) 669–75.

[68] Ibid., 671.

[69] See Michael Phayer, *The Catholic Church and the Holocaust, 1930–1965*, and David Kertzer, *The Popes Against the Jews: The Vatican's Role in the Rise of Modern Anti-Semitism* (New York: Knopf, 2001).

[70] *The Economist* (8 September 2001) 90.

[71] See Kertzer, *The Popes Against the Jews*, 279–83.

conditioned some European Catholics to become part of Hitler's murderous machinery."[72] Phayer claims that during the Holocaust period Pius XII "did not urge, publicly or clandestinely, an institutional response to the Holocaust. . . . Had the leaders of the church urged Catholics to save Jews, there would have been more rescuers and fewer victims."[73] Pius XII believed, argues Phayer, that diplomacy rather than a prophetic stand would be the best way to stop the Nazi persecution of the Jews.[74] Other historians, on the other hand, claim that the Pope did all that was humanly possible.[75] However, the failure of Pius XII to condemn the Nazi atrocities is a complex issue requiring more historical research.[76]

Summary

- Envy and jealousy are destructive emotions; they commonly cause the misuse of power through gossip, scapegoating, and other violence.

- Much violence in the Scriptures against individuals can be traced to these two emotions, e.g., Cain's killing of Abel, Joseph's cruel rejection by his brothers, and the death of Jesus.

- Cultures vary in the ways they foster and control the expression of envy and jealousy; the capitalistic world of modernity uses these to help maintain its production and selling systems.

- Scapegoating (or witch-hunting) is a process of passing the blame for afflictions on to others (who are commonly innocent), thus distracting from the real causes and the efforts necessary to remove them.

[72] Michael Phayer, *The Catholic Church and the Holocaust, 1930–1965*, 1.

[73] Ibid., 132.

[74] Ibid., 41–132.

[75] For example, see Margherita Marchione, *Pope Pius XII: Architect of Peace* (London: Gracewing, 2000).

[76] See comments by Kilian McDonnell, "Pope Pius XII and the Holocaust: Fear of Reprisals and Generic Diplomacy," *Gregorianum*, vol. 83, no. 2 (2002) 329–33; and Michael Walsh's analysis of the historical and theological weaknesses of Daniel J. Goldhagen's book, *A Moral Reckoning: The Role of the Catholic Church in the Holocaust and Its Unfilled Duty of Repair* (London: Little, Brown, 2002), in *The Tablet* (2 November 2002) 17.

- Scapegoating flourishes in modernity; the speed of change and the resulting cultural and personal dislocation encourage people to look for individuals or events to blame.

- The Church's history of support for scapegoating is a sad one, as shown in its relationships with women and Jews over the centuries.

Discussion Questions

1. Read Mark 15:10, followed by Mark 15:16-39 (the death of Jesus). Ponder the terrible violent consequences of uncontrolled jealousy and envy.

2. Read 1 Corinthians 13:1-13. Here St. Paul says the more we love God the less the evils of jealousy and envy will affect us. Why do you think this is so? Have you praised individuals recently for something good they have done?

3. Does your culture encourage you to look down on other peoples, even to blame them incorrectly for the problems of your nation? Think of examples when Jesus condemned this behavior.

Chapter 7

Postmodernity:
Background to New Forms of Violence

The human mind [to the postmodernist] now appears to be anything but a neat thinking machine that—when properly operated—poses right questions and prints out right answers. (Walter T. Anderson[1])

One listens to reggae, watches a western, eats McDonald's food for lunch and local cuisine for dinner, wears Paris perfume in Tokyo and 'retro' clothes in Hong Kong. (Jean-François Lyotard[2])

This chapter explains:

- the meaning of the terms "postmodernism" and "postmodernity";

- that the roots of postmodernity are to be found in movements of the expressive revolution that began in the 1960s;

- the "anti-order" reactions to postmodernism: rejection of "meta-narratives" or cultural mythologies, the loss of history, cynicism;

- the relationship between postmodernism and new forms of violence;

- globalization and some of its negative qualities.

[1] Walter T. Anderson, *The Truth About the Truth: De-Confusing and Re-Constructing the Postmodern World* (New York: Putnam, 1995) 240.
[2] Jean-François Lyotard, *The Postmodern Condition: A Report on Knowledge* (Manchester: Manchester University Press, 1984) 263.

The thesis of the chapter is that postmodernity is an epochal cultural shift from modernity. It involves the rejection of many of the cultural certainties on which the Western world has been built over the last two centuries (see chapter 1, table 1.1). It has legitimized new forms of violence, some referred to in this chapter and others in more detail in the following chapter. At the same time, paradoxically, fundamental aspects of modernity have become stronger, e.g., the Social Darwinist negative policies of the nineteenth century toward the poor have re-appeared in politics and economics. This is why Anthony Giddens refers to postmodernity as "accentuated modernity."[3]

The terms "postmodernity" and "postmodernism" are freely used today, but not defined in any consistent manner. Both terms have become elastic and, for many, disturbingly elusive in their breadth of reference and attributions.[4] Ernest Gellner, professor of social anthropology at Cambridge University, summarizes a general feeling when writing on postmodernism: "it is not altogether clear what the devil it is." With little comfort he says, "clarity is not conspicuous amongst its marked attributes."[5] However, in this book:

- *postmodernity* describes the culture model that actively influences the world today;

- *postmodernism* connotes the movements that produced the culture shift from modernity to postmodernity in the late 1960s and early 1970s, as well as reactions to these movements.[6]

Signs of a postmodern world began to catch the attention of culture-watchers in the early 1970s, its way "paved by the psychedelic, academic, racial and political upheavals of the 1960s."[7] The assumptions that reality is ordered in a way which can be laid bare by the human mind and that it is possible to build a universal human culture upon a

[3] See Anthony Giddens, *The Consequences of Modernity* (Cambridge: Polity Press, 1990).

[4] See Peter Brooker, *A Concise Glossary of Cultural Theory* (London: Arnold, 1999) 174.

[5] Ernest Gellner, *Postmodernism, Reason and Religion* (London: Routledge, 1992) 22; see comments by Stuart Sim, *Postmodernism*, ed. Stuart Sim (London: Routledge, 2001) 3–14.

[6] See David Harvey, *The Condition of Postmodernity: An Enquiry into the Origins of Cultural Change* (Cambridge: Basil Blackwell, 1989) 6–7.

[7] Anderson, *The Truth About the Truth*, 7.

foundation of rational thought are rejected. Assertions of truth and ethics are considered to be without foundation and in their place is a relativistic construction of the world through language and narrative. There is a breakdown of certainty, writes Jean-François Lyotard, "a loss of a central, organizing principle governing society and a unitary standard of cultural excellence or morality, and a decline in the belief of a unitary, coherent self."[8] Today postmodern thought is already passing into a new stage connected "to the explosion of information and communication technologies, the global mass-media economy of images, and the ever-increasing determination of many men and women to reconstruct traditional ideas about sex and gender."[9]

Postmodernity: Characteristics

To unravel some of the complexity of postmodernity, it is helpful to summarize its main characteristics under four headings:[10] economic, social, political, and cultural.

1. Economic: Post-Fordism

Fordism characterized modernity (see chapter 5): the mass production of a standardized and limited variety of goods by large companies, most of which were nationally organized; the employment of a predominantly male workforce; the widespread use of unskilled or semiskilled labor in fragmented jobs; the use of the "assembly-line" production techniques; a hierarchical and centralized management style.[11] In the last twenty years, however, there has been a rapid and significant shift in capitalist production and organization away from Fordism to what is termed *Post-Fordism*, noted for the following qualities:

• computers and other forms of information technology have widely replaced the heavy industry of modernity;

---

[8] Jean-François Lyotard, "The Postmodern Condition," *The Postmodern Turn: New Perspectives on Social Theory*, ed. Steven Seidman (Cambridge: Cambridge University Press, 1994) 27.

[9] Anderson, *The Truth About the Truth*, 7.

[10] See Nicholas Abercrombie and others, *The Penguin Dictionary of Sociology* (Harmondsworth: Penguin, 2000) 272–3.

[11] See Philip Bounds, *Cultural Studies* (Plymouth: Studymates, 1999) 87.

- the labor process is more flexible, specialized, and decentralized;

- individual companies no longer control all aspects of production, but outsource to other agencies;

- an emphasis on variety of goods, rather than mass production of standardized goods, made possible by production systems using programmable automation;

- the size of the blue-collar working class is significantly reduced and replaced by service and white-collar classes; the employment of women significantly increases;

- the rise of multinational companies and the weakening of the state controls over industry; the financial system is increasingly globalized and removed from individual state controls.[12]

2. Social: Sources of Identity Varied

Industrialization and its economic system of capitalism had produced clearly identified and rigid social classes. In postmodernity the social structure is more fluid, fragmented, and complicated. It has been called by Manuel Castells "the network society."[13] The massive extension of transnational information systems and the consequent ability of people to develop social identities which transcend national boundaries, are resulting in sources of social identity additional to class systems based on gender, ethnicity, age, etc.

3. Political: Weakening of the Nation-State

The nation-state, once powerful in modernity, is no longer so dominant in defining people's identities and controlling their lives.

- Given the new technologies, it has become possible for today's states to be subjected to levels of intense surveillance by their citizens and by other states. Cover-ups of corruption or the misuse of power are less and less likely to be sustained.[14]

- Governments can no longer significantly control their finances through their intervention in the economy. States function less as

---

[12] See ibid., 87–8.
[13] Manuel Castells, *The Power of Identity* (Oxford: Blackwell, 1997) 1.
[14] See Castells, ibid., 302.

"sovereign" entities and more as components of an international "polity."[15]

- Ease of communication, vastly improved transportation facilities, and high-tech weaponry are making states more vulnerable to terrorist violence and its potential to cause widespread economic, political, and social consequences.[16]

- In reaction to the big government philosophy of modernity, states are lessening their direct involvement in people's lives by dismantling the welfare state and by privatization.

4. Cultural: Mythological Shifts

Behind the economic and political shifts that characterize postmodernity were radical changes in mythology. In contrast to the optimistic mythology of modernity, postmodernism connotes an extensive cultural malaise noted for its cynicism, pragmatism, deconstructionism, narcissism, skepticism, relativism, and nihilism.

Postmodernity's Roots:
Revolution of Expressive Disorder

To understand this mythological change, it is necessary to appreciate the dynamics and impact of the cultural turmoil of the 1960s, sometimes referred to as the "revolution of expressive disorder." Morris Dickstein is right: "The sixties are over, but they remain the watershed of our recent cultural history; they continue to affect the ambiance of our lives in innumerable ways."[17]

From the early 1960s to the early 1970s, the entire Western world experienced a dramatic, highly intense transformation of its cultural values and behavior patterns that started as a form of cultural revolution among a small group of committed radicals and climaxed by changing some of the most profound habits and assumptions of Western society.

---

[15] See Paul Hirst and Grahame Thompson, *Globalization in Question: The International Economy and the Possibilities of Governance* (Cambridge: Polity Press, 1996) 171.

[16] See Castells, *The Power of Identity*, 302.

[17] Morris Dickstein, *Gates of Eden: American Culture in the Sixties* (New York: Basic Books, 1977) 213.

The catalytic actions of white middle-class youth affected everything: politics, arts, education, and religion.

The Expressive Revolution in the United States

Gerald Howard considers the period as "a spirited, wildly inventive era—a decade of great social and political upheaval when ideas and customs collided in every corner."[18] Within the United States, for example, it cut short the presidency of Lyndon Johnson, eventually killed the imperialist presidency of Richard Nixon, and weakened centuries of discrimination against blacks. Traditions were devalued, censorship dismantled, churches deserted, schools degraded, the family derided. Contemporary art, rock, recreational drugs, women's lib, and gay lib edged their way into the establishment. The cold war, a revulsion against McCarthyism, and the rise of student activism unleashed a whirlwind of violence. Protests on university campuses and riots in the inner cities were merely the outward signs of a nation in ferment captured nightly on television. Helicopters hovering over teargassed protesters outside the White House, national guardsmen firing into crowds of student anti-Vietnam War demonstrators in Alabama, and, most terrible of all, the assassinations of President Kennedy, his brother Robert, and Martin Luther King Jr.[19] The pattern was the same in varying degrees in other parts of the Western world;[20] for example, student riots in France helped to topple President de Gaulle in 1968.

Sociologist Bernice Martin points out that the most common characteristic of the revolutionary liminality was the symbolism of "antistructure," "anti-order," "anti-predictability":[21] gaudy dress, long

---

[18] Gerald Howard, *The Sixties: The Art, Attitudes, Politics and Media of Our Most Explosive Decade* (New York: Washington Square Press, 1982) 4.

[19] See Terry H. Anderson, *The Movement and the Sixties: Protest in America from Greensboro to Wounded Knee* (New York: Oxford University Press, 1995).

[20] See Arthur Marwick, *The Sixties: Cultural Revolution in Britain, France, Italy, and the United States* (Oxford: Oxford University Press, 1998).

[21] See Bernice Martin, *A Sociology of Contemporary Cultural Change* (Oxford: Basil Blackwell, 1981) 27–52.

hairstyles, and new beat music of pop stars like the Beatles, or art forms of painters like Andy Warhol. It was essentially an attack on boundaries, gender differences, limits, certainties, taboos, roles, systems, style, predictabilities, form, tradition. Prior to the revolution men and women had strictly separate places for haircuts, but now there emerged the unisex hair salon. Men and women could also dress alike in jeans. Extravagant, unconventional sexuality and a dramatic increase in the use of drugs like marijuana and LSD were not just ways to satisfy individual desires, but means to attack traditional taboos or moral boundaries. Like all liminalities, the revolution was subversive of the status quo.

Influential People

Friedrich Nietzsche

Friedrich Nietzsche profoundly influenced both modernity and postmodernity. He believed that Western civilization was destroying itself and falling into a moral abyss as a consequence of its functional atheism. Since God no longer existed, everything immoral was possible and the only way for society to survive was for humankind to become its own god; then all its actions would be "beyond good and evil." He believed that all life sought to increase its hold on power. All identities were the result of relations of force.[22] Knowledge, for Nietzsche, was but an expression of the will to be master over reality, and truths were illusions that we have forgotten are illusions.

Contemporary postmodernist writers, influenced by Nietzsche, like Michel Foucault (see chapter 1) and Jacques Derrida (see chapter 10), questioned traditional notions of power and knowledge. Knowledge was not an autonomous body of abstract theorems existing independently of culture; language and culture must be scrutinized to see how they are used by those in power to dominate people's lives.

---

[22] See Fredrich Nietzsche, *The Will to Power*, trans. Walter Kaufmann (New York: Vintage, 1968).

Guy Debord

In France in the 1960s the movement called "situationism" under the leadership of Guy Debord had subversiveness as one of its key aims. Situationists saw the consumer and media cultures as insidious methods of oppression. Authority and its representatives (politicians, parents, trade unionists, or intellectuals) had to be subverted. Firm believers in the power of hedonism as a method of cultural resistance and subversion, situationists created art and theory they expected would stimulate a carnivalesque revolt against a suffocating and falsifying modern world. Situationists emphasized what they termed "drifting" which they explored essentially in terms of urban landscapes. It was thought that cities should be redesigned so that they had separate bizarre, happy, sinister, tragic, and useful quarters that people could drift in and out of.[23]

Writers

Among the writers who significantly influenced the revolution by emphasis on narcissism, self-gratification of desires, and the cultivation of feeling in preference to reason were philosopher Herbert Marcuse, novelist William S. Burroughs, the poet Allen Ginsberg, and the writer Susan Sontag. Marcuse writes in laudatory terms of "a resurgence of pregenital polymorphous sexuality" that "protests against the repressive order of procreative sexuality."[24] For him, the perverse is to be embraced as normal. For Ginsberg, drugs and promiscuous sex are central avenues to total liberation.[25] Sontag champions pornography as an antidote to the meaninglessness of secular modern culture.[26]

---

[23] See *The Economist* (2 May 1998) 81–2, and Andrew Hussey, *The Game of War: The Life and Death of Guy Debord* (London: Jonathan Cape, 2001).

[24] Quoted by Roger Kimball, *The Long March: How the Cultural Revolution of the 1960s Changed America* (San Francisco: Encounter Books, 2000) 168.

[25] Ibid., 200.

[26] Ibid., 90.

Impact on Institutions: Erosion of Legitimacy

During the expressive revolution there was widespread erosion of the legitimacy of traditional institutions: business, government, education, and the family.[27] The outrage of young revolutionaries was grounded in a perceived discrepancy between principles espousing the right of human beings to fulfill themselves and the practices of these institutions.[28] They were seen to have compromised values such as freedom, self-expression, and the dignity of the human person. The continuous and competitive pursuit of money in the capitalist system, or the involvement in foreign wars for questionable reasons, e.g., in Vietnam, conflicted with these values.

The mainline Churches experienced widespread malaise, a loss of institutional vitality and direction; they were ill-prepared to respond to the spiritual and ideological upheavals of the time. Significant numbers of young people felt these Churches had not only compromised with secular values, but had become so bureaucratic and unfeeling that they could no longer provide the desired havens of understanding and meaning. While the demands for social justice that characterized many movements in the revolution conformed closely to the traditions of Judaism and Christianity, the Churches themselves were perceived to have colluded with oppression. Hence they were excluded from influencing the revolution and from developing a following, despite the leadership of religious people like Martin Luther King Jr.

Summary

• The revolution was an attempt to make ambiguity and uncertainty a total way of living in itself. Yet the revolution had a major paradox: on one hand, there was an earnest effort to develop structureless individualism with immediate self-fulfillment and liberation from all constraints on freedom. This became the "anti-order" emphasis of the revolution.

• On the other hand, there was a push toward collectivity, in which the individual became smothered or controlled by the collectivity itself

[27] Robert Bellah, cited by M. Haralambos, *Sociology: Themes and Perspectives* (London: Bell and Hyman, 1985) 489.

[28] See Charles Y. Glock, "Consciousness among Contemporary Youth," *The New Religious Consciousness*, ed. Charles Y. Glock and Robert Bellah (Berkeley: University of California Press, 1976) 361.

pushing for order or predictability, through commune-living, or uniformity in anti-structure clothing or hairstyle. This "pro-order" quality was at first a less obvious emphasis in the revolution. In fact, many colorful rituals of the revolution projected only an image of individual self-expression and freedom from all restraints.

Postmodernism:
Reactions to the Revolution

The two opposing emphases of the revolution resulted in two opposing successor movements (see figure 7.1) in the mythology of postmodernity: "anti-order" movements of freedom and self-discovery, and "pro-order" political and religious movements emphasizing control and rationality. The second is very much a reaction to the malaise of the first. Both claim to liberate people, but are also the origin of new forms of violence.

A. "ANTI-ORDER" REACTIONS

The "anti-order" side of postmodernism has the following characteristics:

- Rejection of the "metanarratives"
- Disillusionment with modernity
- Self: fluid identities
- No history: permanent present: "hyperreality"
- Spatial-disorientation: "hyperspace"

1. Rejection of the "Metanarratives"

Jean-François Lyotard, an influential postmodernist thinker, defines "postmodern as incredulity toward . . . metanarratives"[29] causing the widespread breakdown for people of traditional certitudes and sense of order. "Metanarratives" means foundational theories or founding myths (as explained in chapter 1)—grand stories legitimating modern knowledge, universal morality, and social progress. Christianity and Marxism are examples of metanarratives. Postmodernism undermines

---

[29] Jean-François Lyotard, in Seidman, *Postmodern Turn*, 27.

Figure 7.1 Postmodernity: Reactions to Expressive Revolution

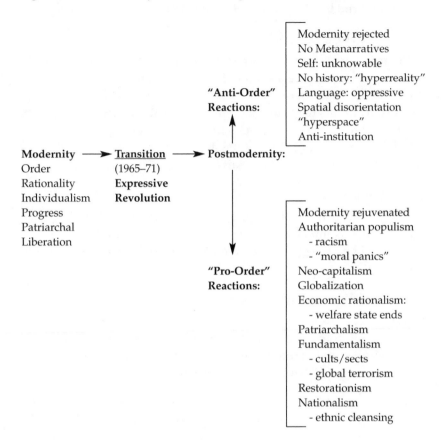

two major assumptions in the Enlightenment mythology: the power of language to mold the world and free people from ignorance and violence, and the power of consciousness to shape the self.

Several factors influenced Jean-François Lyotard and others in their rejection of metanarratives:

• *Disillusionment with Modernity*

A series of events marked the breakup of the self-confidence of modernity's mythology: the horrors of the Holocaust, Hiroshima 1945, the oppression of uprisings in Prague 1959, Budapest 1968, and police brutality and bullying at the Democratic Convention in 1968. They symbolized for Lyotard the bankruptcy of rationality as society's guiding principle, the fallacy of dialectical materialism as a metaphor for history, and the hollowness of capitalism.[30]

• *Orderly World Questioned*

Modern science promised an orderly and rationally led world; the more we trusted science the more closely the promise could be fulfilled. However, the findings of physicists destroyed this belief. When reflecting on the random behavior of atomic and subatomic phenomena, they discovered that classical physics' emphasis on an orderly world could no longer be sustained (hence, the development of what is called the "chaos theory"[31] and the "uncertainty principle").

• *Science Changing*

The rapid expansion of computerization means that scientific knowledge is now as much the result of artificial as of human reasoning. Scientific knowledge no longer has the prestige it commanded in modernity.[32]

• *Particular Critiques of Metanarratives*

Michel Foucault reinforced Lyotard's distrust of metanarratives. Foucault, for example, challenged the assumption that knowledge in modernity led to liberation; on the contrary, knowledge was often a way to gain new and oppressive control over people.[33]

Foucault on Sexuality

Foucault in his *History of Sexuality* argues that modernity has incorrectly encouraged the impression that sexuality is no longer repressed. The mass media is filled with sexual images and discussions about sex, yet Foucault sees this as paradoxically another form of oppressive cultural control. Discussion and examination do not free sexuality; rather, they make it a problem.[34]

---

[30] See ed. Andrew Benjamin, *The Lyotard Reader* (Oxford: Blackwell, 1989) 318.

[31] See Ralph Stacey, *The Chaos Frontier* (Oxford: Butterworth-Heinemann, 1991).

[32] See Bounds, *Cultural Studies*, 91.

[33] See, for example, Michel Foucault, *Madness and Civilization: The History of Insanity in the Age of Reason* (New York: Random House, 1965).

[34] See Michel Foucault, *An Introduction: The History of Sexuality*, vol. 1 (London: Penguin, 1979) 23.

In summary, postmodernists deny it is possible to know objective truth and absolute values such as justice or compassion, because human language and knowledge can no longer be trusted. In their place there is a relativistic construction of the world through language and narrative.

2. Views of the Self: Fluid Identities, Narcissism, Cynicism

• *Identity*

It is no longer possible to depend on mythologies to provide fixed personal and social identities. To replace modernity's view of the self as a coherent being, individuals must become creative storytellers: there are as many selves as there are innovative stories. The idea of the self as "continuously revised biographical narratives"[35] is an attempt to achieve meaning in a world where reality cannot be grasped to any degree. There is a constant, wearying, even manic search for personal identity, but one is always aware that even when it is achieved to some degree, it remains a fiction because there is no way to prove its objective truth. A symbol of a postmodern person is the pop star Madonna, well known for her constant changes of images and identity.[36]

Friedrich Nietzsche: Self-Creation

The influence of Nietzsche on the development of self-centered individualism in postmodernity is profound. For Nietzsche, the individual alone is important. The world has no intrinsic meaning and individuals can either accept this—which is a mark of weakness—or create their own meaning and impose it on others. The more one creates meaning for oneself by dominating others, the more one is able to develop a sense of identity. The struggle must never cease. The Christian ideal of loving one's neighbor is a mark of mediocrity; those who are too weak to dominate others hide their timidity behind proclamations of love and justice for others.[37]

---

[35] Anthony Giddens, *Modernity and Self-Identity* (New York: Polity Press, 1991) 5.

[36] See Michael O'Shaughnessy, *Media and Society* (Melbourne: Oxford University Press, 1999) 265–7.

[37] See Jonathan Glover, *Humanity: A Moral History of the Twentieth Century* (London: Jonathan Cape, 1999) 11–7.

• *Narcissism*

Inevitably the ongoing search by individuals for sustained meaning in life in a rapidly changing world produces many very fragile, insecure, highly narcissistic, and depressed people. Narcissism exists in modernity, but more markedly in postmodernity. Narcissists are focused only on themselves; relationships and commitments of all kinds are highly fragile, for every relationship, even marriage, is dispensable if it fails to serve the self-fulfillment aspirations of the narcissist.[38]

• *Humor and Cynicism*

Richard Stivers argues that cynicism is a consequence of postmodernism: we cannot know reality as it is and there is nothing one can do about it. Cynicism makes things worse in that it renders the current situation permanent, providing no hope of transcending it.[39] The pop art of Andy Warhol, for example, his paintings of soup tins, is an expression of postmodern cynicism. As Mark Taylor asserts, "Pop art is utterly superficial—it is all surface and no depth."[40] What you see is reality. There is nothing beneath it. Warhol encouraged his followers to embrace what they saw, enjoy it without question, even if what people saw were the commodities of capitalism. No room in his art for a God that cannot be seen.

Cynicism, with it fatalistic foundation, breaks out into scorn and derision. Stivers points to contemporary humor, for example, television programs such as *Monty Python* and *Saturday Night Live*, and individual comedians like Roseanne. Their humor has become violent: "It's not enough to point out the foibles and incongruities of human existence and to laugh with the other; instead, one must show contempt for the stupidity and absurdity of the other. The other is a failure; I, the scorner, am the success."[41] The *Mr. Bean* series, though marvelously funny, at times slips into this postmodern form of humor and occasionally is even sadistic.

Readers may like to compare the old television family sitcoms, such as *The Brady Bunch* and the Cunninghams in *Happy Days*, with today's

[38] See Christopher Lasch, *The Culture of Narcissism* (New York: Warner, 1991) and Rollo May, *The Cry for Myth* (New York: Delta, 1991) 15.

[39] See Richard Stivers, *The Culture of Cynicism: American Morality in Decline* (Oxford: Basil Blackwell, 1994).

[40] Mark C. Taylor, "Reframing Postmodernisms," *Shadow of Spirit: Postmodernism and Religion*, ed. Philippa Berry and Andrew Wernick (London: Routledge, 1992) 17.

[41] Stivers, *The Culture of Cynicism*, 90.

popular program, *The Simpsons*. The first two programs represent modern culture where in the ideal family roles are clear and all problems can be resolved and people are open to change. *The Simpsons*, however, reflects postmodern culture: the family is dysfunctional, characters at times show degrees of sadism, members do not change, there is an atmosphere of hopelessness and bullying, and authority figures are presented in ridiculous and cynical ways.

Metaphors: "Vagabond" and "Tourist"

Zygmunt Bauman believes that vagabonds or vagrants offer an apposite metaphor of the postmodernist. What keeps vagabonds moving is their disillusionment with the last place of rest and the hope that eventually the right locale will be found to give them a long-awaited sense of meaning. But meaning is never achieved, though the wandering continues; the postmodernist is a vagabond, without roots or destination, "a nomad without an itinerary."[42] The pilgrim is not a vagabond, because the pilgrim firmly believes there is a destination and wants to know more about it.

The tourist is another metaphor. Tourists live without any commitment to, or any in-depth social or spiritual encounters with, the people they see while traveling. The vagabond and tourist, Bauman claims, share one thing in common: they do not assume there is any particular depth in the world around them that is worth knowing.[43]

---

3. No History: Permanent Present

Some argue that a sense of history is impossible in contemporary society because people are so overwhelmed and confused by the speed of change in fashions and society, exacerbated by the power of the mass media and advertising, that for protection they escape into a "permanent present." Jean Baudrillard explains this by describing "hyperreality," which he calls the self-made present. Hyperreality results from people being bombarded with images from television screens, advertising hoardings, computer terminals, and such like. These images are ubiquitous, they enter our homes and public places and form a kind of

---

[42] Zygmunt Bauman, *Postmodern Ethics* (Oxford: Basil Blackwell, 1994) 240.
[43] Ibid., 242.

parallel world which is different from the "real world" that exists at the same time.[44] Baudrillard claims narcissism in postmodern society exists because people are so trapped by hyperreality that they believe the external world is simply a projection of their own thoughts. They cannot distinguish between the self and anything beyond the self.

4. Spatial-Disorientation: "Hyperspace"

Fredric Jameson, another postmodernist commentator, argues that there is so much change that it is now impossible for individuals to identify perceptually and cognitively any fixed points in space.[45] Little wonder that people to repress their pain of disorientation and confusion escape into world of narcissistic pleasure in the here and now.

Summary: "Anti-Order" Violence

While there are significant positive aspects to the "anti-order" side of postmodernity (to be explained in chapter 10), at the same time it is the source of significant violence toward individuals and society.

- With the rejection of mythologies (metanarratives), it is but a logical step to discard universal values like justice, respect for life (including before birth), and the dignity of the person, mercy, and compassion. John Paul II speaks of the "culture of death," or "a war of the powerful against the weak"—an excellent description of an oppressive culture. He writes: "A person who, because of illness, handicap or, more simply, just by existing, compromises the well-being or life-style of those who are more favored tends to be looked upon as an enemy to be resisted or eliminated."[46]

- For the postmodernist reality is one of sterility, meaninglessness, chaos without hope, a world in which God, rationality, and history have no place. There is a bleakness and an inescapable sadness in much of postmodernism that can lead to depression. Sociologist Mike Presdee argues that in postmodernity, where a sense of powerlessness and disenchantment prevails, "violence . . . has become

---

[44] See Jean Baudrillard, *Selected Writings* (Cambridge: Polity Press, 1988) and Bounds, *Cultural Studies*, 93–4.

[45] See Fredric Jameson, *Postmodernism, or, The Cultural Logic of Late Capitalism* (Durham: Duke University Press, 1991) 44.

[46] John Paul II, Encyclical, *Evangelium Vitae* (25 March 1995) par. 12.

more a way of life in this society. . . . We live in a culture where to express 'hate,' to 'talk' hate, is increasingly encouraged because 'talk' is no longer communication but 'therapy' and 'good for us' and 'crime creates power for the individual to express their individuality.'"[47] Pornography has always been big business, but in the postmodern world computer pornography has dramatically expanded the "industry" at the cost of women's and children's dignity particularly.[48]

• Young people are a particular focus of the negative pressures of postmodernism, as Henry Giroux concludes: "[They] often bear the burden of new, undeserved responsibilities and pressures to 'grow up.' . . . Where can children find narratives of hope, semiautonomous cultural spheres, discussions of meaningful differences, and nonmarket-based democratic identities?"[49]

B. "Pro-Order" Reactions

Within the broad category of "pro-order" reactions come such movements as political and religious fundamentalism; the New Right; new cults and sects; globalization and its consequences; neocapitalism and economic rationalism; revitalized patriarchy; ethnic nationalism and racism. Some of these movements will be considered below and others in the following chapter.

1. The New Right Culture

The New Right is an ideological political reaction to the vagueness and moral malaise of the "anti-order" pole of postmodernity with a distinctive set of values and clear-cut answers to contemporary social and economic challenges.

In the United States the founding figures are people like William F. Buckley Jr. and Barry Goldwater. Ronald Reagan became a highly effective communicator of the movement's beliefs. Widespread support for the New Right comes not just from the rising urban lower middle

---

[47] Mike Presdee, *Cultural Criminology and the Carnival of Crime* (London: Routledge, 2000) 152, 158.

[48] See Terry Gillespie, "Virtual Violence? Pornography and Violence Against Women on the Internet," *Women, Violence and Strategies for Action*, ed. Jill Radford and others (Buckingham: Open University Press, 2000) 40–56.

[49] Henry A. Giroux, *Stealing Innocence: Corporate Culture's War on Children* (New York: Palgrave, 2000) 11.

class, but also from rural, small-town, and religiously fundamentalist citizens who lost their cultural and economic power. They see the breakdown in morality and the increase in government support for welfare services as ways of undermining the nation's local and international strength. For them, it is patriotic to support a laissez-faire market capitalism and decreasing aid to the poor. The New Right movement is an attempt to revitalize and reinforce the creation mythology of the American nation along markedly conservative lines.[50] Similar conservative movements developed in other Western countries. In Britain, Margaret Thatcher and her successors have sought to dismantle the welfare state. For Prime Minister Thatcher the primary purpose of government is to respect the rights of individuals, not the common good.[51]

2. Neocapitalism/Economic Rationalism

Economic rationalism (or market capitalism, neoclassical capitalism, market liberalism) became a powerful mythological support in the emergence of the New Right culture. Profit is the sole measure of value and the economics profession serves as its priesthood.[52] The assumptions are: sustained economic growth is the best way to distribute wealth; free markets, unrestrained by government interference, result in the most efficient use of resources; economic globalization, with the unrestricted flow of goods and finance, will benefit all; lower taxation and reduced government spending are desirable; governments must privatize services; the government's primary task is to support individual initiatives in commerce.[53]

Contained in the mythology of the economic rationalist culture (its operational wing is called the "new managerialism") is the Social Darwinist assumption that the poor are what they are through their own fault; welfare services only make their poverty worse, so they must be reduced. Economic rationalists also aim to change public insti-

---

[50] See Gerald A. Arbuckle, *Earthing the Gospel: An Inculturation Handbook for Pastoral Workers* (Maryknoll: Orbis Books, 1990) 125.

[51] See Annette Scambler, "Gender, Health and the Feminist Debate on Postmodernism," *Modernity, Medicine and Health*, ed. Graham Scambler (London: Routledge, 1998) 103.

[52] See David C. Korten, *When Corporations Rule the World* (London: Earthscan, 1996) 69.

[53] Ibid., 70.

tutions into pseudo-businesses,[54] e.g., healthcare is considered an economic commodity and must be subject to the principles of supply and demand of the marketplace. Thus in the 1990s the planners of healthcare reform in many countries such as Britain, Australia,[55] and New Zealand,[56] are now more commonly economists or accountants, not people with a background in healthcare delivery. The dramatic rise of for-profit hospitals in the United States in recent years is an example of this economic ideology: financial return to shareholders, not the quality of service to patients, is to be the primary aim of healthcare services.

Economic Rationalism: Impact on the Poor

The results are invariably the same: the poor become poorer and more marginalized by society. Since the introduction of economic rationalism in New Zealand, a new underclass of poor people has emerged. Between 1984 and 1993, the percentage of households living in absolute poverty has more than doubled from 4.3 percent to 10.8 percent.[57] Social commentator Michael Moore (now head of the World Trade Organization) points out that "[in New Zealand] it has become fashionable to blame the victims. Bad parents and lazy people are seen as the problems,"[58] but the real causes are to be found in economic rationalist philosophy.

Economic rationalists have adopted the postmodernist distrust of history. As John Saul comments in the 1995 Canadian Massey Lectures, "we have come to so forget our own history that we are now compliantly acting in a suicidal manner, believing that economics can lead— where in the past it has always failed to do so. . . . We have fallen in love with an old ideology that has never paid off in the past."[59]

---

[54] See Cris Shore and Susan Wright, "Coercive Accountability," *Audit Cultures,* ed. Marilyn Strathern (London: Routlege, 2000) 63–85.

[55] See Michael Pusey, *Economic Rationalism in Canberra: A Nation Building State Changes Its Mind* (Cambridge: Cambridge University Press, 1992) 59–75.

[56] See Robert Blank, *New Zealand Health Policy: A Comparative Study* (Auckland: Oxford University Press, 1994) 134.

[57] See Paul Dalziel, "Reaping the Whirlwind of the Economic Reforms," *Tui Motu* (1 August 1998) 3.

[58] Michael Moore, *Children of the Poor* (Christchurch: Canterbury University Press, 1996) 11.

[59] Paul R. Saul, *The Unconscious Civilization* (Toronto: Penguin, 1997) 123.

3. The New Right and Criminal Justice

The authoritarian attitude of the New Right is also obvious in its approach to penal policy. In penal policy as in welfare policy the New Right's philosophy in many Western countries is to emphasize a "law and order" approach and political parties compete with one another in supporting it: increase control and insist on more punishment, prisons, and police numbers while downplaying rehabilitation of prisoners.

Rapid incarceration is a quick way to get the problem cases out of sight, and the judiciary's discretionary powers must be curtailed for the benefit of "decent people." The introduction of mandatory sentencing, the reestablishment of children's prisons, zero tolerance policies, pedophile registers, the movement of young offenders to adult courts— all aimed at restricting the judgments of judges and social workers. Probation represents itself as a punishment in the community, not as a social work alternative to conviction. The populations singled out as the most in need of control and retribution are the welfare poor, urban blacks, the unemployed, and marginalized working-class youth.[60] Since one in three African American males in the United States aged 20–29 is either in prison or under penal supervision, young African American men in urban areas are a group that can expect imprisonment as "normal." Likewise, "the highly disproportionate imprisonment of Indigenous people is a striking feature of Australian imprisonment."[61]

Prisoners: Nonpersons in a Bullying Culture

Calling for justice in prison is hopelessly out of fashion in postmodern political life. Joseph Hallinan, a reporter of the *Wall Street Journal*, commented: "We really don't value inmate life enough to investigate whether a kid doing time for a property crime deserves to be terrorized by a rapist bully."[62] Two studies in the

continued on next page

---

[60] See the excellent analysis by David Garland, *The Culture of Control: Crime and Social Order in Contemporary Society* (Chicago: Chicago University Press, 2001) 175.

[61] *Prisoners As Citizens: Human Rights in Australian Prisons*, ed. David Brown and Meredith Wilkie (Sydney: Federation Press, 2002) xxiv.

[62] Joseph Hallinan quoted in *The Honolulu Advertiser* (28 May 2001) A8. In Australia the national rate of *recorded* prisoner-on-prisoner assaults is about two-and-a-half times the rate of assault in the general community. See Russell Hogg, "Prisoners and the Penal Estate in Australia," in Brown and Wilkie, *Prisoners As Citizens*, 10.

United States have revealed that one in five of the nation's two million male prisoners has been forced into some form of unwanted sexual contact and at least one in fifteen has been raped. Displays of power, racial bias, or the drive of predators taking advantage of weaker inmates are the main causes of inmate-to-inmate rape. An editorial of *The Chicago Tribune* commented: "Many prison systems don't act on reports of rape; many don't want to acknowledge that prison rape occurs. . . . [Prisoners] are assaulted, degraded, sometimes infected with HIV—and then released."[63]

Globalization

> Globalization is not incidental to our lives today. It is a shift in our very life circumstances. It is the way we now live. (Anthony Giddens[64])

Globalization, an element of "pro-order" postmodernity, popularly refers to the process by which the world is considered to be transforming into a single orderly global system. It is a process whereby, "through mass communication, multinational commerce, internationalised politics and transnational regulation, we seem to be moving inexorably towards a single culture."[65]

However, the word "inexorably" is disputed. Robert Holton concludes his study of globalization with the view that it should not be seen "in demonic terms as an unstoppable force, a juggernaut driven by technological change, or as a process whose direction is monopolized from above in a manner that is, in principle, out of reach of the peoples of the globe."[66] The forces pushing for globalization are evoking significant resistances, for example, fierce nationalism, and new expressions of ethnicity, so that there is no certainty that a single culture will finally emerge from the process.

[63] Editorial, *The Chicago Tribune* (28 April 2001) 22.

[64] Anthony Giddens, *Runaway World: How Globalization Is Reshaping Our Lives* (London: Profile, 1999) 19.

[65] Mark Findlay, *The Globalisation of Crime* (Cambridge: Cambridge University Press, 1999) viii.

[66] Robert J. Holton, *Globalization and the Nation-State* (London: Macmillan, 1998) 204.

Globalization: A New Culture of Oppression?

There are positive benefits of globalization but there are also significant negative consequences:

• Nation-States: Loss of Sovereignty

As globalization increases, the ability of national governments to control their economies is reduced; global corporations and financial institutions operate mainly beyond the reach of public accountability so that citizens feel more and more powerless.[67] Even in rich countries, like Australia and New Zealand, governments find themselves with minimal power to control their economies; people refer to their economies as mere branch offices of distant powerful financial and industrial companies.

• Rich Escape Taxation

Governments with economic rationalist policies of privatization and deregulation have less revenue than before; their taxation laws target the middle classes and the poor while the rich transnational companies escape very lightly. Michel Chossudovsky, professor of economics at the University of Ottawa, shows that the WTO's (World Trade Organization) "mandate consists of regulating world trade to the benefit of the international banks and transnational corporations."[68] Little wonder that there are street protests at the annual meetings of the WTO.

• Globalization of Crime

Through money laundering (estimated to be conservatively around $U.S. 800 billion a year) the criminal culture is connected to global financial markets. With such large amounts available, this culture is able to manipulate markets and governments.[69]

• Minorities and Ethnic Cleansing

The revitalization of ethnicity and nationalism in response to globalization's threats to cultural identity or territory can marginalize less

---

[67] See Korten, *When Corporations Rule the World*, 92.

[68] Michel Chossudovsky, *The Globalisation of Poverty: Impacts of IMF and World Bank Reforms* (London: Zed Books, 1999) 35.

[69] See Manuel Castells, *The Power of Identity* (Oxford: Blackwell, 1997) 259–61; Findlay, *The Globalisation of Crime*, 8–11.

powerful groups within a country, even resulting in the ethnic cleansing of minorities (to be explained in the next chapter).[70]

• *Cultural Imperialism*

"Cultural imperialism" means global homogenization through the power of worldwide media forces led particularly by the United States and symbolized by McDonald's restaurants and Coca Cola. This thesis is questioned by significant observers, however, who point to the revitalization of ethnicity and nationalism as a consequence of globalization. They claim that national cultures remain creative and distinctive.[71] Giddens speaks of "reverse colonization," that is, non-Western countries influencing the world, e.g., the sale of Brazilian television programs to Portugal, and the development of a globally oriented high-tech sector in India.[72]

• *World Poverty: The "Fourth World"*

The globalization of world poverty at the beginning of the twenty-first century is unprecedented in world history.[73] Political and social theorist Manuel Castells argues that globalization is producing a global rich and powerful elite in every world city, but at the same time it is creating an ever-increasing reservoir of poor and dispossessed migrant local labor. He uses the expression "Fourth World" to identify those who are excluded from the economic benefits of globalization. The "Fourth World" is "present in literally every country, and every city, in [a] new geography of social exclusion. It is formed of American inner-city ghettoes, Spanish enclaves of mass youth unemployment, French *banlieues* warehousing North Africans, Japanese Yoseba quarters and Asian mega cities' shanty towns. And it is populated by millions of homeless, incarcerated, prostituted, criminalised, brutalised, stigmatised, sick, and illiterate persons."[74]

Political crises even in remote Solomon Islands and Fiji in the South Pacific are frequently consequences of globalization; people feel

---

[70] See Hugh Mackay, "The Globalization of Culture?" *A Globalizing World? Culture, Economics, Politics*, ed. David Held (London: Routledge, 2000) 75.

[71] See John Tomlinson, *Globalization and Culture* (Cambridge: Polity, 1999) 79–105; Mackay, "The Globalization of Culture?" 81.

[72] See Giddens, *Runaway World*, 16–7.

[73] See Chossudovsky, *The Globalisation of Poverty*, 26.

[74] Manuel Castells, *End of Millennium* (Oxford: Blackwell, 1998) 164–5.

manipulated by transnational corporations, dispossessed of lands, their natural resources transported to rich international centers from which they receive only a minimal financial return or none at all.

• *Drugs and the Poor*

The people of the world spend about $500 billion annually on buying drugs in the streets. This is more than the Gross Domestic Product (GDP) of all but the seven richest countries in the world. Approximately 50 percent of all illicit drugs are sold in the United States alone. The United States government spends billions of dollars each year on efforts to encourage countries where the drugs are produced to reduce or stop their supplies, but as long as the demand is there farmers go on producing and criminal gangs continue to sell.[75]

By far the worst effect of the war on drugs in the United States is the imprisonment of thousands of blacks and Hispanics. There are more young black men in prison than in college education. Of the $35 billion or so spent annually on fighting the drug epidemic, at least three-quarters goes not to prevention or treatment but to apprehending and punishing dealers and users. Many of those arrested, notes a survey in *The Economist*, receive mandatory minimum sentences of five to ten years for possession of a few grams of drugs, "a dire punishment rushed through Congress in 1986 amid hysteria about crack cocaine."[76] There is an overall failure in the Western world to tackle the issue of illicit drugs in ways that do not further impose more hardships on the global poor.[77]

• *Slavery*

Slavery and other insidious types of forced labor are growing worldwide because globalization has increased the demand for cheap goods and there is no cheaper labor than slave labor. It is estimated that there are about twenty-seven million people caught in slavery, among them:

• 40,000–50,000 foreign women and girls are bought annually and forced to work as prostitutes or in sweatshops in the United States;

[75] See Richard Clutterbuck, *Drugs, Crime and Corruption* (London: Macmillan 1995) 3–4.

[76] *The Economist* (28 July 2001) 13.

[77] See "A Survey of Illegal Drugs," *The Economist* (28 July 2001) 1–52; Findlay, *The Globalisation of Crime*, 101–4.

- ten million children work in slavery in India, including 300,000 in rug factories; 7.5 million children are in similar slavery in Pakistan;

- between 15,000 and 20,000 children are on cocoa farms in the Ivory Coast helping to make ingredients for half the world's chocolate.[78]

Globalization: Debate

People differ about the long-term trends in globalization. There are two schools of thought:

• Optimists[79]

Optimists are economic rationalists believing that globalization is inevitable and that the world will be a better place provided market forces are given maximum freedom. Traditional nation-states are less and less able to control globalization and that is seen as good. True, only some countries will significantly benefit from globalization, but economic rationalism assumes that the strong have a basic right to succeed, though it be at the cost of the poor.

• Transformationalists

Transformationalists agree that globalization is inevitable but are concerned that worldwide inequality has risen over the past twenty years because of it.[80] Transformationalists, e.g., John Paul II, believe that globalization can and should be controlled by nation-states and by all kinds of people-power or grassroots movements.[81] To counter the oppressive effects of globalization, John Paul II and others insist that there must be debt forgiveness for the poorest countries, the sharing of technology and prosperity, greater efforts in conflict prevention and resolution, and respect for human rights.[82]

---

[78] See International Labor Organization Report, cited in *USA Today* (25 May 2001) 13A; *The Sydney Morning Herald* (4 June 2001) 1, 12; Kevin Bales, *Disposable People: New Slavery in the Global Economy* (Berkeley: University of California Press, 2001).

[79] E.g., see "Globalisation and Its Critics," *The Economist* (29 September 2001) 3–30.

[80] See James K. Galbraith, professor of economics, University of Texas, "Globalisation Fails to Make the Money Go Around," *The Sydney Morning Herald* (26 July 2001) 12.

[81] See Anthony McGrew, "Power Shift: From National Government to Global Governance," ed. David Held, *A Globalizing World?: Culture, Economics, Politics* (New York: Routledge, 2000) 154–64.

[82] See editorial, "Solidarity in Globalization," *America* (3 June 2000) 3.

Summary

- Postmodernism consists of economic, cultural, political, and social movements that reject certainties characteristic of modernity; post-modernity is the culture model that dominates much of the contemporary world.

- Signs of a postmodern world emerged in the early 1970s in reaction to the expressive revolution of the 1960s; the most common characteristic of the expressive revolution was the symbolism of "anti-structure" or "anti-institution"; the legitimacy of every institution was questioned, including the Church.

- Two broad types of reactions to the revolution are identifiable: "anti-order" and "pro-order." Violence-oriented elements of the former include the discarding of universal values such as the respect for the sacredness of life and a loss of meaning and a sense of history.

- In the "anti-order" reactions to the revolution the ongoing search by individuals for sustained meaning in life in the midst of a rapidly changing world produces many very insecure, highly narcissistic, and depressed people. There is a constant, even manic, search for new experiences in the hope that ultimately some persuasive meaning will emerge, but there is the feeling at the same time that this is not possible, merely a fantasy of the imagination. In this sense postmodern mythology is a source of violence to people.

- Among the "pro-order" destructive reactions are: the rise of economic rationalism and neocapitalism; the "law and order" approach to crime, e.g., a move from a welfare to penal modality; mandatory sentencing; and zero tolerance policies. "Pro-order" policies, especially those inspired by economic rationalism, weigh heavily against the poor and in favor of the rich. Economic rationalism has one overriding goal—material wealth. The role of governments is primarily to establish conditions that permit the market to operate without restrictions. Financial aid for the poor interferes with open competition and thus must be severely restricted by governments.[83]

- There is no definitive evidence indicating that globalization, an element of postmodernity, is good or bad,[84] but its oppressive qualities

[83] See Lindy Edwards, *How to Argue with an Economist* (Cambridge: Cambridge University Press, 2002) 64–93.

[84] See Holton, *Globalization and the Nation-State*, 204.

so far include: intensification of world poverty, internationalization of crime, an increase in adult and child slavery.

- The next chapter concentrates on the violence of "pro-order" reactions to postmodernism, e.g., fundamentalism, terrorism, and ethnic cleansing. The institutional Church, in the midst of the chaos of postmodernity, remains aloof and trapped in its own internal chaos. There is a concerted effort to disregard the call of Vatican II to become engaged in dialogue with the contemporary world and to restore the ghetto culture of the precouncil era.

Discussion Questions

1. Pope John Paul II speaks of the "culture of death" that pervades the contemporary world. What does he mean by this? Why do you think it has developed as an "acceptable" culture?

2. In many countries there is an emphasis in criminal justice on insisting on mandatory sentencing, the reestablishment of children's prisons, and the movement of young offenders to adult courts. Why are these trends developing? What are they saying about society's attitudes to the poor? Why can they be unjust? Why is the Church against the death penalty?

3. John Paul II says that despite the problems of the postmodern world there "is no justification for despair or pessimism or inertia" (*Social Concerns*). Why can a believer in Jesus Christ say this?

Chapter 8

Demanding Certitudes: Ethnicity, Fundamentalism, Restorationism

> Fundamentalism originates from a world of crumbling traditions. (Anthony Giddens[1])

> Not only has centralization of decision making accelerated at a breathtaking pace but the Vatican's style often seems more autocratic, less dialogical, and less collegial than ever. (John W. O'Malley, S.J.[2])

This chapter explains:

- the nature and types of ethnicity and their relationship to violence;

- the emergence of "football hooligan" ethnicity and violence;

- the impact of globalization on ethnicity;

- ethnic cleansing;

- New Religious Movements and their potential for violence;

- the rise of fundamentalism and its involvement in violence;

- Vatican II, Catholic fundamentalism, and restorationism.

Throughout history some people have hoped that ethnicity and nationalism would cease to exist. Their hopes reached new heights during

---

[1] Anthony Giddens, *Runaway World: How Globalisation Is Reshaping Our Lives* (London: Profile Books, 1999) 4.

[2] John W. O'Malley, "Interpreting Vatican II: Version Two," *Commonweal* (9 March 2001) 22.

the late 1940s and 1950s; they thought that the process of modernization would inevitably lead to the decline of intercultural differences and bitterness. Since the 1960s and the rise of postmodernity and its accompanying cultural turmoil, however, there has been a dramatic renaissance of nationalism and ethnicity, and increased demands for multiculturalism have destroyed this quixotic dream. In the half-century since the end of the Second World War, some 25 million people have been killed, mostly civilians by their own governments, in internal conflicts and ethnic, nationalist, or religious violence.

Cultures, far from assimilating, are separated by chasms of mutual distrust, and ethnic cleansing is one contemporary result. In Los Angeles, ninety languages are spoken by students in the public schools, and minorities continue to be blamed for all kinds of problems. At the same time, in the California legislature immigrants have been attacked (as they have been in Germany and elsewhere) as "welfare scroungers" or "for taking jobs from local people." Some 300,000 undocumented immigrant children in California, if the law were enforced, would be banned from enrolling in public schools.[3]

The fall of communism and the subsequent painful disintegration of Communist states, e.g., the Soviet Union and Yugoslavia, are further reminders that ethnicity has persisted as long as humankind, and that the assimilationists' "melting pot" is a dream. In fact, globalization, rather than causing a bland monocultural world, is a catalyst for the revitalization of ethnicity as well as for the dramatic rise of fundamentalism and cults. Anthony Giddens, describing the rise of fundamentalism, writes: "In a globalising world, where information and images are routinely transmitted across the world . . . fundamentalists find [globalization] disturbing and dangerous. Whether in the areas of religion, ethnic identity or nationalism, they take refuge in a renewed and purified tradition—and, quite often, violence."[4]

Contemporary ethnicity, nationalism, fundamentalism, New Religious Movements, and Catholic restorationism have one common quality. They are "pro-order" movements. Followers see their world of secure traditions and identities crumbling under the influence of post-modernism, globalization, and "trendy" innovators. Feeling lost, they

---

[3] See Carola Suarez-Orozco, "Identities Under Siege," *Cultures Under Siege: Collective Violence and Trauma*, ed. Antonius C. G. Robben and Marcelo M. Suarez-Orozco (Cambridge: Cambridge University Press, 2000) 205.

[4] Giddens, *Runaway World*, 4–5.

again seek the security of clearly defined certitudes (see axiom 1, chapter 1). Some are prepared to use intimidating tactics, including terrorism in the case of some fundamentalist movements, to get what they want, fearful that there is no other way to achieve their goals. This chapter examines these movements, including Catholic restorationism, a movement to return the Church to the stable structures and attitudes of pre-Vatican II times.

Types of Ethnicity and Violence

Ethnicity derives from the existence of culturally distinctive, self-conscious groups (ethnic groups), each claiming a unique identity based on a shared tradition or common experiences and on social markers such as culture, language, religion, income, and physical characteristics (e.g., skin pigmentation). The social markers may indeed be quite simple, e.g., dress, styles of house building; in other words, whatever a group of people feel particularly distinguishes themselves.[5]

Ethnic Groups:

Involuntary

Voluntary

Indigenous

Migratory

Separatist

Racist

Sporting

Cults/sects

Restorationist

Figure 8.1 Types of Ethnic Groups

The term "ethnic group" is used to refer to minorities whose distinctive qualities are recognized as different from the majority's in ways

[5] See Fredrik Barth, *Ethnic Groups and Boundaries: The Social Organization of Culture Difference* (Boston: Little Brown, 1969).

that set them apart from the dominant national culture. Defined in this way, all kinds of groups may fall within the category of "ethnic groups," e.g., football "tribes," cults and sects, as well as the more traditionally defined ethnic groups such as indigenous and minority peoples. Figure 8.1 lists nine types of ethnic groups and these will be explained in the following pages.

Involuntary or Ascribed Ethnicity

The identity of an oppressed group is called an involuntary, or ascribed, ethnicity; there is little or no escape from this negative labeling and oppression. In cases of ascribed ethnicity, the us/them dichotomy present in ethnic relations is especially strong. The dominant group ("us"), often out of a sense of fear of losing their position of power, pejoratively stereotypes a group ("them") and institutionalizes that oppression. In key areas of life (e.g., employment, education, social relationships) the oppressed are excluded from equality with the dominant group. To develop and legitimize this discrimination the in-group frequently brands the out-group as racially or culturally inferior, e.g., blacks in South Africa, Jews in Nazi Germany, and immigrants in contemporary Germany, Switzerland, Austria (under Jorg Haider's influence), and France (under Jean-Marie Le Pen's National Front).

Voluntary Ethnicity

Shortly after Afro-Americans in the United States in the 1960s began to demand respect for their history and origins, there developed what can be variously termed "voluntary," "symbolic," "defensive," or "backlash" ethnicity among whites. Protests of self-righteous indignation continue, especially as economic conditions worsen and competition for employment intensifies. In consequence of this defensive ethnicity there are demands for university programs in such areas as Irish, Jewish, and Polish studies. Similar but less strong backlash movements are to be found in countries whose governments have been fostering affirmative action programs for minorities, including Australia, New Zealand, and Canada.

In summary, by way of illustration, voluntary ethnicity means:

- White middle-class Americans, in reaction to the growing demands of minority groups in their midst for equality, feel the need to redefine their own identity more precisely by asserting their ancestral right to their power position in society. The ethnicity of whites of European ancestry does not restrict their choice of a spouse, suburb, or friends, or affect their access to employment and political opportunities.

- The socioeconomic and political consequences of being Asian, Hispanic, or black in the United States are real and frequently hurtful and obstructive. These people, unlike white middle-class Americans, are not free to choose their ethnic identity; the crippling boundaries of their ethnicity are defined for them on the basis of color. They are pressured to feel inferior and subjugated to the dominant white power group.

Indigenous Ethnicity

Indigenous peoples who are minorities in their own country may undertake a process of identity revitalization through the rearticulation of their mythology and traditional rituals, e.g., Maori people in New Zealand, Aborigines in Australia, and First Nations in Canada. Their revitalization does not constitute a formal separatist movement from the wider society, but a selective use of traditional mythology while they seek at the same time significant economic, educational, and social integration in the life of the nation as a whole.[6] Two anthropological axioms motivate revitalization movements:

- Only from a position of cultural strength can a people move out with dignity and self-confidence to share with other cultures.

- Only if minority groups have access to the power structures of society, that is, political and economic institutions, will the achievement of full ethnic self-confidence be possible, but their efforts to win equality often arouse animosity, even violent resistance, from the dominant power block.

The following comment to the author by a Maori civil rights leader in New Zealand in the 1970s illustrates the importance of these axioms.

---

[6] See Thomas K. Fitzgerald, *Education and Identity: A Study of the New Zealand Maori Graduate* (Christchurch: NZER, 1977) 70–9.

Reactions to Institutional Bullying

"For over a hundred years we indigenous people have been told our way of life is inferior to [that of] white settlers from Europe. And we came to believe it. Look at what has happened. We do the manual work in this country because we are told we are capable of little else. We have been oppressed for over a hundred years.

Now we demand the world recognize that we have a culture born of the struggle to survive through the centuries. We are a unique people, and this uniqueness gives us a sense of belonging. Without it we are nothing, not human. The more we tell our own story, the more we feel stronger inside to stand on our own feet and demand respect. The more self-esteem we have, the more we feel we can give something of our uniqueness to others. We demand, and are getting at last, a say in the power institutions of this country. For too long we have had to depend on the good will of the whites to give us justice. No more. Many Anglo-Saxons in this country don't like it. Hard luck on them!"

Migratory Supportive Ethnicity

In 1997 almost ninety million people were estimated to be living outside their country of birth and, of these, around seventy five million are international migrant workers and their dependants.[7] Tragically, migrant workers of whatever sex or nationality are easily exploited.[8] The loneliness and exploitation that migrants experience in a foreign land encourages them to develop a supportive ethnicity amongst themselves.[9]

Separatist Ethnicity

Some Afro-Americans in the 1960s and 1970s preached separatism because they became convinced that the dominant political system could not be justly changed in their favor. Thus, Malcolm X of the Black Muslims could bitterly remark on the need for blacks to go it alone: "It

[7] See Peter Stalker, "Refugees and Migration," *Internet* (28 August 2001) 1.
[8] See *The Economist* (10 September 1988) 25–8.
[9] See Nina Glick Schiller, "Citizens in Transnational Nation-States," *Globalisation and the Asia-Pacific*, ed. Kris Olds (London: Routledge, 1999) 202–8.

is not necessary to change the white man's mind. We have to change our own mind."[10]

The Parti Quebecois political movement in Quebec Province, Canada, believes that their French-speaking identity is threatened by the anglophone majority in Canada and only political separation will provide protection. At the same time non-francophone speakers in Quebec complain that they are objects of cultural bullying because the emphasis on the French language is excessive and discriminatory.[11]

Racist or Hate Ethnicity

Since 1945 millions of people from the Third World have migrated to Western countries, usually in search of work. For example, Western Europe has absorbed immigrants coming from Southern Europe, North Africa, Turkey, Finland, Asia, and Ireland, mainly in response to local labor shortages. There are 7.3 million foreigners in Germany, together with another four million ethnic Germans of foreign origin, many of whom did not speak German when they arrived.

Powerful, often vociferous, movements have developed against immigrants and other minority groups. These movements come within the category of voluntary ethnicity but they are built on implicit or explicit racism. People try to maintain their privileged power positions through discriminatory action, violence, or threats of verbal or physical violence.[12]

The growth in these white racist movements is not in reaction to immigration alone. As Stephen Castles and Alastair Davidson point out, the catalysts for extremist views and organizations are frequently falling living standards and increasing insecurity caused by the speed of globalization and economic restructuring. Social and economic turmoil resulting from these changes causes people to feel personally and culturally lost. Immigrants become the scapegoats for people's frustrations.[13]

[10] See Gerald A. Arbuckle, "Understanding Ethnicity, Multiculturalism, and Inculturation," *Human Development*, vol. 4, no. 1 (1993) 6.

[11] See Jack D. Eller, *From Culture to Ethnicity to Conflict: An Anthropological Perspective on International Ethnic Conflict* (Ann Arbor: University of Michigan Press, 1999) 297–347.

[12] See Barbara Perry, *In the Name of Hate: Understanding Hate Crimes* (London: Routledge, 2001) 3.

[13] See Stephen Castles and Alastair Davidson, *Citizenship and Migration: Globalization and the Politics of Belonging* (London: Macmillan, 2000) 145.

In countries like France, Belgium, Austria, Canada, and Australia,[14] there are antiminority political parties—polling between 10 and 15 percent of the national vote—pushing for the expulsion, not only of foreigners, but of recently naturalized immigrants.[15] There are violent extremist groups like the Ku Klux Klan and other white supremacist groups in the United States and neo-Nazi organizations in European countries. Immigrants, Jews, nonwhites, and homosexuals[16] are subjected to appalling abuse in many European countries. As the victims are often powerless to act, many crimes go unreported. Neo-Nazi groups, often referred to as skinheads, are well organized (including making use of the Internet) and growing; they are part of a loose network that links far-right parties, "white power" rock music, and football hooligans.

Football Hooligan Ethnicity

From about the late 1970s, especially in Europe, a new youth ethnic group emerged called "football hooligans" noted for its physical violence. There has always been a tendency for football fans to show aggressive and disorderly behavior, but football hooligans now exemplify a far more rowdy and disruptive pattern than ever before. Rioting at big sporting matches has occurred from time to time in the United States but there has been little or no ethnic-type bonding among rioters.[17] In Europe and Britain, rioters, generally from working-class backgrounds and wearing distinctive hair and clothing styles, disrupt major international games, fight against similar groups of different nationalities, vandalize trains after games, assault minorities, and ransack shops.

1. Postmodernism

Zygmunt Bauman speaks of a distinctive postmodern "tribe."[18] Premodern tribes and modern ethnic groups are held together on the basis

[14] See Rob White, "Immigration, Nationalism and Anti-Asian Racism," *Faces of Hate: Hate Crime in Australia*, ed. Chris Cunneen and others (Sydney: Hawkins Press, 1997) 15–43.

[15] See Castles and Davidson, *Citizenship and Migration*, 144; Nicholas Fraser, *The Voice of Hatred: Encounters with Europe's New Right* (London: Picador, 2000) 7.

[16] See Perry on antigay violence, *In the Name of Hate*, 105–16, and *Faces of Hate*, ed. Chris Cunneen and others, 115–36.

[17] See Varda Burstyn, *The Rites of Men: Manhood, Politics, and the Culture of Sport* (Toronto: University of Toronto Press, 1999) 194.

[18] See Zygmunt Bauman, *Intimations of Postmodernity* (London: Routledge, 1992) 198–9.

of blood ties; boundaries are clearly identified and rules of rites of passage are sharply defined. However, postmodern tribal groups are the result of individuals seeking identity and self-definition; there is little cohesion, structure, or mutual obligation. Football groups, with their proneness to mass violence or hooliganism against rival football fans, fit this postmodern ethnic description: they are fluid, open to all, permitting individuals to construct their own meanings and to participate under their own terms.[19]

2. Globalization: Consequences

In modernity, in Britain, the transition from boyhood to manhood for working-class youth was ritualized through obtaining employment and acceptance in an all-male atmosphere, under the guidance of their elders, e.g., being taken to the local pub for their first beer after a day's work. With the decline of traditional, unskilled industrial occupations as a consequence of globalization, and the ending of exclusively male employment, "the one surviving facet of masculine credibility that has come down to the current group of young men is the ability to fight, and via that, the ability to hold a reputation."[20] Football hooliganism is a rite of passage into adulthood, a substitute for the rituals of initiation into manhood of former times.

Hooliganism: Class Resentment

One controversial view of the origins of hooliganism is that downwardly mobile working-class youth, feeling increasingly pushed aside by economic rationalist policies, resent the transformation of football into a middle-class, international game, under the direction of powerful business tycoons and mass media interests. Spectators are increasingly middle class. In addition, players are enticed away from their working-class roots into a jet-set, upper-middle-class lifestyle. Hooliganism is a violent protest against these trends, a mass statement of resentment against the loss of the game's working-class origins, as well as the failure of the protesters to have a satisfying work and class identity.[21]

---

[19] See Gary Armstrong, *Football Hooligans: Knowing the Score* (Oxford: Berg, 1998) 306.
[20] Ibid., 156.
[21] See I. Taylor, "Football Mad: A Speculative Sociology of Football Hooliganism," *The Sociology of Sport: A Collection of Readings*, ed. E. Dunning (London: Frank Cass, 1971).

3. Football: Ritual of Violence

Sport draws people together to witness, identify with, or participate in a contest where the predominant perception is of people struggling against one another. One of the most striking features of football, no matter what form it takes, is its violent nature. Books and commentators on football use symbolic references to warfare, and the wider public approves of this.[22] Football hooliganism, such as that experienced in Europe, merely mimics what spectators see in front of them but in a more dramatic form (see axiom 5, chapter 1).

Nationalism and Ethnic Cleansing

The relationship between nationalism, ethnicity, and ethnic cleansing is complex and clarification is necessary.

A *nation* is a group of people who have a common cultural inheritance and consider themselves a political community, and *nationalism* is a mythology that assumes the nation is the pivotal principle of political organization.[23] This is where historically a nation has differed from an ethnic group. An ethnic group has a common identity and a feeling of cultural pride, but, unlike a nation, it may not have collective aspirations for political autonomy. A nation may contain many ethnic groups but all are expected to accept symbols of national unity;[24] if groups refuse a common identity, they will be discriminated against. The case of Northern Ireland illustrates the tragic consequences when nationalism and ethnicity are in conflict, resulting in so much violence.

Case Study: Nationalism and Ethnicity in Conflict

Many Protestants in Northern Ireland claim that they are the only true nationalists because they are loyally committed to the British nation. They regularly parade their allegiance to powerful symbols like the Union Jack and the Queen. Catholics are an

continued on next page

---

[22] See Kendall Blanchard and Alyce Cheska, *The Anthropology of Sport* (South Hadley, Mass.: Bergin and Garvey, 1985) 57.

[23] See Andrew Heywood, *Politics* (London: Macmillan, 1997) 408.

[24] See *Key Concepts in Cultural Theory*, ed. Andrew Edgar and Peter Sedgwick (London: Routledge, 1999) 254–5.

ethnic group, unwilling to be part of the British nation, according to this Protestant mythology.[25] Catholics assert they are the authentic nationalists, because the land belongs historically to them, and the Protestants are an imposed foreign ethnic group, whose ancestors came from Scotland and England precisely to force Catholics to be loyal to Britain.[26]

Since the late 1960s, peoples such as Quebecois in Canada, Basques in Spain, Chechens in the Russian Federation, the ethnic Albanians in Kosovo, Croats in Bosnia-Herzegovina, the Tamils in Sri Lanka, and Ibos in Nigeria,[27] claim that ethnic *and* political boundaries must be congruent. Other ethnic groups must be forced to leave the territory or suffer extreme discrimination. Hence, the expression "ethnic cleansing." It is a form of vicious cultural bullying whereby an advancing army of one ethnic group expels other ethnic groups from towns and villages it conquers in order to create ethnically pure enclaves for members of their own group. Ethnic cleansing in Bosnia and Croatia in the former Yugoslavia has resulted in more than two million refugees and displaced persons, with over two hundred thousand civilians killed.

Example: Ethnic Cleansing Outside Europe

In other countries ethnic cleansing may not be as ruthless nor as "successful" as it has been in the case in the Balkans. In Ethiopia authorities are arbitrarily expelling persons of Eritrean origin, irrespective of their nationality. In Fiji, during the coup attempt of 2,000 led by ethnic Fijians, many Indian Fijians (descendants of indentured labor from India in the nineteenth century) fled the country and those remaining were often terrorized by ethnic Fijian gangs. The aim of the coup leaders was to alter the constitution to prevent Indian Fijians from ever being able to achieve significant political power.

---

[25] See Gillian McIntosh, *The Force of Culture: Unionist Identities in Twentieth-Century Ireland* (Cork, Ireland: Cork University Press, 1999).

[26] See Colin Coulter, *Contemporary Northern Irish Society: An Introduction* (London: Pluto Press, 1982) 198.

[27] See Heywood, *Politics*, 97.

New Religious Movements and Violence

The breakdown of tradition in the late 1960s created a meaningless vacuum open to fundamentalist groups[28] and controversial New Religious Movements (NRMs), variously called "sects" or "cults," that proliferated at that time. Fundamentalist movements will be explained later in the chapter.

Definitions

1. Sects and Cults

A *sect* is a small, voluntary, exclusive religious grouping demanding total commitment from its followers and stressing its separateness from and rejection of society, e.g., the Unification Church (Moonies). A *cult* tends to be a more spontaneous and open movement, lacking specific membership requirements, offering particular concrete benefits to its adherents rather than the comprehensive worldviews and conceptions of salvation typical of religious sects. There are political cults as in a group of people attached to a particular charismatic leader; religious cults, such as followers of Indian gurus; and self-improvement or therapy cults. A more recent example of a self-improvement cult is the New Agers.[29]

2. New Religious Movements (NRMs) and "The Cults"

The religious movements following the expressive revolution were labeled by journalists and others pejoratively as "the cults," confusing the above distinctions between sect and cult. These "cults," e.g., the Hare Krishna and Scientology, are more accurately "sects" in the traditional sense described above because of their elitism and their vigorous efforts to make and retain converts. In recent years, because of the emotional connotations of the words "cult" and "sect," new, more neutral terms have been introduced to describe contemporary movements: "New Religious Movements," "New Religious Groups," "Alternative Religions."[30]

[28] See Samuel P. Huntington, *The Clash of Civilizations and the Remaking of World Order* (London: Touchstone, 1998) 98.

[29] See John A. Saliba, *Christian Responses to the New Age Movement* (London: Geoffrey Chapman, 1999) 1–38.

[30] See James A. Beckford, *Cult Controversies: The Societal Responses to the New Religious Movements* (London: Tavistock, 1986) 18–9.

Origins of NRMs

Young people in the 1960s, particularly in the English-speaking world, disoriented in consequence of the expressive revolution and mostly from fairly prosperous middle-class families, either rejoined the structures of society and accepted its competitive values and/or they enrolled in various New Religious Movements or in conservative Evangelical nonmainline Christian Churches.[31]

The NRMs (including the Evangelical conservative Churches) offered postmodern people what they most desired: experiential religion unencumbered with theological dogma; intimacy in community life; clarity of meaning and direction in life; therapeutic services—many in the drug culture wanted help that was understanding and non-judgmental.[32]

Types of NRMs

There are two major types of NRMs: "self-help sects" and "total" or "world-rejecting" sects.[33]

1. Self-Help Sects

These claim to offer individuals therapeutic, supposedly scientific services, so that they have improved personal identities that allow them to survive in a competitive and changing world. Examples are encounter and rebirthing groups, Scientology,[34] Zen, and Ananda Marga.

2. Total or World-Rejecting Sects

In these groups, emphasis on individual identity and self-direction give way to the dominance of the group; the individual's sense of belonging and identity will come, not so much from internal self-discipline, but from submission to the demands of the group. For example, in the

[31] See J. Gordon Melton, "How New is New? The Flowering of the 'New' Religious Consciousness since 1965," *The Future of the New Religious Movements*, ed. David G. Bromley and Phillip Hammond (Macon, Ga.: Mercer, 1987) 46–52.

[32] See descriptions in "Vatican Report on Sects, Cults and New Religious Movements," *Origins* (22 May 1986) 1–10.

[33] This helpful distinction is made by Bernice Martin, *A Sociology of Contemporary Cultural Change* (Oxford: Basil Blackwell, 1981) 202–33.

[34] Roy Wallis, "Thoughts on the Future of Scientology," Bromley and Hammond, *The Future of the New Religious Movements*, 80–4.

Hare Krishna[35] and the Unification Church, there is an explicit hierarchy
of command, firm control, and radical restriction of both personal pri-
vacy and choice.[36] Some of these anti-world sects demand from their
followers absolute obedience to the leader/group. In fact, many movements require the renunciation of family ties to be a test of the sincerity
of submission to the group.

NRMs and Violence

Generalizations about the use of violence by NRMs against members
and outsiders are inappropriate. There developed what has been called
"the new bigotry" or a militant anticult movement.[37] Modern mass
communications, encouraged by politicians, church people, and legis-
lators, began to scapegoat these movements, blaming them for all
kinds of society's illnesses.

The movements have been charged with brainwashing their followers
so that they were never free to join or leave. While there are instances of
serious coercion, e.g., in the mass suicide by members of the Peoples
Temple in 1973, it is unfair to generalize. Eileen Barker, in her study of the
Moonies, comments that people joined more often for rational reasons
than because they were brainwashed.[38] Sociologist John Saliba concludes
that the "evidence adduced to support the tenet that new religious
movements in general are destructive organizations that invariably
ruin one's life and warp one's personality is just not strong enough."[39]

In summary, not all NRMs use bullying techniques; some in fact
have achieved beneficial results for members.[40] However, violence and

[35] See Shirley Harrison, *Cults: The Battle for God* (London: Christopher Helm, 1990)
104–16; E. Burke Rochford, *Hare Krishna in America* (New Brunswick: Rutgers
University Press, 1985).

[36] See Eileen Barker, *The Making of a Moonie: Brainwashing or Choice* (Oxford: Basil
Blackwell, 1984).

[37] See J. Gordon Melton and Robert L. Moore, *The Cult Experience: Responding to the
New Religious Pluralism* (New York: Pilgrim Press, 1982) 95–100.

[38] See Barker, *The Making of a Moonie*, 250–1.

[39] John A. Saliba, *Perspectives on New Religious Movements* (London: Geoffrey
Chapman, 1995) 97. See also J. Gordon Melton and David G. Bromley, "Challenging
Misconceptions about the New Religions—Violence Connection," *Cults, Religion
and Violence*, ed. David G. Bromley and J. Gordon Melton (Cambridge: Cambridge
University Press, 200) 42–56.

[40] See Villa Appel, *Cults in America: Programmed for Paradise* (New York: Holt, Rinehart and Winston, 1983) 178.

coercion against their members and society are endemic to some move-ments; for example, child and sexual abuse were pervasive in the Peoples Temple under the leadership of Jim Jones, and in the Branch Davidians, led by David Koresh, Waco, Texas.[41] Intimidating tactics by outside agencies can encourage leaders to be dictatorial in relating to members of movements: in the face of an "enemy" they demand total loyalty to themselves. Federal government agents in the United States contributed through their confrontational style to the violent ending of the Branch Davidians. It seems this style also provoked Timothy McVeigh to destroy the federal office building in Oklahoma City in revenge against the federal government.[42]

Fundamentalism, Violence, and Terrorism

Definitions and Qualities of Fundamentalism

Fundamentalism, a historically recurring tendency within Judeo-Christian-Muslim religious traditions,[43] occurs today as an authoritarian reaction to the fears of chaos evoked by postmodernism and globaliza-tion. Patrick Arnold defines fundamentalism as

> an aggressive and marginalized religious movement which, in re-action to the perceived threat of modernity seeks to return its home religion and nation to traditional orthodox principles, values, and texts through the co-option of the central executive and legislative power of both the religion itself and the modern national state.[44]

R. Scott Appleby defines fundamentalism in a similar way, but intro-duces the notion of militancy:

> a specifiable pattern of religious militancy by which self-styled true believers attempt to arrest the erosion of religious identity,

---

[41] See March Galanter, *Cults: Faith, Healing, and Coercion* (Oxford: Oxford University Press, 1998) 167–71.

[42] Ibid., 171.

[43] See Patrick Arnold, "The Rise of Catholic Fundamentalism," *America* (11 April 1987) 298.

[44] Patrick Arnold, "The Reemergence of Fundamentalism in the Catholic Church," *The Fundamentalist Phenomenon*, ed. N. J. Cohen (Grand Rapids, Mich.: W. B. Eerdmans, 1990) 174.

fortify the borders of the religious community, and create viable alternatives to secular structures and processes.[45]

James Hunter calls fundamentalism a form of "organized anger" and says that all fundamentalist groups "share the deep and worrisome sense that history has gone awry,"[46] the result of modernity and post-modernity.

In brief, fundamentalists:

- believe their task is to make history accord with the orthodox principles of their religion;

- are anti-intellectual and intolerant of opposition;

- are absolutely certain that they are right;

- are led by male charismatic or authoritarian leaders;

- draw their following from professional and working classes, though disproportionate numbers come from among the young, educated, unemployed, or underemployed males;[47]

- select particular statements from the sacred texts of their religion or tradition to legitimate their actions

- and ignore other important points.

Fundamentalists tend to form themselves into sects in the traditional sense described above, rather than cults. They believe that people in an established religious group have lost their original truth and zeal, so their task is to purify the group. If resistance is too great, fundamentalists may form a schismatic group. Fundamentalism in the Western world has generally tended to be confined to the middle class, whereas in India and Israel its mix of nationalism and religion has attracted people from all sections of society.

In Islamic countries fundamentalism has appeared as the mouthpiece for the oppressed and marginalized and as the scourge of the decadent and materialist West.[48] Fundamentalists scapegoat objects,

---

[45] R. Scott Appleby, *The Ambivalence of the Sacred: Religion, Violence, and Reconciliation* (Oxford: Rowman and Littlefield, 2000) 86.

[46] James Hunter, in Cohen, *The Fundamentalist Phenomenon*, 59.

[47] See Appleby, *The Ambivalence of the Sacred*, 87–8.

[48] See Walter Laqueur, *The New Terrorism: Fanaticism and the Arms of Mass Destruction* (London: Phoenix Press, 2001) 154.

individuals, or groups of people for the breakdown of "orthodoxy," e.g., video machines, Hollywood, feminists demanding equality, card players. Modernity and postmodernity in their many forms are the "Great Satan" for Islamic fundamentalists (see chapter 7).[49] In a reaction against the modernization and secularization that the mullahs believe have corrupted the purity of Islam, Ayatollah Khomeini outlawed as "satanic" all those elements that symbolize corruption in Iran.[50]

Fundamentalists and Terrorism

Fundamentalists seek to co-opt the central executive and legislative power either through democratic processes or recourse to extreme violence.

1. Democratic Fundamentalists

Democratic fundamentalists, for example, the Moral Majority in the United States, are prepared to work through political and legislative processes to achieve their goals.

In the United States fundamentalist Evangelicals were traditionally seen as "anti-political soul-savers who waited for the second coming of Christ, wanted to live decent lives and be left alone except when they would convert others."[51] This dramatically changed in 1979 when Evangelical fundamentalist Jerry Falwell recognized that, "In spite of everything we are going to turn the nation back to God . . . the national crisis [is] growing quickly out of hand."[52] Organized political action was seen as the only way to achieve the traditional aims of Evangelicals and fundamentalists. Falwell formed the Moral Majority, dominated by Protestant fundamentalists, but drawing together Protestants of all kinds, Jews, and Roman Catholics. Its platform was sharply focused: pro-life, pro-traditional family/morality, pro-American, pro-national defense, and pro-Israel.

At the same time, the New Right,[53] as described in the previous chapter, emerged in the political scene as an ideological political movement

---

[49] See Steve Bruce, *The Rise and Fall of the New Christian Right: Conservative Protestant Politics in America 1978–1988* (Oxford: Clarendon Press, 1990) 110–8.

[50] See Appel, *Cults in America*, 17.

[51] M. E. Marty, "The New Christian Right," *The Tablet* (23 April 1988) 462.

[52] Jerry Falwell, *Strength for the Journey* (New York: Simon and Schuster, 1987) 358.

[53] See Bruce, *The Rise and Fall of the New Christian Right*.

with distinctive values, a strong emphasis on maintaining the American way of life and America as the world's capitalist superpower, and with clear-cut answers to contemporary social and economic challenges. Senator Barry Goldwater, an early leader of the New Right, could confidently declare that "extremism in defense of liberty is no vice."[54] The presidencies of Ronald Reagan and George Bush were deeply influenced by this political philosophy, for example, in their secret weapon sales to Iran and their undeclared war on the Nicaraguan government. President Bush, when he pardoned officials for their involvement in these activities, claimed that they had been inspired by patriotism that made their deeds pure.[55] Niccollo Machiavelli, the fifteenth-century political philosopher, would have agreed with this political fundamentalism: "You should adopt wholeheartedly the policy most likely to save your homeland's life and preserve her liberty."[56]

The Moral Majority supported the New Right, giving it religious legitimation; the revitalized conservative ideology was pronounced to be God's will for America. Both political and religious ideologies saw the breakdown in morality, the excesses of postmodernity, and growing government support for welfare services as undermining the nation's local and international strength. It became a religious and patriotic duty to support laissez-faire market capitalism and decreasing aid to the poor.

2. Violent Fundamentalists and Terrorism

Violence can range from manipulating facts and truth to physical assault on people and property. Fundamentalists who commit themselves to violence believe they are living in exceptional times that threaten their beliefs, and this permits them to suspend normal requirements of their religion, such as respect for human rights.

Toward the end of his life, Ayatollah Khomeini explained why fundamentalists are able to use terrorism even though this is normally against their religious beliefs. He claimed that since the very survival of the Islamic Republic of Iran was threatened, parts of the Islamic law gov-

---

[54] Barry Goldwater cited by Theodore White, *The Making of the President 1964* (Toronto: Signet Books, 1965) 261.

[55] See S. L. Sutherland, "Retrospection and Democracy," *Cruelty and Deception: The Controversy over Dirty Hands in Politics*, ed. Paul Rynard and David P. Shugarman (Orchard Park: Broadview Press, 2000) 218–20.

[56] *Niccollo Machiavelli, Selected Political Writings*, ed. David Wooton (Indianapolis: Hackett, 1994) 215.

erning it were to be bypassed in favor of the supreme jurist's (i.e., Khomeini's) own decisions.[57] In this way he justified the establishment of state terrorism in Iran and his support of Islamic terrorists in other parts of the world. Likewise, the fundamentalist Taliban in Afghanistan and "pro-lifers" who kill abortionists or blow up their buildings claim that exceptional times demand ruthless responses. White supremacists in the United States, who destroy property and kill, assert that the laws of the land no longer apply to them, for governments are corrupt and evil. God is calling them to be his special prophets and all previous laws are suspended.

3. Political Terrorism

Political terrorism is "criminal behavior designed primarily to generate fear in the community, or a substantial segment of it, for political purposes."[58] The primary motivation of terrorist organizations may be nationalist (e.g., Basque Nationalism, the Irish Republican Army), ideological (e.g., the Red Brigade), or religious (e.g., the Taliban, Hamas, Hezbollah—the Lebanese Shiite movement). All have one thing in common, namely, to create enough fear in the population to force governments to make desired political changes.[59] Terrorist movements have existed for centuries, sometimes involving thousands of members, but in recent times there has been a radical change in their character. Now, given the increasing availability of sophisticated technology, a small group or even one individual can terrorize thousands, even millions of people. Small groups are difficult to detect and infiltrate.[60]

Political terrorists have instrumental and primary targets. For example, in the case of the attacks on the World Trade Center in New York and the Pentagon the primary target of the terrorists was the people of the United States; the instrumental target was the people trapped in the planes and buildings. Terrorism has at least three strategic objectives:

- to gain publicity for the terrorists' cause;

- to show that a government cannot protect the people;

---

[57] See Appleby, *The Ambivalence of the Sacred*, 89.

[58] Chalmers Johnson, *Revolutionary Change* (Stanford: Stanford University Press, 1982) 154.

[59] See Bruce Hoffman, *Inside Terrorism* (New York: Columbia University Press, 1998) 43.

[60] See Laqueur, *The New Terrorism*, 4–6.

- to force a government to overreact by turning the situation into a military one with the aim of so restricting a population's freedom that people will eventually turn against their government and impel it to submit to the terrorists' demands.[61]

With the availability of weapons of mass destruction and advanced technology, terrorists can now imagine a further aim, namely, to paralyze and undermine a nation's economic infrastructure, even the global economy itself. The terrorist attack on the United States illustrates that this aim is now a real possibility.

Islamic Fundamentalism and Violence [62]

Following the bombings in New York and Washington in September 2001, there was rejoicing on the West Bank and in Palestinian refugee camps, among the Taliban in Afghanistan; and praise to Allah among Muslims in Pakistan and northern Nigeria, overwhelmingly among the poor and the dispossessed in the Muslim world. Some Westerners find this jubilation difficult to understand.

The Muslim peoples have an old and proud culture, but have long felt under attack from the West. Islamic radicalism draws its power from a deep sense of injustice. Since the early nineteenth century scarcely a decade has passed without some Muslim area in Asia or Africa being threatened by Western Christian powers. There are efforts to build states on Islamic foundations—some radical, e.g., Iran; some less so, e.g., Pakistan, Malaysia, and Indonesia.

Islamic fundamentalists[63] feel that so much has been destroyed by contact with the West: Qur'anic education, a sense of community, social coherence, the old religious legal system; above all, respect for ancient Muslim culture and values. Globalization has intensified this feeling of lostness, e.g., the Internet's pornography, the atomization of families, the neglect of religious values. The West is blamed, but the United States in particular is seen as the "Great Satan" leading the destruction

---

[61] See Johnson, *Revolutionary Change*, 156–68.

[62] See Michael Binyon, "How the Islamic World Learnt to Hate the US," *The Times* (13 September 2001) 13.

[63] For explanation of contemporary Islamic fundamentalism see *Islamic Fundamentalism*, ed. Abdel S. Sidahmed and Anoushiravan Ehteshami (Boulder: Westview Press, 1996), and Malise Ruthven, *Islam in the World* (London: Penguin, 2000).

of all that is considered sacred. Political terrorism draws on this bitter resentment, and terrorists have a perverted hope that in the violent downfall of the "Great Satan" the world will be put right again

As regards Afghanistan, the policies of the United States over the last twenty years have helped to create both Osama bin Laden and the fundamentalist Taliban regime that protects him.[64] The idea of *jihad*, or holy war, had almost stopped in the Islamic world after the tenth century but was revived, with American backing, in order to create a pan-Islamic movement following the Soviet invasion of Afghanistan in 1979. The United States sent billions of dollars' worth of weaponry to groups fighting the Soviets. The aid succeeded and the Soviets were forced to withdraw, but the results are everywhere to be seen: huge supplies of arms, powerful local warlords, and extreme religious zealotry. Now the *jihad* has been taken into Pakistan, to the unjust kingdoms of the Gulf, the repressive states of the southern Mediterranean, and to the West itself.

The uncomfortable truth for the West is that much of the contemporary hostility of fundamentalism in the Islamic world is the result of its own past political failures resulting in violence and injustice for innocent people. Many of the world's most troubling problems have their roots in decisions made at the treaty of peace at Versailles in 1919 following the defeat of Germany. Among them are the creation of Burundi, Rwanda, and Iraq, the instability of the Balkans, and above all, the feud between the Arabs and the Israelis.[65]

Similarly, in recent times, there are Palestinian exiles in refugee camps in Lebanon, Syria, and Jordan living in poverty and overwhelmed with a sense of hopelessness. Frustration is attracting growing numbers of refugees to Islamic extreme groups; violence in defense of their political and religious rights, these dispossessed refugees believe, is the only way out of their oppressive conditions.[66]

As long as the West continues to contribute to the volatile atmosphere, and unless the injustices are addressed, we can expect more violence and terrorist activity.

[64] See Richard Mackenzie, "The United States and the Taliban," *Fundamentalism Reborn? Afghanistan and the Taliban*, ed. William Maley (London: Hurst, 2001) 90–103.

[65] See *The Economist* (15 September 2001) 69.

[66] See *The Economist* (8 September 2001) 51.

Fundamentalism: Summary

Fundamentalism is a response of religious traditionalists to situations that threaten their identity; fundamentalists are fearful of the uncertainties and challenges of rapid change caused by modernity and postmodernity (see axiom 3, chapter 1).

- Militant fundamentalists seek to reshape the world according to their understanding of orthodoxy; this commonly involves coercion, including physical violence or terrorism, e.g., the actions of the Taliban in Afghanistan,[67] and Hamas against Israel.

- "Democratic fundamentalism" normally acts within the law, but is open to politically bullying tactics to ensure that religious orthodoxy is restored and maintained.

- Islamic fundamentalism is a reaction to modernization and to ongoing economic and cultural domination by the West.

- Fundamentalists reject the separation of politics and religion and aim to capture the state and to use it to enforce their understanding of orthodoxy.

- For fundamentalists the end may at times justify the means; religious imperatives, e.g., justice and love, are temporarily suspended.

- Fundamentalists choose passages from a sacred text selectively, but depend on an authority or charismatic figure to interpret them, as happened with Ayatollah Khomeini in Iran, David Koresh for the Branch Davidians, Mohammad Omar for the Taliban, Sheikh Fadlalla for the Hezbollah in Lebanon, and Ahmed Yassin for Hamas.

- Fundamentalists, like all witch-hunters (see chapter 7), search for secret connections or conspiracies; for example, Ian Paisley, leader of the Democratic Unionist Party, claims that Jesuits (and therefore all Catholics) are not Christians because their symbol, "HIS" ("Jesus Savior of Humankind"), really stands for some divinities of an ancient Egyptian religion and there is a conspiracy to impose this religion on others.[68]

- Fundamentalism is a symptom of a threat to, or destruction of, cultural and personal identity. Arguments against the fundamentalist

[67] See Steve Bruce, *Fundamentalism* (Cambridge: Polity, 2000) 63.
[68] Ibid., 111.

position, no matter how cogently reasoned and presented, will have no impact on fundamentalists. Such arguments will be seen as examples of the enemy's "cunning and evil" ways.

• The rage of "violent fundamentalists" often has its roots in past and present injustices. Until the injustices are openly acknowledged and addressed, it is impossible to begin dialogue.

Catholic Restorationism and Fundamentalism

John Paul II, in his speeches and praxis, strives to relate the faith to everything that is positive in today's world, fearlessly naming issues and practices that run contrary to the Gospel message.[69] The moral leadership of the papacy has never been so high for centuries. For the Pope, "the council documents have lost nothing of their value and brilliance. They . . . [are] normative texts of the Magisterium. . . . We find a sure compass [in the council] by which to take our bearings in the century now beginning."[70] The Pope has also reaffirmed the fact that he is not a monarch and bishops are not his delegates: "the whole body of Bishops . . . are also 'vicars and ambassadors of Christ.' The Bishop of Rome is a member of the 'College,' and the Bishops are his brothers in the ministry."[71]

There are, however, in and throughout the Church, well-orchestrated attempts to restore the opposition-to-the-world mentality of the pre-Vatican II times. Restorationism is an undefined, but nonetheless powerful movement within the Church toward *uncritical* reaffirmation of pre-Vatican II structures and attitudes in reaction to the theological and cultural turmoil of the changes of the council and in the modern world at large. Restorationism takes many forms, some fanatically aggressive, e.g., fundamentalist movements, and others less so.[72] The following are some examples of restorationist movements.

---

[69] See O'Malley, "Interpreting Vatican II: Version Two," 19.

[70] John Paul II, *At the Beginning of the New Millennium* (Vatican, 2001) par. 57.

[71] John Paul II, *Ut Unum Sint* (Boston: Pauline, n.d.) 102.

[72] For example, John R. Quinn, *The Reform of the Papacy: The Costly Call to Christian Unity* (New York: Herder/Crossroad, 1999); Bernard Häring, "The Church I Want," *The Tablet* (28 July 1990) 944–5; Franz Konig, "In Defence of Fr Dupuis," *The Tablet* (16 January 1999) 76–7; and "My Vision for the Church of the Future," ibid., (27 March 1999) 424–6.

Episcopal conferences and the bishops' synod are structures established by Vatican II to express collegiality between papal Rome and
local churches. However, their initiatives and effectiveness have weakened. For example, the Rome Curia informed the episcopal conference
of the United States that it did not have the authority to write a pastoral
letter on peace.[73] The bishops' synods have also lost their original
authority intended by the council. A synod was "to demonstrate that
all the bishops . . . share in the responsibility for the universal
Church."[74] This collegial involvement by bishops has not been fully
developed; at present its role is an advisory one.[75]

Rome's involvement in local churches is especially marked in matters
of liturgy, though the council restored the right to episcopal conferences to regulate liturgy in their territories.[76] Nathan Mitchell of Notre
Dame University critiques this form of intervention: "Fueled by fear,
fantasy and misinformation, stalwarts in the Roman dicasteries seem
to feel they can bully both bishops and believers into submission [in
matters liturgical]. . . ."[77]

Case Study: Liturgical Issues—Roman Domination

In 1991 the bishops of the United States approved a new Lectionary that favored the use of inclusive language, but approval was
suddenly revoked by Rome in 1994. Texts retaining many of the
most controversial uses of masculine vocabulary were reintroduced
by a small group in Rome. Its members had minimal experience

continued on next page

---

[73] See Peter Hebblethwaite, *The Tablet* (30 April 1983) 400–1; the bishops of England and Wales complained in 1985 that they had to refer matters to Rome that
should have been within their own competency to decide; *The Tablet* (3 August 1985)
816. For an analysis of Rome's efforts to restrict the laity's role to pre-Vatican II
times see J.-G. Vaillancourt, *Papal Power: A Study of Vatican Council Control Over Lay
Catholic Elites* (Berkeley: University of California Press, 1980).

[74] "Decree on the Pastoral Office of Bishops," *The Documents of Vatican II*, ed.
Walter Abbott (London: Geoffrey Chapman, 1966) par. 5.

[75] See Gerald A. Arbuckle, *Refounding the Church: Dissent for Leadership* (Maryknoll:
Orbis Books, 1993) 61–2; Quinn, *The Reform of the Papacy*, 110–6.

[76] See "Constitution on the Sacred Liturgy," *Documents of Vatican II*, ed. Walter M.
Abbott (London: Geoffrey Chapman, 1966) pars. 22.2.

[77] Nathan D. Mitchell, "Troubling Assertions from Rome about ICEL," *America*
(1 July 2000) 21.

of the American culture, no women were involved, and only one member had a graduate degree in Scripture.[78] Rome subsequently asked that members of the International Commission on English in the Liturgy (ICEL) appointed by the episcopal conferences of English-speaking countries require its *nihil obstat*—an action in defiance of the powers of local churches.[79]

In 2001 Rome issued a document, *Liturgiam Authenticam*, without consultation with the episcopal chairman of ICEL, reaffirming a ban on gender-inclusive language.[80] The document asserts that Rome has the right to intervene in liturgical matters. This evoked some strong reactions from commentators. For example, John Allen, a liturgical commentator, writes: "[The document] strikes at the heart of Vatican II ecclesiology by centralizing power in the curia and by insisting that local cultures adopt an essentially Roman style of worship."[81]

Official Apologies

In the deeply moving papal apologies, it is never the institutional Church that has erred, just its "sons and daughters." It is always the sins of the children, not of the mother.[82] What is required, however, is the admission "that some official policies and practices of the church have been objectively in contradiction to the Gospel and have caused harm to many people."[83] One has but to think of Rome's long hesitancy in speaking out against issues such as slavery, the persecution of Jews, the Crusades, and gender inequality, to support this point.

[78] See John L. Allen, "On the Lectionary, Eleven Men Made a Deal," *National Catholic Reporter* (25 September 1998) 3–5.

[79] See Donald W. Trautman, "Rome and ICEL," *America* (4 March 2000) 7–11; Jorge A. Medina, "ICEL Controversy," ibid. (13 May 2000) 17–9; Ronald D. Witherup, "ICEL and Liturgical Translations," ibid. (7 October 2000) 17–21.

[80] See *The Tablet* (12 May 2001) 704–5.

[81] John L. Allen, "New Document Replaces 35 Years of Liturgy Work," *National Catholic Reporter* (25 May 2001) 13; see also Donald Trautman, "'Authentic Liturgy' Fails the Mission of the Church," ibid. (9 November 2001) 17–8.

[82] See Garry Wills, "The Vatican Regrets," ibid. (25 May 2000) 19.

[83] Francis A. Sullivan, "The Papal Apology," *America* (8 April 2000) 22; see also analysis by Bradford E. Hinze, "Ecclesial Repentance and the Demands of Dialogue," *Theological Studies*, vol. 61, no. 2 (2000) 207–38.

Vatican II as a Revolution

As a theologian, I am grateful for the documents of Vatican II and regret that the council did not happen earlier, but as an anthropologist I believe the council fathers were naïve in not recognizing the inevitably disorienting impact on Catholics of their decisions. The fact is, the council's efforts to reform the Church and its governmental structures amounted to a cultural revolution. "Revolution" here means sudden, radical changes in key areas of a culture so that an established government or way of life is dramatically replaced by another.

There are three reasons why the term "revolution" can aptly be applied to the council's decisions:

1. Myth Change

As explained in axiom 6, chapter 1, it is impossible to change the mythic structure of any organization without catastrophic consequences. For centuries Catholics had been treated in a premodern culture like dependent children, being told by a clerical leadership exactly how to win salvation by obeying a list of detailed rules. Suddenly the council says Catholics must stand on their own feet and make decisions for themselves in the light of the Gospel and the needs of the world. Personal and cultural malaise were the inevitable consequences.

2. Ambiguities in Documents

The council reintroduced theological balance to the Church's mythology; for example, the theology of the local church and the principle of collegiality were reaffirmed in order to counter the centuries-long emphasis on its opposite, papal authority. The restored theological balance left significant and fundamental ambiguities and tensions evident in the following summary statements of the council's documents:

> The Church is an institution under the leadership of the bishops; *but* it is also the People of God, pilgrims not concerned about rank. The Church is universal, *but* it is to be incarnated within local churches and reflect their diversities of culture.
>
> Priesthood is a sacrament and ministry established by Christ, *but* all who are baptized are priests.
>
> The aim of liturgy is to help us adore God our Creator, *but* it must reflect the needs and customs of different peoples and cultures.

Nowhere in the documents does the council spell out precisely *how* these polar opposites are to be balanced in real life, and in fact it could not do so. Immediately following the council, the process of mythology-splitting started, and it has not stopped (axiom 7, chapter 1). People opted with emotional intensity for one pole or the other of the theological statements. One group would say, "The council says that the Church is universal—this must be respected above everything else!" Another would say, "Particular churches must take precedence because that is what the council says!" Others became overwhelmed with grief, confused, feeling pressured on all sides into change, angry, benumbed, and hurt by the chaos within the Church. The joyful hopes of the council disintegrated into sadness.

3. Secular World in Turmoil

The council called Catholics to leave religious and cultural ghettoes and dialogue with the secular world around them, itself in revolutionary turmoil. It would have been difficult enough for Catholics to have related to modernity, but they were expected at the same time to understand and evangelize postmodern societies. No wonder many felt confused.

Responses to Vatican II

Historically, there are three possible ways of reacting to a revolution. First, there is the formation of a new status quo with appropriate structures and power systems based on a new or reformed mythology. This is a long and arduous process demanding patience, leadership, and the ability to live in the ambiguity of the here-and-now as the new mythology is slowly and hesitantly owned and structures are built on its value system.

The second is counterrevolution—the often intolerant, even violent, attempts to restore former values and power structures. Sometimes there is a short period of concessions to change by those in power, then a growing rigidity and insistence on widespread conformity/uniformity builds frustration to breaking point for people who want to move forward.

The third is the breakdown of the revolution into general disorder in which diverse, conflicting groups flourish. Some actively support the revolution's values but do not have access to appropriate power structures; others form sects characterized by elitism, quick-fix authoritarian solutions to the malaise, and witch-hunting crazes to identify the "unorthodox." Others, weary of the infighting, withdraw entirely from the society to go underground. All three reactions to the council's revolution are evident in the Church today, particularly the second and third.

In the revolutionary turmoil it is possible to identify at least three distinct ways of being Catholic. First, there is a model of the Church based on the balance between the hierarchical and collegial values of the council. The United States Bishops Conference uses this model when constructing their pastoral letters: the Holy Spirit is in all members of the Church, hence the hierarchy must establish appropriate consultative channels to listen to the faithful before making authoritative statements. Secondly, there is the counterrevolution or restorationist model that today is in the ascendancy. Its adherents stress the need for orthodoxy over pastoral creativity, a monocultural, Rome-centered Church rather than a multicultural one. Thirdly, there is the "Protest Church." This comprises a growing number of Catholics who, because they can no longer tolerate restorationism, have ceased to be actively involved in contemporary Church structures. Claiming to be Catholics loyal to the council's values, they search for parishes where they can participate in well-prepared Eucharists and, if they do not find them, form faith groups of their own. Followers of this model of the Church can succumb to sectarianism, for example, in their zeal some condemn everything of the precouncil Church, refusing any dialogue with those who disagree with them.

Catholic Fundamentalism

Catholic fundamentalists belong to a particularly aggressive form of restorationism noted for:[84]

- A concern for the dangers of secular humanism, that is, the *assumed* undermining of the religious heritage and purity of the Church and nation through a conspiracy of liberals, media, government, and so-called leftists in theology and ecclesiastical administrations.

- An elitist assumption, as in all sects, of a kind of supernatural authority and right to pursue and intolerantly condemn those who disagree with them, even bishops or theologians.

---

[84] See Patrick Arnold, "The Rise of Catholic Fundamentalism," *America* (11 April 1987) 297–302, and T. C. Ross, "Catholicism and Fundamentalism," *New Theology Review*, no. 1 (1988) 74–87.

- A highly selective approach to the Church's teaching: statements on ecclesiastical authority, private sexuality or incidental issues are obsessively emphasized, but the papal or episcopal pronouncements on social questions are ignored or considered matters for debate only. After the publication of John Paul II's encyclical letter *Sollicitudo Rei Socialis* in 1987, and the 1986 Catholic Bishops' (USA) Pastoral Letter on the USA Economy, which criticized liberal capitalism and Marxist collectivism, fundamentalists like Richard Neuhaus and Michael Novak denounced these documents for containing, they asserted, a swing toward, or acceptance of, leftist/Marxist thinking. These critics believe that the capitalist system must be defended as the only authentic method to protect the freedom of the people.[85]

- Concern for accidentals, not for the substance of issues, e.g., the Lefebvre sect stresses Latin for the Mass, failing to see that this does not pertain to authentic tradition.

- Attempts by fundamentalist groups, e.g., Opus Dei, to infiltrate governmental structures of the Church in order to obtain legitimacy for their views and to impose them on the whole Church.

- The vehemence and intolerance with which they attack coreligionists.

Development of Catholic Fundamentalism [86]

Fundamentalists believe that the secularist values of the 1960s' expressive revolution found their way into the Church through Vatican II. On the one hand, the revolution's followers supported increased aid for the poor, civil rights, the rejection of the capitalist system, and antiwar rallies, and on the other hand, the relaxation of existing antiabortion and antipornography laws. Fundamentalists point to the "insidious" impact of the revolution's secular humanism in such documents as The Church in the Modern World (Vatican II), the encyclical *Populorum Progressio* (1967) on social justice by Paul VI, and *Justice in the World* by the Synod of Bishops (1971). If the Church became too

---

[85] See Gregory Baum, "Neo-Conservative Critics of the Churches," *Neo-Conservatism: Social and Religious Phenomenon*, ed. Gregory Baum (New York: Seabury Press, 1981) 43–50.

[86] This section is a revision of material from my book *Refounding the Church*, 51–4.

closely allied with the poor it would lose support of the politically powerful, it was said, and where would it all end!

Jesuit Fr. Thomas O'Meara defines Christian fundamentalism as "an interpretation of Christianity in which a charismatic leader locates with easy certitude in chosen words, doctrines and practices, the miraculous actions of a strict God saving an elite from an evil world."[87] This is an apt description of Catholic fundamentalism. Sects like Catholics United for the Faith (CUF) were formed to defend the Church against the "evils of secular humanism," "the loss of orthodoxy," or the "liberalizing excesses that Vatican II inspired." The Latin Mass movement gave some Catholics the nostalgic support they craved, and some eventually moved out of the Church to join the Lefebvre sect. A wide variety of cults developed around supposed apparitions of the Mother of God and commonly their message was: the world is basically evil; return to traditional practices of the Catholic faith; divine chastisement is imminent if the revelations are not listened to. In brief, the message was: return to the pre-Vatican II Church or face dire consequences! The Catholic Charismatic Renewal Movement developed from within North America in 1967 and became one of the major movements of the 1970s. It often fostered sect-like qualities contrary to Vatican II values, e.g., opposition to social justice programs, elitism, fundamentalism with regard to the interpretation of the Scriptures, and authoritarian male leadership.[88]

Examples of Fundamentalist Movements

1. Opus Dei and Communion and Liberation

Opus Dei is a movement that evokes strong feelings in people. For example, Andrew Greeley views it as "a devious, antidemocratic, reactionary, semi-fascist institution, desperately hungry for absolute power in the church. It ought to be forced either to come out into the open or be suppressed."[89] It is decidedly anti-Vatican II, not only because it has

[87] Thomas F. O'Meara, *Fundamentalism: A Catholic Perspective* (New York: Paulist Press, 1990) 18.

[88] See *The Catholic Pentecostal Movement: Creative or Divisive Enthusiasm* (Brussels: Pro Mundi Vita), bulletin no. 60 (1975) 30–4.

[89] Cited by Penny Lernoux, *People of God: The Struggle for World Catholicism* (New York: Penguin, 1989) 320. For a critical analysis of Opus Dei, see Michael J. Walsh, *The Secret World of Opus Dei* (London: Grafton Books, 1989). William J. West claims

retained a Latin liturgy, but because it has uncritically supported right-wing political movements in Latin America and Asia, and capitalistic structures in the West. Earlier, the organization backed the authoritarian regime of Ferdinand Marcos in the Philippines.[90] Its members claim that liberation theology, involvement in social justice issues, and the development of Basic Ecclesial Communities undermine the authority and secular power of the Church. Archbishop Fernando Saenz Lacalle, an Opus Dei member and successor of martyred Archbishop Oscar Romero in San Salvador, has publicly stated that "liberation theology no longer has any place" in his country.[91] A less secretive movement of Italian origin is Communion and Liberation, like Opus Dei, openly hostile to Vatican II theology.[92]

2. "Neo-Catechumenate (The Way)"

As with the previous movements, the Neo-Catechumenate offers thousands of people a challenging Christian vision in their lives. However, this group also has sect-like features and can be oppressive both to its members and the people they minister to. Gordon Urquhart, who has studied the organization, comments that the Way's "world-rejecting stance is so extreme that little interaction with the wider society is possible. The emphasis is on the spiritual life and detachment from all worldly cares. . . . All attempts to change or influence society are actively discouraged as presumptuous."[93] In summary, some of the Way's sect-like qualities are:

- It demands total and unquestioning commitment from its members and submission to the authority of its organizers.

- It is elitist and frequently divisive within parishes, e.g., it demands an excessive amount of time from members who are priests and/or religious and often acts without reference to existing parish structures.

---

to counter the criticism in his book *Opus Dei: Exploding a Myth* (Sydney: Little Hills Press, 1987), but he avoids the real grounds for concern.

[90] See Appleby, *The Ambivalence of the Sacred*, 227–9.

[91] Quoted by Marianne Johnson, "The Hand of Opus Dei in El Salvador," *The Tablet* (18 November 2000) 1552.

[92] See Lernoux, *People of God*, 302–46, and Michael J. Walsh, "The Conservative Reaction," *Modern Catholicism: Vatican II and After*, ed. Adrian Hastings (London: SPCK, 1991) 283–8.

[93] Gordon Urquhart, *The Pope's Armada* (London: Bantam Press, 1995) 270.

• It rejects the Gospel call, repeated in Vatican II and subsequent ecclesial documents, to struggle for justice in society.

• It sees no necessity for inculturation, yet, as John Paul II says: "the Church's dialogue with the cultures of our time [is] a vital area, one in which the destiny of the world . . . is at stake."[94]

In their enthusiasm to preach the Good News, the Way's followers adopt a Eurocentric model of the Church and evangelization. This is precisely the oppressive approach that Peter and Paul condemned at the Council of Jerusalem (Acts 15:1-35). The rituals and catechetical material of the Way's evangelizers are prepackaged in Europe and then imposed on other cultures.[95] Furthermore, there are no concerted attempts among the Way's evangelizers to prepare themselves for work in cultures different from their own. Yet simple trust in the Holy Spirit is no substitute for the serious cultural openness and respect for diversity, for the discernment and pastoral competence that Paul VI considers essential for inculturation.[96]

In short, fundamentalism is a quality of all the above grassroots movements. Fundamentalists actively look to the Church's central authority to use its coercive power "to put things right" in the Church.[97] Rome, however, while continuing to support these movements, has at times expressed reservations about them: Pope John Paul II spoke of "questions, uneasiness and tensions" at the level of local churches because of "presumptions and excesses"[98] of members.

Summary

• The mythology of a culture provides people with a sense of security and belonging. Any dramatic change in this mythology, as occurred

[94] John Paul II cited by Aylward Shorter, *Toward a Theology of Inculturation* (London: Geoffrey Chapman, 1988) 230.

[95] See Urquhart, *The Pope's Armada*, 287.

[96] See Paul VI, *On Evangelization* (Vatican: Sacred Congregation for Evangelization, 1975) par. 20.

[97] See "These Paths Lead to Rome: Six Cardinals supporting Right-Wing Governments," *National Catholic Reporter* (2 June 2000) 13–5; Jeffrey Klaiber, *The Church, Dictatorships, and Democracy in Latin America* (Maryknoll: Orbis Books, 1998) 11–5.

[98] Cited by Gordon Urquhart, "Movements in the Church," *The Tablet* (26 June 1999) 877.

through postmodernism in the secular world and Vatican II for Catholics, can throw people into chaos. They can react in a variety of ways, for example, by supporting pro-order movements which promise them a return to being in control of their lives.

- Among the pro-order reactions to postmodernism, involving at times considerable violence, are: the rise of nationalism and ethnicity in many forms; racist groups in response to immigration and globalization; football hooligan "tribes"; and fundamentalism. Nationalism constructs culture into an object and a thing of worship.

- Ethnic nationalism is the belief that ethnic and political boundaries must be congruent and people who do not belong to the dominant grouping must be forced to leave the territory. This process is called ethnic cleansing.

- New Religious Movements (NRMs) emerged as a consequence of the postmodern Revolution of Expressive Disorder: self-help sects aim to provide new individual identities for individuals; total sects aim to give individuals group-oriented identities. Some subject their followers to considerable violence.

- Fundamentalism is a form of organized religious anger in reaction to secularism, secularization, and globalization; it often intimidates or coerces people unduly to achieve its ends. "Violent" fundamentalists, e.g., Islamic extremists, use terrorism for their purposes. They claim that the killing of innocent people is justified because there is no other way to protect their sacred heritage in the postmodern world.

- Catholic restorationism is an ill-defined but powerful movement in the Church to restore pre-Vatican II structures and attitudes; it is often an aggressive reaction to the anxiety-creating turmoil caused by the council and the impact of postmodernity.

Discussion Questions

1. What points in this chapter do you feel relate to your experience?

2. Many millions of innocent people are being displaced through globalization and become unskilled migrants and refugees. The environment is also being gravely undermined through pollution. What can you do to make these injustices better known in your community?

3. Often sects and cults are spawned because Christians have not welcomed people into their midst. What are you and your parish doing to make strangers and young people welcome?

Chapter 9

Paramodern Culture: "Signals of Transcendence"

Violence will no longer be heard of in your country, nor devastation and ruin within your frontiers. (Isa 6:18)

[Postmodernism] can support the Church. (Bishop Jeremiah Newman[1])

This chapter explains:

- that a new culture is hesitantly emerging, paramodernity, with a distinctive mythology;

- some positive aspects of postmodernist "deconstructionism," the distrust of metanarratives, multiculturalism, and holistic health policies;

- that postmodernity offers an environment for the Church to collaborate with people wanting to build a paramodern culture;

- the positive strengths and biblical foundations of nonviolence.

The many varieties of violence listed in this book may leave readers with a sense of hopelessness about the future of humankind. Is there any mythology that is not open to the misuse of power? Walter Anderson, a commentator on postmodernism, answers the question

---

[1] Jeremiah Newman, *The Postmodern Church* (Dublin: Four Corners Press, 1990) 151.

optimistically: "The time is, for all its complexity and dissonance, a moment of great beauty and opportunity. We glimpse new ways of thinking about ourselves, new possibilities for coexisting with others— even profoundly different others."[2] Peter Berger speaks of "signals of transcendence," that is, people cooperating with God in transforming the world. There is no need to submit to violence "as an irresistible tyranny," he writes. There are "signals of transcendence" and we need to find them and regain hope in "openness in our perception of reality."[3]

Both observers correctly note: There is an identifiable culture— paramodernity—emerging with the distinctive mythology that people acting together can create justice and peace in the world. Among its symbols are: nonviolence, interdependence, systems thinking, collaboration, liberation from oppression, spirituality, gender equality, reconciliation, accountability, and deconstructionism. Some of the people who have influenced the development of this mythology and culture in recent times are theologians such as Fr. Teilhard de Chardin, S.J., Fr. Karl Rahner, S.J., Fr. Gustavo Gutiérrez, Elisabeth Schussler Fiorenza, Rosemary Radford Ruether, prophets such as Mohandas Gandhi, "the Mothers of Plaza de Mayo" in Argentina, Martin Luther King Jr., Nelson Mandela, Popes Paul VI and John Paul II, Lech Walesa, Archbishop Oscar Romero, Cory Aquino, Aung San Suu Kyi, Cesar Chavez, philosophers Jacques Derrida, and cross-cultural scholars Mircea Eliade and Raimon Panikkar.

Signals of Transcendence

In the following section we examine some signals of transcendence that give new hope of justly and peacefully existing with others.

- Benefits of deconstructionism

- Systems and chaos thinking

- Critique of metanarratives

- Awareness of evil within

- Discovery of otherness

[2] Walter T. Anderson, *The Truth about the Truth: De-confusing and De-constructing the Postmodern World* (New York: Putnam, 1995) 11.

[3] Peter Berger, *A Rumor of Angels: Modern Society and the Rediscovery of the Supernatural* (New York: Doubleday, 1970) 95.

- Medical model questioned
- Yearning for a spirituality
- Nonviolent movements

Benefits of Deconstructionism

According to the philosopher Jacques Derrida, deconstructionist methodology is a process "of unceasingly analysing the whole conceptual machinery"[4] of language to see how it manipulates power to the disadvantage of people. Examples of deconstructionism in action are:

- Deconstructionists challenge the postmodern assumption that the inner self can never be known. In the process of deconstruction people peel aside layers of stories to expose the reality beneath. Then they are able to construct a reality-based sense of self. Deconstruction is not necessarily negative but can be used to *construct* authentic reality.[5]

- Contemporary feminism, as expressed in the writings of people like Judith Butler, Rowena Chapman, and Donna Haraway, has used deconstructionism to weaken the binary model inherent in the masculine/feminine dyad that culturally legitimizes male oppression of women. Masculinity must no longer be defined in terms of a man's ability to resort to violence.[6]

- In management studies cultural deconstructionism uncovers ways in which patriarchal values dominate organizational life. Once patriarchal patterns are identified, appropriate action can be taken to allow feminine qualities of mutual responsibility, compassion, gentleness, and love to take root in organizations.

- Scripture scholar Walter Brueggemann sees that deconstructionism can be a liberating force in the use of the Scriptures. Under the influence of modernity, he argues, we made biblical texts fit our orderly

[4] Jacques Derrida, "This Strange Institution Called Literature," *Acts of Literature*, ed. D. Attridge (New York: Routledge, 1992) 109.

[5] See M. Blanchot, "The Absence of the Other," *Deconstructionism in Context: Literature and Philosophy*, ed. M. C. Taylor (Chicago: University of Chicago Press, 1986) 390.

[6] See Sophia Phoca, "Feminism and Gender," *Feminism and Postfeminism*, ed. Sarah Gamble (Cambridge: Icon Books, 1999) 55–65.

modes of knowledge and control. Deconstructionism allows the text in all its prophetic radicality to speak to us without our imposing meanings on it.[7]

Systems and Chaos Theory

Instead of the machine-like universe of Cartesian imagination, scientists are discovering that all organisms, from the smallest bacteria to humans, are integrated wholes and living systems, interdependent and interrelated. The greater whole is the biosphere itself, a dynamic and highly integrated web of living and nonliving forms.[8] In an effort to describe this reality scientists have evolved what is popularly called the *chaos theory*, simply explained as "the science of process rather than state, of becoming rather than being . . . [resulting in] a science of the global nature of *systems*."[9] Systems thinking in organizations recognizes that all aspects of an organization are interrelated or connected: touch one relationship and all are affected to some degree.[10] Systems and chaos theory have helped people to become sensitive to the following:

• *Environmental Issues and World Poverty*

Protest movements show how the greed and selfishness of postmodern economic rationalists impoverish the poor and the environment.

• *Need for Collaborative Skills*

Chaos theory concludes that one cannot cope alone with the unpredictability of the contemporary world. Nor is it possible to solve problems with the use of rational thinking only; hence, the importance of developing collaborative skills and intuitive, imaginative thinking.[11] Research shows that coercive leadership, that is, leadership that creates "a reign of terror, bullying and demeaning [staff],"[12] has disastrous

[7] See Walter Brueggemann, *Texts Under Negotiation: The Bible and the Postmodern Imagination* (Minneapolis: Fortress Press, 1993) 11.

[8] See Gerald A. Arbuckle, *From Chaos to Mission: Refounding Religious Life Formation* (Collegeville: The Liturgical Press, 1996) 56.

[9] James Gleick, *Chaos: Making a New Science* (New York: Penguin, 1987) 5.

[10] See Gerald A. Arbuckle, *Healthcare Ministry: Refounding the Mission in Tumultuous Times* (Collegeville: The Liturgical Press, 2000) 114-5.

[11] See Ralph Stacey, *The Chaos Frontier: Creative Strategic Control for Business* (Oxford: Butterworth-Heinemann, 1991) xi.

[12] Daniel Goleman, "Leadership That Gets Results," *Harvard Business Review* (March 2000) 82.

commercial consequences, but that leadership that recognizes the need to involve people at all levels of an organization in order to tap their imaginative and creative skills has the best results.[13] According to this research, postmodern managerialism and authoritarianism in the Church are incapable of responding to the needs of people today.

Suspicion of Metanarratives:[14] Benefits

Postmodernists believe that metanarratives (see chapter 8), that is, stories that claim to give a total explanation of reality, lack legitimacy. While their condemnation of metanarratives is too sweeping, nonetheless, there are benefits for the Church in questioning some of its traditional metanarratives.

For example, one popular metanarrative of the Church is the assumption that people can be led through objective rational arguments to an understanding and acceptance of our faith. Paramodernists question this assumption and claim that faith and witness, not reason, must be center stage in theology. As Huston Smith comments: "Instead of 'These are the compelling reasons, grounded in the nature of things, why you should believe in God,' the approach of the Church to the world today tends to be 'This community of faith invites you to share in its venture of trust and commitment.'"[15] Paul VI in his 1975 apostolic letter *Evangelisation* accepts the paramodern emphasis: "for the Church, the first means of evangelization is the witness of an authentically Christian life. . . . [Today] people listen more willingly to witnesses than to teachers, and if they do listen to teachers, it is because they are witnesses."[16]

Another metanarrative is the assumption that the Church is not subject to human failings. For centuries its frailties have been glossed over, yet its history is characterized not just by grace but also by malpractice.[17] Today paramodernists critique the institutions of the Church

[13] See Jim Collins, "Level 5 Leadership: The Triumph of Humility," *Harvard Business Review* (January 2001) 67–76.

[14] Bruce Lescher provides a helpful summary of positive aspects of postmodernism: "Spiritual Direction: Stalking the Boundaries," *Handbook of Spirituality for Ministers*, ed. Robert J. Wicks, vol. 2 (New York: Paulist, 2000) 316–7.

[15] Huston Smith, *Beyond the Post-Modern Mind* (New York: Crossroad, 1982) 12.

[16] Paul VI, *On Evangelization* (Vatican: Sacred Congregation for Evangelization, 1975) par. 42.

[17] See James D. Whitehead and Evelyn Whitehead, *Method in Ministry: Theological Reflection and Christian Ministry* (Kansas City: Sheed and Ward, 1995) 8.

with "love, patience, kindness . . . gentleness and self-control" (Gal 5:22), a healthy consequence of postmodernism.

Discovery of "Otherness"

Metanarratives of cultural superiority and patriarchalism in pre-modern and modern cultures were used to silence the voices of cultural minorities and women. In paramodernity these metanarratives are critiqued with positive consequences, e.g.:

• *Internationalism Confronts State Violence*

International organizations are rejecting the long-standing principle of noninterference in domestic matters of states by intervening to protect minority rights. Up to this point, states alone held the right to determine how violence could be inflicted or controlled within their borders. The following are examples.

France

The European Parliament intervened in France to protect the *sans papiers*, that is, foreigners who did not meet the national requirements for residency. The forced repatriation of Muslims or blacks to places like Algeria would have meant mass unemployment, starvation, and in some cases death.

Balkans

After the bloody break-up of Yugoslavia, outsiders intervened to protect the rights of the dispossessed minorities: the American-led peacemaking effort in Bosnia and NATO in Kosovo and Macedonia.

Mexico

Following the inauguration of the North American Free Trade Agreement in 1994, three thousand mainly local peasants (Zapatis-

continued on next page

tas), descendants of those who had been ejected from their lands in the 1940s, stormed several municipalities in the state of Chiapas, Mexico, and a number were killed by the army. The cause of the revolt was the destruction of the fragile economy of the peasants by the government's economic rationalist principles. The Zapatistas mounted a highly effective international and national mass media campaign to alert people to what had happened, and as a result the government was forced to stop its coercive actions. This triumph over oppression has been called the "first informational guerrilla movement" against globalization.[18]

• *Multiculturalism*

Paramodern thinkers are prepared to respect others for what they are, with their own unique stories and rights to justice; they reject the Cartesian duality, the us/them dichotomy, and recognize the value of multiculturalism. Bhikhu Parekh provides a helpful working definition of multiculturalism:

> [It] doesn't simply mean numerical plurality of different cultures, but rather a community which is creating, guaranteeing, encouraging spaces within which different communities are able to grow at their own pace. At the same time it means creating a public space in which these communities are able to interact, enrich the existing culture and create a new consensual culture in which they recognize reflections of their own identity.[19]

In this definition, two inadequate definitions are rejected, namely, *demographic* and *holistic* multiculturalism. The former connotes that a particular society merely contains different cultural groups, saying nothing about how they are to relate to one another; the second means that a society values cultural diversity, but gives higher priority to group-wide cohesion. The definition supports the initiatives of political multiculturalists to establish structures that permit minority peoples *by right* to be fully involved in decisions that affect their lives. They foster

---

[18] See Jim McGuigan, *Modernity and Postmodern Culture* (Buckingham: Open University Press, 1999) 118.

[19] Bhikhu Parekh as cited by Henry Giroux, *Multiculturalism: A Critical Reader*, ed. David T. Goldberg (Oxford: Blackwell, 1994) 336.

a balance between the demands of overall group cohesion and cultural diversity.[20]

Case Study: Canada

A major report released in 1996 showed that the administration of indigenous affairs had been dominated by colonialist and racist attitudes, causing the First Nations grievous social, cultural, and economic harm for two centuries.[21] In recent years, decisions of the Canadian Supreme Court have recognized the rights of the indigenous societies (First Nations) to their cultural distinctiveness and self-government.[22] These changes are due primarily to pressure applied by the First Nations themselves.[23]

An Awareness of Inner Evil

The widespread belief of modernity that human beings had become increasingly civilized had been shattered by the events of the Second World War and subsequent horrors. Postmodernists alert us to the reality that, in the words of Alexander Solzhenitsyn, "the line dividing good and evil cuts through the heart of every human being."[24] Every person is capable of deliberately depriving others of their humanity, from small-scale assaults on their dignity to outright murder. This understanding is a gift of postmodernity to paramodernists. Thomas Merton, meditating on the growing acknowledgment of the potential for evil within every person, expressed his gratitude in this way: "Now it begins to dawn on us that it is precisely the *sane* ones who are the most dangerous. . . . If modern man [sic] . . . were a little less sane, a little more doubtful . . . perhaps there might be a possibility of his survival."[25]

---

[20] See Arbuckle, *From Chaos to Mission*, 179–81.

[21] See Ken Coates, "The 'Gentle' Occupation: The Settlement of Canada and the Dispossession of the First Nations," *Indigenous Peoples' Rights*, ed. Paul Havemann (Auckland: Oxford University Press, 1999) 141–61.

[22] See Michael Asch, "From Calder to Van der Peet: Aboriginal Rights and Canadian Law, 1973–96," Havemann, *Indigenous Peoples' Rights*, 428–46.

[23] See Augie Flleras, "Politicising Indigeneity: Ethno-politics in White Settler Dominions," Havemann, *Indigenous Peoples' Rights*, 201–3.

[24] Alexander Solzhenitsyn quoted by Jonathan Glover, *Humanity: A Moral History of the Twentieth Century* (London: Jonathan Cape, 1999) 401.

[25] Thomas Merton, *Thomas Merton on Peace* (London: Mowbray, 1971) 84.

Medical Model Questioned

In the paramodern model there is a marked shift away from the modernistic optimism that scientific medicine has all the answers to sickness. In brief, the paramodern culture, with its new physics and systems view of living organisms, is a return to the holistic thinking of premodern culture. Holistic health emphasizes the following qualities:[26]

- the unity of the psyche and soma: there is a need to get beyond the presenting of mere external symptoms of sickness to explore the history and circumstances of the patient's life.[27]

- the dignity of life: political and social campaigns are developing, often across traditional denominational boundaries, e.g., anti-euthanasia and anti-abortion campaigns, the hospice movement, respect for the rights of people with disabilities.

- the recognition that the causes of disease are far more complex than germs: cultural and economic factors are of critical importance.

- radical political and socioeconomic policies are required to reduce disease, unemployment, and levels of poverty.[28]

- the patriarchal hold over healthcare services is being increasingly challenged.

- the small-group movement as testimony to people's desire for community in the midst of an abstract and dehumanizing postmodern society. People want to experience a sense of belonging. Small groups offer "friendships, forums for discussing values, and links with wider institutions."[29]

- personal storytelling: people want to be able to tell of their own experiences, of their search for personal meaning, and to be free to share this with others.[30]

[26] See Gerald A. Arbuckle, *Healthcare Ministry*, 38–41.
[27] See Sarah Nettleton, *The Sociology of Health and Illness* (Cambridge: Polity Press, 1995) 230.
[28] See Basiro Davey and Jennie Popay, *Dilemmas in Health Care* (Milton Keynes: Open University Press, 1993) 184–99.
[29] Robert Wuthnow, *Sharing the Journey: Support Groups and America's Quest for Community* (New York: Free Press, 1994) 365.
[30] See Arbuckle, *Healthcare Ministry*, 35–6.

- healing through meditation and spirituality, understood as "a perpetual process of becoming, a continual unfolding of the human spirit."[31]

Church: Some Inculturation Opportunities

Paramodernists are creating a new, secular way of thinking that the Church can dialogue with and build upon.[32] The Church can offer paramodernists:

- a deeper appreciation of spirituality;
- tradition: diversity of models for living;
- acknowledgment of death;
- insights into holistic healing;
- an appreciation for aging.

• *Appreciation of Spirituality*

Paramodernists speak of a world yearning for a spirituality, but there is often a vagueness about what this means. As Chris McGillion says, most people assume spirituality to be "a path to enlightenment that is exciting (as distinct from well-trodden and predictable), intimate (rather than public and thus remote), and informal (which is to say free of rules, regulations and authority)." It has come "to signify everything that religious faith is not."[33] Believers have the chance to respond to this yearning and lack of clarity by offering people Jesus of the Scriptures who gives meaning to all that we do.

The same opening and challenge exists with the small-group movement in paramodernity. Robert Wuthnow of Princeton University, in his critique of the small-group movement in the United States, notes: "[The movement] should be understood as a distinct product of our times. We want community, but nothing very binding. We want spir-

---

[31] Ian I. Mitroff and Elizabeth A. Denton, *A Spiritual Audit of Corporate America* (San Francisco: Jossey-Bass, 1999) 184–5.

[32] See Newman, *The Postmodern Church*, 151.

[33] Chris McGillion, "Faith, Not Spirituality the Answer," *The Sydney Morning Herald* (22 February 2000) 14.

ituality, but we prefer the sacred to serve us instead of requiring our service."[34] He says the movement is at a crossroads: people are on the verge of disillusionment because the groups cannot hold together if participants' primary concern is their own personal needs. This is the time for the Christian insight of "community for others, not for me."

• *Tradition: Diversity of Models of Living*

People may be repelled by the institutional Church or formal religion[35] but be open to Christian tradition.[36] The latter is filled with stories of people (Jesus of Nazareth, Paul of Tarsus, St. Francis of Assisi, St. Teresa of Avila, Dorothy Day, Martin Luther King Jr.) who provide road maps through darkness to light. People can ponder the lives of these pilgrims and come to recognize that God's love is also searching for them in their own unique experiences of life. God will not respond in some prepackaged manner, but in forms that respect each person's life. Bruce Lescher advises: "The great mystics have traveled many paths; . . . they have been nuns, husbands, bishops, dissenters, hermits, activists. Thus beginners can be encouraged to try different prayer styles and spiritual practices until they find some that 'fit' for them."[37]

• *Acknowledgment of Death*

One gift of postmodernity to paramodern culture has been an increasing acknowledgment of the reality of death in reaction to modernity's denial. The writings of Michel Foucault, Zygmunt Bauman,[38] and Jean Baudrillard, for example, significantly dwell on this point. The widespread open expressions of grief after the bombing in Oklahoma City, and after the death of Princess Diana and the terrorist attacks in the United States in 2001, testify to the fact that people are less prepared than before to deny death and their own sadness at loss. Bishop Jeremiah Newman, commenting on Baudrillard, writes that "in spite of its exaggerations, Postmodernism does acknowledge the fact of death

[34] Wuthnow, *Sharing the Journey*, 365

[35] See Mitroff and Denton, *A Spiritual Audit of Corporate America*, 184.

[36] I am grateful to Bruce Lescher for beginning my thinking on this point, "Spiritual Direction: Stalking the Boundaries," 322–3.

[37] Lescher, "Spiritual Direction: Stalking the Boundaries," 323.

[38] See Zygmunt Bauman, "Postmodern Adventures of Life and Death," *Modernity, Medicine and Health*, ed. Graham Scambler and Paul Higgs (London: Routledge, 1998) 216–31.

in a way that the modernism of the Enlightenment did not. To that extent, whether it intends it or not, it leaves an opening for religion."[39]

We have a rich heritage to offer people. The Scriptures are filled with calls to sorrow over what has been destroyed or broken down, if there is to be new life; through the psalms we are even taught *how* to grieve. Particularly in the lament psalms we are reminded that no matter how chaotic our condition may be, God has the power to do the humanly impossible—to lift us through hope out of "the seething chasm, from the mud of the mire" (Ps 40:2).

• *Holistic Healing*

The Christian tradition offers a deep understanding of the meaning of holistic healing. Christian healthcare is not confined to physical sickness, but focuses on the spiritual, social, and economic health of individuals and communities. Holistic healthcare is a process whereby people are liberated from whatever political, physical, psychological, or spiritual oppression constrains them from being fully human and being responsibly in control of their lives.

The Scriptures acknowledge deep tensions in the living out of this process, and offer no ready-made solution to them. Biblical writers often return to the problem, especially in prayer, where ultimately resolution occurs. Christ, overwhelmed with the mystery of his own death and resurrection in Gethsemane, ponders and resolves the tension creatively in prayer (Mark 14:36). Hence, the value of small faith-based groups (e.g., Basic Ecclesial Communities) in which people are able to reflect prayerfully on their own experiences of these tensions in light of the Scriptures.

• *An Appreciation for Aging*

Whenever Western medicine follows the medical model it loses its caring touch. For example, the dying increasingly find themselves unwelcome anomalies in the system of high-technology medicine that emphasizes successful physical cures. The aged cannot be cured of their infirmities, so they have no place left in a society that places an emphasis on successful curing. At the heart of the Christian hospice and palliative care movement is a network of values and attitudes that tries to lessen the indignities of dying so as to maximize the human potential of the dying and their families. Emphasis is placed on using

---

[39] Newman, *The Postmodern Church*, 143.

skills based on the most up-to-date scientific knowledge, and at the same time recognizing the importance of a truly caring attitude and approach.[40]

Nonviolent Responses to Cultures of Violence

Nonviolence is not for power but for truth. It is not pragmatic but prophetic. . . . Nonviolence . . . does not say, "We shall overcome" so much as "This is the day of the Lord, and whatever may happen to us, He shall overcome." (Thomas Merton[41])

The purpose of this section is to:

- name the qualities of authentic nonviolent movements;
- examine the scriptural foundations for nonviolence;
- recount examples of nonviolent movements.

Nonviolence is a quality of paramodernity. People movements against political and institutional violence have been common in history, but in the twentieth century the application of nonviolent methods gave birth to a different way of confronting and even overthrowing an unjust order.

Within the Church this emphasis on nonviolence has led to a radical rethinking of the centuries-old support for "holy war," that is, the use of force or violence to defend the rights of God, and the "just war" tradition. In his closing address to the meeting of bishops following the Gulf War, Pope John Paul II declared, "There can be no such thing as a holy war."[42] In the second draft of the United States Catholic bishops' peace pastoral of 1983,[43] nonviolence is recommended as a standard Christian reaction to war. This is the first time in a major Church document that such a recommendation has been made; in the final edition it

---

[40] See Cicely Saunders, "Hospice Worldwide: A Mission Statement," *Hospice Care on the International Scene*, ed. Cicely Saunders and Robert Kastenbaum (New York: Springer, 1997) 3–12.

[41] Thomas Merton, "Peace and Revolution," *Peace and Nonviolence*, ed. Edward Guinan (New York: Paulist Press, 1973) 127.

[42] John Paul II quoted by Patriarch Michel Sabbah, *Origins*, vol. 23, no. 31 (1994) 550.

[43] National Conference of Catholic Bishops, *The Challenge of Peace: God's Promise and Our Response* (Washington: U.S. Catholic Conference, 1983).

was significantly modified to give prominence again to the tradition of the just war.[44]

The dramatic nonviolent movements in the twentieth century are especially remarkable in light of the fact that the century saw violence under Marxist influence raised from instrumental to something akin to sacramental: revolution had to be violent, or it would not be transformational. Nonviolence has shown, however, that while violence can change events, even radically, it does not give power to people.[45]

Defining Nonviolence: Its Qualities

Staughton and Alice Lynd warn against a too rigid definition of nonviolence, but point to four guidelines: *first*, the refusal to retaliate; *secondly*, acting out of conviction by demonstrative action; *thirdly*, the vision of love as an agent for radical change; *fourthly*, deliberate lawbreaking for conscience's sake (i.e., civil disobedience).[46] In the case study below, the actions of Arturo and his friends followed the first three guidelines. People in nonviolent movements, as in the tragic incident below, refuse to respond to violence through verbal, physical, or psychological violence, but aim to build a new positive power equilibrium by disarming their adversaries through the inner strength of love and courage.

Case Study[47]

While working in the Philippines, I heard the story of a poor sugar plantation worker named Arturo, on the island of Negros. He lived with his wife and four children in a small hovel surrounded by fellow workers and their families, receiving unjust wages from the sugar estate. One day the local priest offered Arturo a copy of the New Testament and Arturo opened it at

continued on next page

---

[44] See Robert R. Beck, *Nonviolent Story: Narrative Conflict Resolution in the Gospel of Mark* (Maryknoll: Orbis Books, 1996) 16–7.

[45] See Peter Ackerman and Jack Duvall, *A Force More Powerful: A Century of Nonviolent Conflict* (New York: Palgrave, 2000) 466.

[46] Staughton Lynd and Alice Lynd, *Nonviolence in America: A Documentary History* (Maryknoll: Orbis, 1998) xii.

[47] See Arbuckle, *Healthcare Ministry*, 257–8.

random, noticing the text from the Beatitudes: "Blessed are those who hunger and thirst for uprightness: they shall have their fill. . . . Blessed are the peacemakers: they shall be recognized as children of God" (Matt 5:6, 9).

Arturo then called his male companions for a meeting and read the text to them saying: "What do you think this text means?" One replied: "I think it means that if we are to follow Christ, then we must search for justice and peace. We have no option but to try." "What are the implications?" said Arturo. They all agreed that they must go together to the manager of the large sugar estate and ask for an increase of wages, because the Gospel required that they not submit to injustices. They went, but the manager chased them off the property with vicious dogs. Arturo tried again, this time alone, failing once more. A rock was thrown at the door of Arturo's house with a note attached: "Stop the agitation or we kill you!" Arturo called his friends together and showed them the note seeking their advice, but a companion asked him to reread the biblical texts out aloud. Then they prayed together to the Spirit for strength to do what was right. Arturo then said and they all agreed that in order to follow Christ they could not stop the struggle for justice, but it had to be in peaceful ways. As a group they tried again, but with the same lack of success. Shortly later a jeep carrying masked men and guns swept past Arturo's house spraying it with machine-gun fire. Arturo and most of his family were killed.

For Martin Luther King Jr., love of one's neighbor is at the heart of nonviolence.[48] As John Paul II commented when speaking of the success of nonviolence in Eastern Europe: "the masses won by eschewing violence in favor of winning their oppressors over with love. . . . They appealed to the conscience of the adversary, seeking to awaken in [them] a sense of shared human dignity."[49] For Arturo the model of nonviolence was Jesus Christ. Like Christ, he and his companions were prepared out of love to search for justice and die if that was necessary.

[48] Martin Luther King Jr. quoted by Lynd and Lynd, *Nonviolence in America: A Documentary History*, 217.

[49] John Paul II, encyclical letter *Centesimus Annus*, par.23.

Visible results were not the issue, but only the search for truth and justice.

Compassion is the particular form of love that is at the heart of non-violence. Biblically, compassion is a value founded in kinship obligations, whether natural or fictive; the Hebrew word for compassion is derived from the word for womb, implying the need to feel for others because they are born of the same mother. Yahweh is that mother, and we are all children of that womb and must accordingly feel with, and care for, each other as brothers and sisters. Compassion is an opposite to violence; as violence imposes malicious images on an opponent, compassion accepts that such evil forces exist within oneself. We can judge someone without condemning the person because we are aware of our own inner weaknesses. Rollo May puts it this way: "Compassion is felt toward another . . . because he [*sic*] *doesn't* fulfill his potentialities—in other words, he is human, like you or me, forever engaged in the struggle between fulfillment and nonfulfillment."[50]

Nonviolent movements aim to remove the fundamental source of power of tyrannical authorities, namely, the consent or acceptance of the people they are dominating. People refusing to be subjugated slowly remove the oppressor's ability to control, for example, through strikes and boycotts. In brief, nonviolence directs energy at the most exposed quality of hierarchical institutions and governments—dependence on the governed. As long as people collude with oppression, the bullies remain in charge.[51]

Nonviolence and Scripture

Though the New Testament writers place nonviolence at the heart of Christ's message and life, paradoxically much of our history is about the use of violence by Christians against nonbelievers and against one another. They legitimize their actions by drawing on the image of God in the Old Testament as the divine warrior leading Israelite armies to victory against enemies who would destroy the chosen people. Why this paradox?[52]

[50] Rollo May, *Power and Innocence: A Search for the Sources of Violence* (New York: Norton, 1998) 251.

[51] See Ackerman and Duvall, *A Force More Powerful: A Century of Nonviolent Conflict*, 494–5.

[52] See Leo D. Lefebure, *Revelation, the Religions, and Violence* (Maryknoll: Orbis, 2000) 55–129.

1. Old Testament

An understanding of God is only slowly revealed to the Israelites.[53] On the one hand, they project onto Yahweh their own violent methods of resolving conflicts. Yahweh is expected to proclaim his holiness and power by acting violently against Israel's enemies (Num 16:30; 1 Kgs 18:40; Ps 10:15); on the other hand, God is progressively revealed as condemning violence. For example, the prophets condemn acts of violence perpetrated by Israel: "There is no loyalty, no faithful love, no knowledge of God in the country, only perjury and lying, murder . . . and violence" (Hos 4:1-2). Physical force is of no avail: "For human strength can win no victories" (1 Sam 2:9), but "your salvation lay in conversion and tranquility, your strength in serenity and trust" (Isa 30:15). The prophecy of the "Suffering Servant" in Isaiah prepares the Israelites for Jesus of the New Testament, the nonviolent One who suffers but refuses to be personally subjugated to evil (Isa 53).

2. New Testament

Jesus Christ by word and action condemns violence as a way to achieve power over others or even in defense of one's rights. In his vision Jesus goes beyond the dreams of the Israelite prophets and declares that the fullness of the reign of God means the end of all suffering, violence, and injustice, the coming of a new community of perfect love and justice (Rev 21:1, 4). His mission from the Father is to proclaim in speech and action what must be done to realize this vision (Luke 4:18). In Old Testament times Yahweh was one with those who suffered, but in Christ there is total identification with the violated. Jesus is himself the poor one, born in a stable (Luke 2:7) because structures of poverty condemn him and his family to no better. He the Poor One accepts death that others might live (Luke 27:35).

The universal guideline in relating to others is: "So always treat others as you would like them to treat you" (Matt 7:12). And love must be the motivating force: "But I say this to you, love your enemies and pray for those who persecute you. . . . For if you love those who love you, what reward will you get?" (Matt 5:44, 46). Love for one's persecutors, not the "eye for an eye" directive of premodern culture, is to be the principle of action: "You have heard it said: *Eye for eye and tooth for tooth*. But I say this to you: offer no resistance to the wicked" (Matt 5:38).

---

[53] See Sabbah, *Origins*, vol. 23, no. 31 (1994) 549–51.

But Jesus is quick to explain that "no resistance" is not synonymous with accepting powerlessness. The violator wants the violated precisely to agree that they are powerless, insignificant, less than human. To be in control of one's life, even under violence, is a fundamental right of every person, for it is the source of one's self-esteem and the foundation of the belief that one has significance.[54] Jesus is so insistent on this point that he uses several concrete cases to explain what he means. In the following colorful examples, explained by Walter Wink, Jesus is saying to his listeners that nonviolence does not mean passivity but claiming one's rightful power to self-respect through nonviolent means.[55]

- Roman soldiers could by law bully people to carry their baggage a limited distance only and if a person offered to carry the burden an extra mile, this placed the soldier in the embarrassing situation of violating Roman practice. So, Jesus says to victims of bullying: "And if anyone requires you to go one mile, go two miles with him" (Matt 5:41).

- Likewise, if someone takes one's tunic, let them have the cloak as well (Matt 5:40). A person is left naked if their tunic and cloak are handed over to the oppressor, but to be naked in public is a violation of Jewish law, and the intimidator would be shamed.

- Similarly, to turn one's cheek to be hit can be embarrassing for the assailant. An open-handed slap by the right hand can be given only to the left cheek of the recipient. If one turns the right cheek, the intimidator cannot use his right hand and would be forced to use his left, which is forbidden. To use the right fist on the right cheek this is also wrong because only friends would do this (Matt 5:39).

The Beatitudes have been commonly misinterpreted to mean that people should be passive in the face of violence. In Matthew's text (Matt 5:3-12) Jesus speaks of two groups of people especially loved. First, the *anawim* ("the little people"). Their attitudes and lifestyle are contrary to the oppressive culture around them. For them wealth,

---

[54] See Rollo May, *Power and Innocence: A Search for the Sources of Violence* (New York: Norton, 1988) 243.

[55] See Walter Wink, *Engaging the Powers: Discernment and Resistance in a World of Domination* (Minneapolis: Fortress Press, 1992) 175–84.

power, and selfishness have nothing to do with true happiness, which is to be found only in the reign of God and in righteousness. Their example is a form of nonviolence because it challenges the oppressors to see that their behavior is wrong.

The second are those advocates who stand up to protect the rights of the powerless and, suppressing self-love and ambition, show mercy. They struggle in nonviolent ways to develop peace in an unjust and oppressive culture, and are prepared to suffer in defense of justice: "the kingdom of Heaven is theirs" (Matt 5:3). The verse "Blessed are the gentle: they shall have the earth for their inheritance" (Matt 5:4) makes gentleness synonymous with love. Those motivated by love will not give way to a violator, because they have an inner strength to protest injustice.

The ministry of Jesus consists of nonviolent public protests against cultural violence. For example, he

- challenges oppressive ritual regulations that forbid healing on the Sabbath (Luke 14:3);

- associates with the ritually impure, e.g., tax collectors and prostitutes (Luke 15:1-3);

- associates publicly with women, who were considered inferior to men (Luke 23:55);

- speaks with Samaritans, who were thought to be racially and religiously impure (John 4);

- heals people marginalized because of disease (Mark 10:46-52).

Out of love he seeks to dialogue with his enemies. While strongly disagreeing theologically with the scribes and Pharisees, denouncing their purely external observances of the Law, their multitude of oppressive formalistic rules and regulations, and their self-righteousness, he nonetheless seeks to remain friendly and unprejudiced towards them. Finally, by forgiving his executioners, he confronts violence with love. The cross, the most powerful Jewish symbol of violence and death, becomes instead a symbol of peaceful, active protest against everything that seeks to degrade and subjugate humankind and the universe. And the Resurrection is the hope that ultimately the violated "shall have the earth as inheritance" (Matt 5:4).

For St. Paul nonviolence is central to Christ's teaching. To the Corinthians he writes: "I am glad of weaknesses, insults, constraints . . . for

Christ's sake. For it is when I am weak that I am strong" (2 Cor 12:10). Without inner conversion and the power of Christ within oneself non-violence is impossible (Eph 6:12-3).

Examples of Nonviolent Movements

Christian nonviolent movements are led by pathfinding dissenters[56] who draw their authority and power to act from the mythology of the Gospels; they see oppression as contrary to the teachings of Christ and are prepared to work together in peaceful ways to achieve a just society. Not only do they dream up appropriate ways of being nonviolent, but they actually move to implement them. Gifted with pragmatic imaginations, a shrewdness for timing and organizing, pathfinding dissenters are dreamers who do.

1. Basic Ecclesial Communities

Liberation theology is a people-power movement that developed in Latin America in the 1960s and spread to many other parts of the world, especially Asia. It is founded in the experience of the poor, particularly that of Basic Ecclesial Communities (BECs). While other theologies seek an understanding of revelation, liberation theologians seek to bring about the reign of God—a reign of peace and justice. It requires that evangelizers totally immerse themselves in the culture of the poor, otherwise dialogue and action are impossible. Traditionally, the Church in Latin America belongs to the culture of the elite, or oppressing class, and it is for this reason that the first act of liberation must be to liberate the Church itself.[57]

A BEC is a group of individuals or families that know, care for, and share with one another, worship together, and seek to center their life, relationships, and activities on the Word of God. The poor together discover within the context of oppression that the Scriptures can be the source of empowerment and liberation.[58] The poor, long trapped in the

---

[56] See Gerald A. Arbuckle, *Refounding the Church: Dissent for Leadership* (Maryknoll: Orbis Books, 1993) 5–7.

[57] See "Medellin Documents" (1968), *The Gospel of Peace and Justice*, ed. Joseph Gremillion (Maryknoll: Orbis Books, 1976) 471–6.

[58] See Gerald A. Arbuckle, *Earthing the Gospel: An Inculturation Handbook for Pastoral Workers* (Maryknoll: Orbis Books, 1990) 86–8; Robert J. Schreiter, *The New Catholicity: Theology Between the Global and the Local* (Maryknoll: Orbis Books, 1999) 16–8, 105–14.

patron-client mentality that has traditionally characterized class relations in Catholic societies, are able to discover that they do not have to be passive in the presence of violence.[59] This is just what happened to Arturo and his friends in the case study above.

The initiative to begin BECs often comes from bishops, priests, or religious. However, once these lay-centered communities become self-moving, they inevitably begin to critique traditional ecclesiastical structures according to Gospel values; hence, a "renaissance of the very church itself"[60] as the People of God generally involves the bishop and priest in a healthy identity crisis: the erstwhile master becomes the disciple of his own disciples.[61]

However, once the poor empower themselves, there is always the risk of opting for violence to overcome sinful structures. The Conference of Latin American Bishops meeting at Medellin in 1968 spoke directly to this point, assenting to the traditional theories in favor of just war, but coming out somewhat more strongly in support of the theology of nonviolent action against injustice. They write "that violence or 'armed revolution' generally generates new injustices, introduces new imbalances and causes new disasters; one cannot combat a real evil at the price of a greater evil."[62] Liberation theologians also have come to recognize that the "Christian can triumph, even where circumstances do not change, even when liberation does not come. Liberation and salvation overlap . . . to a significant degree, but they do not overlap totally."[63]

Suffering has been an inevitable experience for many pathfinders involved in BECs, especially in countries controlled by dictatorships. For example, in Chile during the Pinochet regime, they were targeted by the government, and between 1973 and 1979 nearly 400 foreign priests were expelled and local members of BECs were harassed. In El Salvador Archbishop Oscar Romero and other supporters of BECs were murdered. At times even members of the Catholic hierarchy, e.g., in

[59] See Jeff Haynes, *Religion in Third World Politics* (Buckingham: Open University Press, 1993) 106.

[60] Leonardo Boff, *Ecclesiogenesis: The Base Communities Reinvent the Church* (Maryknoll: Orbis Books, 1986) 1.

[61] See G. Deelan, *Basic Christian Communities in the Church* (Brussels: Pro Mundi Vita, 1980) 5.

[62] See Gremillion, *The Gospel of Peace and Justice*, 461.

[63] David J. Bosch, *Transforming Mission: Paradigm Shifts in Theology of Mission* (Maryknoll: Orbis Books, 1991) 446.

Colombia, have strongly criticized the emergence of the "people's Church" as expressed in the BECs.[64]

BECs have also emerged within the First World, though usually with less focus on poverty. Bernard Lee estimates that there are 37,000 small Christian communities in the United States and, except for Hispanic/Latino communities, Catholic members are better educated and financially better-off than the average Catholic.[65] Lee concludes his study with this comment: "As a result of explicit attention to church issues, many members become more critical of the church but also practice a greater sense of charity toward it."[66]

2. "People Power" Revolution: Philippines, February 1986

The dictator Ferdinand Marcos in 1986 attempted to hold onto power through a fraudulent election process, supported by the American government,[67] and political murders and oppression. The Catholic Bishops Conference in response urged Filipinos to use nonviolent action to protest: "This means active resistance to evil by peaceful means. . . . Our acting must always be according to the Gospel of Christ, that is, in a peaceful, nonviolent way."[68] Over a million Filipinos then lined the streets to protest in a nonviolent way. Marcos ordered his troops to fire on a small group of rebel soldiers that the people sought to protect. Despite the threat to their own lives, the people did not withdraw.[69] Protesters with extraordinary bravery approached the soldiers of the dictator offering them flowers, food, and cigarettes. They even tied yellow ribbons on the rifles, others knelt in prayer before them. Eventually the army crumbled and joined the protesters, leaving the dictator powerless and fleeing the country.

The most inspiring sight of the event was the intense religiosity of the people as they invoked the aid of Divine Providence in hymns and devotional prayer, the rosary in particular. Liberation theologians have

[64] See Haynes, *Religion in Third World Politics*, 106.

[65] Bernard J. Lee, *The Catholic Experience of Small Christian Communities* (New York: Paulist, 2000) 10–1.

[66] Ibid., 145.

[67] See Ackerman and Duvall, *A Force More Powerful: A Century of Nonviolent Conflict*, 383.

[68] Ibid.

[69] See Marcelo A. Ordonez, *People Power* (Quezon City: Sampaguita Press, 1986) iii; Patricio R. Mamot, *People Power: Profile of Filipino Heroism* (Quezon City: New Day, 1986).

at times ignored popular religiosity, but the experience of the Philippines illustrates that it can be of singular importance in mobilizing people for nonviolent action.[70] Popular religiosity at its core "is a storehouse of values that offers answers of Christian wisdom to the great questions of life. . . . It creatively combines the divine with the human, Christ and Mary . . . intelligence and emotion."[71]

3. Nonviolent Collapse of Communism

Pope John Paul II had a critical role in the peaceful collapse of communism in Eastern Europe. His triumphal return to Poland as Pope in June 1979 exceeded any such experience in the history of contemporary Europe. Approximately twelve million people saw him. The government's power weakened as the Church controlled the cities through which the Pope passed.[72] He challenged in his speeches the oppressive political system at two levels: he reaffirmed the Christian faith's opposition to Marxist atheism, and implicitly condemned the violations of human rights and the Soviet control over Poland.[73] His message of nonviolence during this visit gave people hope and energized them to act collaboratively for justice: "Whatever the miseries of sufferings that afflict us, it is not through violence, the interplay of power and political systems, but through the truth [of the Gospel message] that we journey toward a better future."[74] After the Soviet empire collapsed without hardly a shot being fired, Mikhail Gorbachev commented that "nothing that happened in Eastern Europe would have happened without the Polish Pope."[75]

4. Protesting a School for Terrorists: USA

The School of the Americas (now called the Western Hemisphere Institute for Security Co-operation) was established in the United

---

[70] See Michael R. Candelaria, *Popular Religion and Liberation* (Maryknoll: Orbis Books, 1990) xii.

[71] "Final Document of the Third General Conference of the Latin American Episcopate, Puebla," *Puebla and Beyond*, ed. John Eagleson and Philip Scharper (Maryknoll: Orbis Books, 1979) 185–6.

[72] See H. Stuart Hughes, *Sophisticated Rebels: The Political Culture of European Dissent: 1968–1987* (Cambridge, Mass.: Harvard University Press, 1990) 79–93.

[73] See Ackerman and Duvall, *A Force More Powerful: A Century of Nonviolent Conflict*, 133–4.

[74] John Paul II address to Latin American Bishops, *L'Osservatore Romano* (5 February 1979) 8.

[75] Mikhail Gorbachev cited by John Wilkins, *The Tablet* (12 October 2002) 11.

States in 1946 as a terrorist training camp for military personnel from Latin American countries. Graduates of this facility have been responsible for the deaths of four American nuns, Archbishop Oscar Romero, Bishop Juan Gerardi of Guatemala City, as well as countless rapes and massacres in Latin America, especially during periods of military dictatorships.[76] Civilians have frequently protested in nonviolent ways in an effort to draw national attention to the school's activities. Recently, Franciscan Sister Dorothy Hennessey, aged eighty-eight, and twenty-five others were jailed for trespassing in protest.[77]

Summary

- Key symbols in the mythology of paramodernity are: respect for the person and cultural identity, interdependence, systems, collaboration, holistic health, imagination, spirituality, gender equality, accountability, reconciliation, and nonviolence. These are "signals of transcendence" in a world where violence is frequently assumed to be normal.

- This emerging culture offers rich opportunities to the Church for inculturation—to purify and transform the mythology into a "new creation" (2 Cor 5:17).

- In many parts of the world the Church must grapple with a pre-evangelization environment; evangelizers will have an impact to the degree that they are personally alive in Christ and their lives mirror their words.

- Nonviolent action is not synonymous with passivity, submissiveness, and cowardice. It is a skill of struggling to use social, economic, and political power to remove the violator's legitimacy and ability to dominate. At the same time the heart of nonviolence is never to destroy or injure another person's sense of self-worth, no matter what the provocation.

- Nonviolent action has been effectively used not only within democratic societies, for example, through strikes, but also against totali-

---

[76] See George Monbiot, "Looking for a Terror School to Bomb?" *Sydney Morning Herald* (1 November 2001) 12.

[77] See Patrick O'Neill, *National Catholic Reporter* (1 June 2001) 5.

tarian systems; it is no magic solution to violence, but it is an imperative of the Scriptures.[78]

- Nonviolence recognizes the reality of the human condition, namely, as Hannah Arendt writes, that the "danger of using violence . . . will always be that the means will overwhelm the end . . . the practice of violence changes the world, but the most probable change is to a more violent world."[79]

Discussion Questions

1. What do you admire most in leaders? Read Matthew 20:20-8 where Jesus describes "servant leadership" and how it differs from the behavior of a bully. In what way could you be a better servant leader at home or work over the coming week?

2. In paramodernity people are claiming their own authority to be respected as persons. Can you identify examples in your own life where this is happening? In the lives of others? What do you feel when you refuse to be bullied by others? What biblical text gives you personal support in your stand against violence?

[78] See Gene Sharp, *The Politics of Nonviolent Action—Power and Struggle* (Boston: Porter Sargent, 1973) 70–1.

[79] Hannah Arendt, *Crises of the Republic* (New York: Harcourt, Brace, 1972) 177.

Epilogue

A Parable for Our Time

Psalm 143 is about violence. The psalmist has been assaulted and for the moment has escaped the violator, but feels utterly helpless and unable to defend himself if attacked again. His ability to control events is shattered, his secure world destroyed. Fear haunts him. Feel the lostness, fear, hopelessness, and powerlessness in his words:

> An enemy is in deadly pursuit,
> Crushing me into the ground, forcing me to live in darkness . . .
> My spirit is faint, and within me my heart is numb with fear . . .
> my spirit is worn out . . . (Ps 143: 3-4, 7)

The terrorist attacks on the United States in September 2001, in Bali and Moscow in October 2002, changed the world. No one, no place is ever safe from violence. Weapons of mass destruction in the hands of terrorists are capable of destroying millions, even the world itself. The fact that an aggressor cannot be readily identified and captured adds to the sense of fear and powerlessness. Military strength alone is no guarantee of peace and security: "An enemy is in deadly pursuit . . . within me my heart is numb with fear . . ."

The Church in its own way is also in a dangerous liminal stage, like the Israelites under Moses in the desert—the darkness of the betwixt-and-between period, in which the securities of Egypt have disappeared and the peace and order of the promised land have yet to be achieved. The pre-Vatican II Church has yet to be boldly assigned to history, and the new Church of Vatican II values has yet to take confident shape. It is a phase of uncertainty, bickering, scapegoating, and intense pain. Restorationist and fundamentalist forces are so fearful of the darkness that they will not let the old Church go. Pastoral pathfinders wanting to engage creatively with the contemporary world often feel unsupported and even rejected by restorationists "in deadly pursuit."

The Church fled in fear from the challenges of modernity. It is in danger of doing the same when confronted with postmodernity. People yearn for meaning in their lives in the midst of violence, a yearning that can only be satisfied with the message of Gospel peace that does not come from escaping the challenge to bring Christ to the cultures of our time.

What are we to do? Remain bystanders and do nothing? Give way to despair? The psalmist in a spirit of hope in the darkness of uncertainty and chaos cried out to Yahweh: "Show me the road I must travel for you to relieve my heart" (Ps 143:8). What road are we to travel to relieve our hearts in the darkness of uncertainty and the violence within and outside the Church? In times of chaos (see axiom 6, chapter 1) we need to rearticulate eagerly and re-own the founding mythology of our mission as Christians. This is the way to avoid being consumed with fear and trapped in fundamentalism and restorationism.

The mission of Jesus is contained in the narrative of the Good Samaritan which is about how to react to violence in ways that are nonviolent and filled with hope (Luke 10:29-37). The incident has three parts:

• the setting

• the Good Samaritan as a healer of violence

• the command to imitate the aid-giver.

The Setting: Types of Violence

The story begins with a lawyer who questioned Jesus and the bullying style was the incident's first act of violence. "And who is my neighbor?" (v. 29). In the premodern world of that time, questions were rarely requests for help, but rather public challenges to personal honor (see chapter 4, above). The lawyer hoped that Jesus could not answer the question and so would be shamed. This is what is meant by the words "But the man was anxious to justify himself" (v. 29).[1]

---

[1] See John J. Pilch, *The Cultural World of Jesus, Cycle C* (Collegeville: The Liturgical Press, 1997) 109.

The second act of violence was physical and social, namely, the assault by bandits of an innocent man (v. 30). At the time it was common for gangs of thugs to terrorize well-off travelers, rob them and often give the proceeds to the poor.[2] The victim may well have been a wealthy man. Not only was he robbed and left to die, but he was also stripped naked. To strip a person naked, as Jesus was on the cross, was the ultimate act of subjugation and social marginalization.

The third act of violence was ritual. The priest and the Levite, two pillars of Jewish culture, represent religious fundamentalism of their times. The Israelite tradition required that people must show compassion, especially to the poor and marginalized, but Jewish fundamentalists had forgotten this obligation and had developed a religion that focused on external conformity to rituals of accidental importance. The priest would have been returning from the Temple in Jerusalem to his home in the country. He refused to help for two reasons: he feared being attacked by bandits if he delayed, but, more importantly, he was not prepared to be defiled by touching what looked like a dead person. If he touched him he would have to undergo lengthy rituals of purification and be a social outcast during this period (v. 31).

The Levite, who belonged to an order of cultic officials "devoted to the Lord" (Exod 32:28), inferior to the priests but nonetheless a privileged group in Jewish society, also refused to help, for the same reasons, although he is pictured as slightly hesitating before making his decision (v. 32). The priest and Levite by their failure to act betrayed the founding mythology of the Israelite people: compassion and justice to the poor and socially powerless (Isa 58).

The figure of the Samaritan traveler highlighted a fourth form of violence in the incident: racial violence. Jews looked on Samaritans in a racist manner; they pictured them as stupid, lazy, and heretical, and the Samaritans had similar views of their Jewish neighbors, as scriptural scholar John McKenzie points out: "[T]here was no deeper break of human relations in the contemporary world than the feud of Jews and Samaritans, and the breadth and depth of Jesus' doctrine of love could demand no greater act of a Jew than to accept a Samaritan as a brother."[3]

---

[2] See Bruce J. Malina and Richard L. Rohrbaugh, *Social-Science Commentary on the Synoptic Gospels* (Minneapolis: Fortress Press, 1992) 404.

[3] John McKenzie, *Dictionary of the Bible* (London: Geoffrey Chapman, 1968) 766.

The story contains a fifth example of violence: occupational violence. The Samaritan as a trader would have been subjected to prejudice and discrimination from Jews and his own people, because all traders were thought to have become rich through shady dealings. Yet, this man, considered racially and occupationally inferior, risked aiding the dying man (vv. 33-35).

The Samaritan: Lessons

Jesus detailed the actions of the Samaritan. The aid-giver was a brave and courageous person because he risked his own life by getting off his mount—his only form of protection—and exposing himself to attack by bandits. He then "bandaged his wounds, pouring oil and wine on them" (v. 34). In order to bandage the wounds, the Samaritan would have had to touch the victim. Jewish people distinguished between disease and illness: the former is what one can see, e.g., the cancer; the latter is the inner pain of lostness and powerlessness that a victim feels in consequence of the disease. It is this inner pain—the illness—that the brutally wounded man would have especially felt, that is, the pain of having been marginalized as a nonperson.[4] By touching him the Samaritan compassionately bonded with the victim but at the same time he himself became ritually impure in the eyes of the Jews and his own people.

The Samaritan used his shrewd business experience in the service of healing. He led the injured man on his mount to an inn to obtain further help. An inn at that time was not a place of safety and security, it was a violent and dangerous place, a den of thieves, and innkeepers were particularly skilled thieves. One risked one's life and possessions to enter and stay at an inn. The aid-giver, knowing this, refused to expose himself and his patient needlessly to violence and bribed the innkeeper to take care of the patient temporarily (v. 35).

The parable is about the holistic healing of violence and implicit in the story are six lessons.

• All life must be respected as a gift of God. Scapegoating people because of their race, ethnicity, gender, or occupation is contrary to this sacred gift of life. The giving and receiving of mercy transcends national and racial barriers.

[4] See Gerald A. Arbuckle, *Healthcare Ministry: Refounding the Mission in Tumultuous Times* (Collegeville: The Liturgical Press, 2000) 14–5.

- The response to violence must not stop at the symptoms, but focus also on knowing and relating to its causes. The Samaritan out of love of a fellow human being, went to the roots of violence by touching the victim—in that one act, he broke the ritual and racial barriers. In responding to the need, he also used his own capital in the form of oil and wine he had intended to sell at the market. This was an expression of justice and hospitality: "You will treat aliens as though they were native-born and love them as yourself" (Lev 19:33). All goods ultimately belong to God, and when we receive a stranger we are but sharing what rightly belongs to all.

- For compassion to be shown to both victim and violator a healer needs to be aware of his or her own inner potential for violence. The psalmist did not condemn the violator, but the violence. He could do this because in the midst of his suffering he was conscious of the grave and universal character of human violence, and so of his own violent tendencies: "do not put your servant on trial, for no one living can be found guiltless at your tribunal" (Ps 143:2). In the Gospel story the Samaritan also knew not only what it was like to be racially and socially marginalized, but to be tempted to violence against his oppressors. This admission of his own inner weakness gave him empathy and compassion for victim *and* violator.

- Seek a method of dialoguing and collaborating with people even when they are known violators. The Samaritan was a realist. He accepted that the innkeeper was a thief, but he treated him respectfully, while protecting himself and the patient from further violence. He provided the innkeeper with an example of compassion.

- The Samaritan risked being attacked by bandits as he bandaged the victim and walked him to the inn, yet he trusted in God. Even if he was killed, he still knew that he was doing God's will in helping the victim and God would be with him: "Rescue me from my enemies, Yahweh, since in you I find protection" (Ps 143:9). To build the Church anew, as John Paul II defines the challenge, means risking the unknown in faith and hope. We may falter and fail, but we must try and leave the rest to God. The basis for our hope is not our faithfulness to God, but rather God's faithfulness to us (Ps 143:1; 1 John 4:10). With this belief in mind fundamentalists and restorationists in the Church are not to be condemned for their anxieties about embracing Vatican II. They, like all pilgrims, are on a journey of discovery and they need the understanding and compassion of fellow-pilgrims—two virtues that the Samaritan knew are necessary for dialogue and mutual growth. This is what John Paul II refers to as "a spirituality of communion." It means, he writes, "'mak[ing] room' for our brothers and sisters, bearing 'each other's burdens' (Gal 6:2) and resisting the selfish temptations which . . . provoke . . . distrust and jealousy."[5]

- We are not to be passive in the presence of violence. Jesus refused to be bullied by the lawyer who attempted to publicly shame him. The trap set by the lawyer to embarrass Jesus failed, and the questioner had himself to answer the question he had asked of Jesus (v. 37).

The parable ends with Jesus commanding the lawyer to travel the same journey in the footsteps of Samaritan: "Go, and do the same yourself" (Luke 10:37). For Christians today the command remains in force. The parable calls for prophets to heal violence within and outside the Church. Prophets were Israel's creative, dynamic, and questioning memory. While listening to Yahweh and to the people's violence against Yahweh and one another, they dared to point out the violence in society; and they repeatedly called fellow Israelites to re-own the founding myth of the nation, that is, Yahweh loved his people who needed to respond with sincerity of heart, worship, justice, and love. With imagination they pointed to ways for people to heal violence.

Contemporary prophets do not settle for outdated pastoral methods but search for ways to present the unchanging message of the Gospel in language and action relevant to the ever-changing needs of our times. They do not give up trying in the face of opposition. There is a cost to this—the risk of being rejected both by victims and violators. The ultimate model and source of courage is Christ: "Yes, I will go further because of the supreme advantage of knowing Christ. . . . I count everything else as loss . . . that I may come to know . . . the power of his resurrection, and partake of his sufferings by being molded to the pattern of his death. . . ." (Phil 3:9-10).

When readers contemplate the violence described in this book and their own inner temptations to hostility and hatred they may be close to despair. However, Christ the Good Samaritan has traveled that road, for he was tempted to despair: "My God, my God, why have you forsaken me?" He knew the feeling of abandonment that victims of vio-

---

[5] John Paul II, *Novo Millennio Ineunte* (Sydney: St. Paul's Publications, 2001) par. 43.

lence experience, but he turned in hope to his Father: "Yet you, the Holy One . . . in you our ancestors put their trust" (Ps 22:1, 3, 4). The biblical vision of suffering is not one of cynicism, despair, or passive resignation, but of hope of union with the one who became a victim that there might be life: "God will dwell with them, and they shall be his people. . . . God will wipe away every tear from their eyes . . . neither shall there be mourning nor crying nor pain anymore. . . . I am making the whole of creation new" (Rev 21:3-4).

Index